Traditions Of The Arikara

By

George A. Dorsey

Double 9
BOOKS

Traditions Of The Arikara
by George A. Dorsey

ISBN: 978-93-59959-13-9
Published by

DOUBLE 9 BOOKS
2/13-B, Ansari Road
Daryaganj, New Delhi – 110002
info@double9books.com
www.double9books.com
Tel. 011-40042856

ABOUT THE AUTHOR

George Amos Dorsey (February 6, 1868 – March 29, 1931) was an American ethnographer of indigenous peoples of the Americas, with a particular focus on the Great Plains Caddoan and Siouan tribes. While working as curator at the Field Museum in Chicago from 1898 to 1915, he is credited with helping to create the anthropology of Plains Indian nations. From 1907 to 1915, he was also Professor of Anthropology at the University of Chicago. Dorsey was one of the first anthropologists to testify as an expert forensic witness in the murder prosecution of Adolph Luetgert in Chicago in 1897, when he examined what he established were human remains. Why We Behave Like Human Beings, his cultural study, became an unexpected blockbuster in 1925. This prompted the release of his 1917 novel, as well as the publication of several other volumes on anthropology and culture. One book that was in the works when he died in 1931 was published posthumously. Edwin Jackson and Mary Emma (née Grove) Dorsey raised Dorsey in Hebron, Ohio. Prior to college, he attended local schools. In 1888, he got a Bachelor of Arts degree from Denison University, and in 1890, he received a second bachelor's degree in anthropology from Harvard University.

CONTENTS

INTRODUCTION

The Arikara traditions in this volume were collected during the year 1903, with funds provided by the Carnegie Institution. The work was part of a systematic and extended study of the mythology and ceremonies of the various tribes of the Caddoan stock. All of the tales here presented were secured through James R. Murie, of the Skidi band of Pawnee. The slight differences in language between the Arikara and Skidi were soon overcome by Mr. Murie, who, when a boy at school, had learned to speak Arikara fluently.

The Arikara belong to the Caddoan linguistic stock, and were formerly closely allied with the Skidi band of Pawnee, from which tribe they separated about 1832. After that time they made their home at various points along the Missouri River until, in 1854, they were placed on what is known as Fort Berthold Reservation in North Dakota, along with the Mandan and Minitaree or Grosventres, the latter two tribes being of Siouan stock. With the Mandan the Arikara had been closely associated even before their removal to the Fort Berthold Reservation. Their dwellings and general mode of life had much in common with the Skidi. Like the Skidi, they constructed the earth-lodge, and their social organization and religious ceremonies in general were also similar to those of the Skidi. Inasmuch as the author has prepared a somewhat extended discussion of the Skidi in his introduction to the "Traditions of the Skidi Pawnee," it will not be necessary here to do more than to refer to that volume.[1]

The Arikara to-day number about 380, as against 435 in 1890, and 725 in 1880. Owing to the continued severe hostility of the Indian Department, but little evidence of their former method of life remains. It is said that the last earth-lodge in use fell into ruins in 1900. In possession of certain members of the tribe are some of the sacred bundles or altars; but the people have been so intimidated that their religious ceremonies are, as a rule, held secretly.

In physique they seem hardier than their Skidi brethren on the south, and in disposition, more tractable. In dealings with the Government they have, as a rule, proved themselves men of high honor, and not since about 1820 have they manifested an unfriendly disposition toward the whites.

An examination of the tales here presented shows, as we might expect to find, many points of resemblance with those of the Skidi and other Pawnee tribes. It is apparent at once, however, that the mythology of the Arikara contains many elements not found among the Skidi. This is possibly due to contact with the Mandan, and perhaps, though to a less extent, with the Minitaree. To what extent the Mandan have influenced the Arikara can not be known, as no extended account of their mythology is available.

Inasmuch as investigation is now being carried on among additional tribes of the Caddoan stock, the usual references to the mythologies of other tribes have been omitted in the present volume. At the completion of this investigation the tales of all the tribes of the stock will be considered from a comparative point of view, while other resemblances to the traditions of other tribes will, at the same time, be pointed out. It seems sufficient at present merely to indicate in a general way the character of the tales here presented.

In the first and second tales, each of which tells of the creation of the earth by the Wolf and Lucky-Man, as well as in the creation of people by the Spiders, through the assistance of the Wolf, we have a story of origin not known to any of the other bands of Caddoan stock, and it is possible that this account is due to foreign influence. The story of the appearance of people upon earth, or of the emergence, is presented in a number of variant forms (Nos. 3 to 13). All these myths are of undoubted Arikara origin, and apparently are uninfluenced by the mythology of any other tribe. The difference of these tales from all similar tales among the Skidi is very interesting, and shows that the Arikara possessed a well-defined mythology of their own before their separation from the Skidi. The next two tales (Nos. 9, 10) bear additional testimony to the importance of the cultivation of corn among the Arikara, while in tales 11, 12, and 13 is related, in varying versions, the escape of the Arikara from the buffalo. The fundamental principle of this myth is wide-spread and extended to many of the Plains tribes.

In the next series of tales (Nos. 14 to 28) we have a general account of the period of transformation following the emergence, and which may be characterized in general as transformer legends. As with the Skidi, the poor boy among these tales is the culture hero, while Coyote, the great transformer of the Northwest, takes a very inferior part. At least three well-defined transformers appear in this series; the first in importance is the boy offspring of the woman who climbed to heaven and married a Star. His greatest work is freeing the land from the presence of the four destroying monsters. Only second to Star-Boy in importance is Sun-Boy (No. 16), whose special merit consists in the fact that he made long life possible, though only after a series of memorable contests with his powerful father. The third transformer is Burnt-Hands, the Burnt-Belly of the Skidi. Like Burnt-Belly, this poor boy, through the aid of certain animals, becomes powerful, kills the mean chief, and calls the buffalo, thus saving his tribe from despotism and famine, and at the same time furnishing by his life a perpetual example to the poor of the Arikara of the value of honest and long-continued effort. In tale No. 20 are related the deeds of two boys who slew the water-monster, one of whom, perhaps, was Burnt-Hands. The deeds also of two brothers, and perhaps the same as those just referred to, are related in the next two tales (Nos. 21 and 22), where we have the additional element of one of the boys turning into a water-monster and taking up his home in the Missouri River, an incident which is of wide-spread distribution among the Pawnee tribes. The first of these two stories might also be considered as a rite myth, for it has certain reference to the origin of the ceremony of the medicine-men. In the next tale (No. 23) the value of the deeds of the poor boy, who, as in a similar Skidi tale, recovers a mouse's nest and so receives power from the mice and rats, is not so apparent. To be sure, for a while, his power is used advantageously, and he is instrumental in fighting the enemies of his tribe, but he finally abuses his power, and in an encounter with the bear this power comes to an end. A similar fate befalls the hero of another tale (No. 34), who, in befriending some young hawks, obtained the power of the hawks, which power, for a while, was rightly used, but eventually, abusing it, he suffered death. This tale, also, might be considered a rite myth. In tales Nos. 25 and 26 is related how the young man recovered the young women from the power of the bear, through the assistance of the magic flute of the elk. In the second of these two tales some of the women become elks. The story of the man who obtained the elk power is related in tale 27, which also relates how certain people, after entering the water, became animals. In a number of tales presented Coyote figures prominently, but only in No. 28 does he appear as a transformer, where, by his action with the magic windpipe, the seven brothers become bumblebees.

Tales Nos. 29 to 42 may be considered rite myths, inasmuch as they refer either to the origin of a ceremony or of a particular rite or to incidents, which were perhaps connected with a ceremony. Myths of this nature apparently are not as common among the Arikara as among the Skidi. It is possible, however, that this apparent difference will not prove to be real, for as yet no extended and systematic study has been made of the Arikara ceremonies.

In tale No. 29 is found an interesting account of the origin of the well-known ring and javelin game of the Plains, which among the Arikara, as among the Skidi and Wichita, is really part of the ceremonial calling of the buffalo. The tale also relates to the origin of the buffalo dance. In the next three tales (Nos. 30–32) is related the origin of the wolf dance and of the medicine-men's dance and of the special medicine of one of the medicine-men. In tale No. 33 is related the origin of the rabbit power, presumably the tale of the origin of some special medicine. In tale No. 34 we have perhaps the account of the origin of some band. Here, as in certain other tales, we have the magic power, derived in this instance from the water-dogs, which led to the separation of the people. Tale No. 35 appears to relate to certain incidents of the buffalo dance, while the next tale gives a mythical account of the well-known musical instrument consisting of a stick which was rubbed by another stick or by a bone, one end of the first stick resting upon a hollow object acting as a resonator. Tale No. 38 has reference to some personage in the medicine-men's ceremony. In Nos. 38 and 39 we have an account of the man and the woman who turned to stone and who as such afterward played a prominent part in the medicine-men's lodge. In tales Nos. 40 and 41 we have an account of magic power derived from scalped-men, presumably being accounts of the origin of some special medicine. Tale No. 42, which tells of the power given a young girl through the skull and corn of the altar, which she used for replenishing the impoverished stores of her tribe, seems to be the fragment of some rite myth.

Tales Nos. 43 to 48 are of miscellaneous character, and are not easily referred to any of the categories above mentioned. The first two in this series, which recount contests between the Arikara and the snakes and the Arikara and the bears, are perhaps rite tales, or they may relate to a still earlier time in the mythologic era. The next tale tells of the wife who married the elk and afterward rendered great assistance to her people. This tale in its general features is similar to a wide-spread myth found among the Plains tribes. The story of the four girls who were pursued by the mountain-lion, as told in tale No. 46, is also equally wide-spread, though it is here presented in an abbreviated form. The next tale, which tells of the boy who could transform himself into an eagle, and who became a great chief and warrior, is similar in general to No. 32, but contains no rite element. The story of the whirlwind girl (No. 48) contains certain elements not yet known to exist among any of the Plains tribes.

Tales Nos. 49 to 59 relate almost exclusively to animals, and in all of them the Coyote plays a prominent part, always as a mean trickster, not as a transformer, and committing deeds which generally result disastrously to himself. These tales in general are similar to those of the Skidi and other bands of the Pawnee.

Tales Nos. 60 to 68 may be characterized in general as traditions, in which the element of superstition or strange beliefs play a prominent part.

Tales Nos. 69 to 82 possess no element of magic power. They are to be considered as traditions or war tales, from which may be gained certain information interesting in a general study of the Arikara. Tale No. 71, and the last of the series, No. 82, are especially interesting, as relating the story of the medicine war shield and the personal experience of a member of the Bear society.

George A. Dorsey.

Chicago, July 1, 1904.

FOOTNOTES:

[1] Traditions of the Skidi Pawnee, Volume 8, Memoirs of the American Folk-Lore Society, 1904.

1.
THE WOLF AND LUCKY-MAN CREATE LAND.[2]

There was a big lake. On this lake were two Ducks swimming around. They saw the Wolf coming from the southwest. Then they saw in the north, Lucky-Man coming. The Wolf and Lucky-Man met on the shore of the lake.

The Wolf challenged Lucky-Man to see who could endure the rain the longest. The Wolf hung up his own skin, while Lucky-Man hung up all kinds of feathers on a long stick. It commenced to rain. The Wolf finally gave in. He said: "I am beaten, but now I want you to create with me. I want to make land. I want you to make land, and whatever things should live on it." Then the Wolf said, "I will take the north side of the Missouri River, and I will make land." The Wolf called a Duck, and said, "Now, Duck, can you dive away down under the lake and fetch me some dirt from the bottom?" The Duck said, "Yes." The Duck dived and brought up mud and placed it before the Wolf. The Wolf then threw the mud in the north, and said, "Form into land, and let it be prairie, and let the buffalo roam over this prairie!" And it was done.

The Wolf told Lucky-Man that it was now his turn. Lucky-Man then turned and called the Duck and told it to bring up the mud from the lake. He brought up even more than he had brought up for the Wolf. Lucky-Man threw this dirt on the south side of where the Wolf had made his land. Hills and mountains were formed. The buffalo were seen on the land. Lucky-Man said: "When the people come they shall choose to live on the south side of the Missouri River, for there are hills and valleys, so that their ponies, dogs, and buffalo can find shelter in the hills and mountains. You made your country level; in the winter time the buffalo will be driven away from there by the storm."

The Wolf made the land on the north side, and Lucky-Man made the land on the south side; so there was a channel between the two countries, and that is where the Missouri River bed is. The first thing they knew, the stream of the Missouri began to flow along the dividing line of the two countries they had created.

FOOTNOTES:

[2] Told by Yellow-Bear.

2.
THE SPIDERS GIVE BIRTH TO PEOPLE.[3]

There was once an old Spider-Man who lived by himself with his wife. One day the Wolf and his friend went to visit these old folks. The Spider-Man was dirty, his eyes were red, he had no hair on his head, and he was very dirty all over, and he emitted a bad odor. His wife also was very dirty; her hair was thin and very coarse. The Wolf had never seen people who looked like these people.

Lupus ab homine quaesivit quem ad modum cum uxore concumberet. Homo respondit: "Non dicere sed ostendere volumus." "Recte," dixit Lupus. Cum autem hominem mulieremque conspexisset, ilium tantum genitalia esse, itemque mulierem repperit; quocirca fetorem emiserunt. Atque uterque de genere araneo fuit.

Deinde Lupus: "Efficiemus ut pulchriores videamini, et concumbere aliter ac nunc possitis."

The Spider-Man and the woman were both willing. So the Wolf and his friend went and got some wild sage and fixed up some medicine. They dipped the wild sage into the water and rubbed it all over the two Spider people. As he rubbed the wild sage over them they became very different, they looked better, and they did not smell bad. Deinde Lupus virum docebat quem ad modum cum uxore concumbere conveniret, quidque facere oporteret ut liberos gignere posset. Nisi Lupus haec fecisset, ut aiunt, nulli de genere humano geniti essent. Namque ille Araneos docuit quem ad modum concumbere oporteret ut liberos gignerent. Qui autem ex eis geniti sunt humani fuerunt, unde homines omnes sunt.

FOOTNOTES:

[3] Told by Two-Hawks.

3.
THE ORIGIN OF THE ARIKARA.[4]

There were large people living upon the earth long ago, who were so strong that they were not afraid of anybody, but they did not have good judgment. They made fun of all the gods in the heavens.

Nesaru looked down upon them, and was angry. Nesaru said: "I made them too strong. I will not keep them. They think that they are like myself. I shall destroy them, but I shall put away my people that I like and that are smaller."

So the animals were made to assist some people to turn into corn and they were taken under ground into a cave, which was so large that animals and people lived down there together. The large people were killed by the flood. The people who were taken in under the ground knew nothing of the flood, for they were not people; they were grains of corn.

Nesaru in the heavens planted corn in the heavens, to remind him that his people were put under ground. As soon as the corn in the heavens had matured, Nesaru took from the field an ear of corn. This corn he turned into a woman and Nesaru said, "You must go down to the earth and bring my people from the earth." She went down to the earth and she roamed over the land for many, many years, not knowing where to find the people. At last the thunders sounded in the east. She followed the sound, and she found the people underground in the east. By the power of Nesaru himself this woman was taken under ground, and when the people and the animals saw her they rejoiced. They knew her, for she was the Mother-Corn. The people and the animals also knew that she had the consent of all the gods to take them out.

Mother-Corn then called upon the gods to assist her to lead her people out of the earth. There was none who could assist her. She turned around to the people, and said: "We must leave this place, this darkness; there is light above the earth. Who will come to help me take my people out of the earth?" The Badger came forth, and said, "Mother, I will help." A Mole also stood up, and said, "I will assist the Badger to dig through the ground, that we may see the light." The long-nosed Mouse came, and said, "I will assist these other two to dig through."

The Badger began to dig upwards. He became tired, and said, "Mother, I am tired." Then the Mole began to dig. The Mole became tired. Then the long-nosed Mouse came and dug until it became tired. It came back. The long-nosed Mouse said, "Mother, I am tired." The Badger began to dig upward. When he became tired the Mole went up. The Mole said, "I was just about to go through when I became tired." The long-nosed Mouse then ran up, and said, "I will try." The long-nosed Mouse stuck its nose through the earth until it reached up to its ears, and it could see just a little light. It went back, and said, "Mother, I ran my nose through the earth, and it has made my nose small; all the people that I shall belong to shall have these long noses, just like mine, so that all the animals will know that it was I who dug through the earth first, making my nose small and pointed."

The Mole was so glad that it tried again. It went up to the hole, dug through the hole and went through. The sun had come up from the east. It was so bright that it blinded the Mole. The Mole ran back, and said, "Mother, I have been blinded by the brightness of that sun. I can not live upon the earth any more. I must make my home under the earth. All the people who wish to be with me will be blind, so that they can not see in the daytime, but they can see in the night. They shall stay under the ground in the daytime." The Mother-Corn said, "Very well."

The Badger then dug through, making the hole larger, and, as it went out, the Badger closed its eyes, but, as he stuck his feet out, the rays of the sun struck him upon the face so that he got a streak of black upon it, and he got black legs. The Badger went back into the hole, and said, "Mother, I have received these black marks upon me, and I wish that I might remain this way, so that people will remember that I was one of those who helped to get your people out." The Mother-Corn said, "Very well, let it be as you say."

The Mother-Corn then led the way and the Mole followed, going out of the hole; but, as they were about to go out from the hole, there was a noise from the east, and thunder, which shook the earth, so that the earth opened. The people were put upon the top of the earth. There was wailing and crying, and, at the same time, the people were rejoicing that they were now out upon the open land. As the people stood upon the earth, the Mother-Corn said, "My people will now journey west. Before we start, any who wish to remain here, as Badgers, long-nosed Mice, or Moles, may remain." This was then done. Some of the people turned back to the holes of the earth and turned into animals, whichever kind they wanted to be.

The journey was now begun. As they journeyed, there seemed to come up in front of them a mountainous country. There was a deep chasm. Here the people could not get down, and if they should get down there was, on the other side, another steep bank, and there was no way for the people to get up. Mother-Corn turned to the heavens, and cried for help, "Any of you gods, come, help." But there was no one to come. Now there came from among the people a little bird, who said, "Mother-Corn, I will be the one to point out the way for you." The bird was the Kingfisher. The bird flew to the other side of the steep bank, stuck its bill into the bank, going through the hill and going out on the other side, so that the earth fell into the chasm. The bird came back again, and flew into the side of the steep bank, where the people were and came out on this side, so that the earth fell into the chasm, so that by the bank's falling there was formed a bridge. The people rejoiced, and the bird said, "All the people who want to join me may remain here, and we will stay and make our homes in these banks." Some of the people went back, stopped and turned into this kind of bird.

Again the people journeyed, and again they came to an obstacle. This obstacle was the timber. The timber was somewhere near the sun. Mother-Corn turned to the gods and asked for help, for the timber before them was very thick. There were thorns all over the timber, so that even animals could not go through. The gods in the heavens had agreed to help Mother-Corn. They gave power to the Owl to clear a way through the timber for the people. The Owl came and stood before Mother-Corn, and said, "Mother, I will help to make a pathway for your people to go through this timber. Any of the people who wish to remain with me may become as I am, and we shall remain in this timber forever." The Owl then flew up through the timber. As it waved its wings it removed the timber to one side, so that when it flew through the timber there was a pathway, so that the people could go through. Mother-Corn then led the people through the timber and passed onward.

As they were journeying through the country, all at once they came to a big lake. They looked around for help, but they could see none. They could not turn back, for Nesaru had instructed Mother-Corn to lead the people towards the west. A bird came and stood in front of Mother-Corn, and said, "I will make a pathway through this water. Let the people stop crying. I shall help them." Mother-Corn looked at the bird, and said, "Make a pathway for us, and you shall have some of my people to remain with you here." The bird flew and jumped into the water. The bird was so swift that it parted the waters wherever it went, and came out on the other side of the water and left the waters parted. This bird was the Loon. The people went over on dry land and crossed to the other side. Some of the people turned back, and as they went into the water they turned into Loons. The other people journeyed on.

When they had crossed the lake they had no implements, for the people at this time had no sense, as they were still animals. Here at this place some of the people were cut off, as the waters came together and left them on the other side of the big waters. At this place the people saw a man who was very tall and whose hair from his mouth reached down to his waist, and they exclaimed, "Wonderful!" And they were afraid of him. They thought that this man was from the heavens.

At this place Mother-Corn brought the people together and said, "I am Mother-Corn; you shall have my corn to plant, so that you, by eating it, will grow and also multiply." Then Mother-Corn also said, "I will have to divide up things among you people," for here at this place they had had their village for some time. Mother-Corn now returned to the heavens.

They made games at this place. The first game they played was the shinny ball and four sticks. The land was marked out by four sticks, which enclosed an oblong extending from east to west. Each side tried to force the ball through the other's goal. When one side was beaten it immediately began to kill those of the other side. At other places they had long javelins to catch a ring with. The side that won began to kill the people who were on the other side, and whose language they could not understand. All this was done while Mother-Corn was away, up in the heavens.

When Mother-Corn returned from the heavens she brought with her a man who said that Nesaru was displeased with their doings; that now he was to give them rules and laws to go by; and that the people were to select a man whose name should be Nesaru, chief.

After a man had been selected as chief the man and Mother-Corn sat down and she commanded that all the animals and people should come to her. The man with Mother-Corn stood up, and said, "I shall go off. I am strong." This man came back with a scalp. "This," he said, "the chief must have, and this other bunch of hair, for the man who takes the most scalps and captures the most enemies shall become a chief. You must put the scalp on your right arm. The next scalp you take, put upon your left arm; the next scalp put on the right breast; the next put on the left breast; the next put on the right leg; and the next put on the left leg. Now, that man becomes a chief."

Mother-Corn then made a bundle, made songs, made the ritual, and gave the people the ceremonies. The medicine-men were instructed by the man, and also were taught sleight-of-hand, and were told to make a village.

They did not stay long in the village, for Mother-Corn led them away on through the country to what is known as the Republican River, in Kansas, where there is only one mountain. Here they were to make their village, for

Nesaru had placed roots and herbs for the medicine-men. All the people now moved on, and the Awaho people came last; for the others had gone on and had their ceremonies, but the Awaho people, coming last, received the ceremonies from Mother-Corn.

At this place, while the ceremonies were going on, Mother-Corn had the people offer smoke to the different gods in the heavens, and to all animal gods. Just as they were about to move on, a Dog came running into the village, frothing at the mouth, and fell down calling upon Mother-Corn, and saying that she had done wrong by leaving it behind; that Mother-Corn had remembered all the gods and all the animals, without remembering him, the Dog; that now he had caught up with the people; that he knew that not only himself, but the Whirlwind was left out; and that the Whirlwind was mad, and was coming to scatter the people; that the Dog had come from the Sun and that the Sun had given it curative powers; that the Dog would help them; that as the Whirlwind was coming to destroy the people, the Dog let them know that the Whirlwind was a disease, and wherever the wind touched the people, disease would be left; but if, when the Whirlwind should come, they would kill a dog and let the dog meat be the first to be offered as a sacrifice to the different gods in the heavens, then the gods would send a storm that would drive away the disease from the villages.

As the Whirlwind came the people cried to the Dog: "Let it be as you say. You shall be the first meat in all our offerings in our ceremonies, and you shall be meat for us to eat when there is disease in the villages, but let the Whirlwind stop." The Whirlwind stopped blowing. Then the Dog appeased the gods, and said, "I shall always remain with the people. I shall be a guardian for all their belongings."

After this was done, Nesaru had gathered in from his garden the crop of corn he had planted. Nesaru then gave three things to the people—Mother-Corn, the office of chief, and the medicine-men. Then Mother-Corn said, "The gods in the heavens are the four world-quarters, for they are jealous. If you forget to give smoke to them they will get mad and send storms." Then she said, "Give smoke to me last. The Cedar-Tree that shall stand in front of your lodge shall be myself. I shall turn into a Cedar-Tree, to remind you that I am Mother-Corn, who gave you your life. It was I, Mother-Corn, who brought you from the east. I must become a Cedar-Tree to be with you. The stone that is placed at the right of the Cedar-Tree is the man who came and gave you order and established the office of chief. It is Nesaru, who still exists all the time, and is watching over you. It will keep you together and give you long life."

FOOTNOTES:

[4] Told by Hand.

4.
THE ORIGIN OF THE ARIKARA.[5]

A long time ago, people lived in the ground. Mother-Corn engaged the animals to help her to get these people out of the ground. The animals came, and said, "Mother-Corn, we will help." There was a Badger, a Gopher, the long-nosed Mouse, and a Mole.

The Badger was the first to stand up, and he said, "Mother-Corn, I will be the first to dig." So the Badger went to work digging through the earth. The Badger gave out. He came back, and said, "Mother-Corn, I am tired." The next animal went and dug, became tired, and came back. The Mole then went to work, but the long-nosed Mouse was the last to go. He dug through the earth with his nose. Then the Mole asked to see the light, and it went through and was blinded. The Mole went back, and said, "Mother-Corn, I will stay under ground always."

The next animal to try was a Gopher. He went up, and tried to go out of the hole. It was late in the evening, so that this animal received only a black streak across his eyes. The Badger then went to work and dug the hole larger, and went out, and it was morning, for the sun was up. The sun burned the fore legs of the Badger, also around his face, but he was not blinded. The long-nosed Mouse stood up, and said, "Mother-Corn, in trying to open the doorway of the earth for the people, my nose was squeezed, and made pointed. My snout has been made small, and I shall keep this shape always, so that the people will know that I was the one that opened the doorway of the earth for the people."

The Mole stood up, and said, "Mother-Corn, I am blinded. I can not go with you, and your people will have to allow me to remain here, that I may always stay under the ground." Mother-Corn gave her consent, and that is why the Mole is in the ground. If it comes out, it will come out in the night, and if the sun comes up on it, it has to sit still all day, until the night comes, then it will travel again.

The people now came out from the ground and stood outside. They saw other pathways, where other people had gone out from the ground, by the help of the Buffalo.

Now the people started upon a journey. This journey was stopped; for the leaders said, "Here is an obstacle, a deep crevice. What shall we do, Mother-Corn?" Mother-Corn said, "Help! Hurry!" And she called upon the gods. The gods sent a Kingfisher, who said, "Mother-Corn, I will be the one to make a way for you and your people." The Kingfisher flew and shot through the side of the bank, and the bank fell. The Kingfisher flew around to where the company of people were, and shot through the other bank, and this bank also fell, so that the two banks, meeting, formed a pathway. Some of the people who saw these banks torn up, turned to Mother-Corn, and said, "Mother-Corn, we want to stay here in the banks, as Worms." So Mother-Corn allowed some of the people to remain in the banks as Worms. The people started, and when they got across this crevice they started on their journey.

Again they met another obstacle—thick timber—and Mother-Corn called on the gods, and said, "Hurry! Help!" So the gods sent the wonderful Owl to the people. This wonderful Owl flew and lighted by Mother-Corn, and said, "Mother, I will be the one to make a pathway." The Owl flew through the timber, and there was a pathway. The people went through the timber, and some of them liked the timber, and they turned to Mother-Corn, and said, "Mother, we want to stay with the wonderful Owl." So some of the people turned into animals and birds, and they stayed in the timber.

Again the people started to journey, and they came to another difficulty. This time they came to a lake, whose banks were mountains, but they managed to get down to the lake. Then the people said, "Mother-Corn, what shall we do, for the lake is in the way?" Mother-Corn called upon the gods, and said, "Hurry! Help!" The gods sent a Loon. The Loon came down and stood by the people, and said, "Mother-Corn, I will help to make a pathway for your people." The Loon flew down to the lake, and flew through the waters, and the waters opened, leaving the bottom of the lake dry so that the people could cross; some drank from the lake, turned into fish, and remained behind. When they had crossed the lake, some of the people said, "Mother-Corn, we want to stay with the wonderful bird, the Loon." Mother-Corn gave her consent. Some of them turned into Loons, and they stayed behind. The obstacles were overcome.

It was now time for Mother-Corn to smoke to the gods. The smoke was ready. Animals and birds were sent out to find offerings.

When the pipe was made the animals and the birds went out to find the offering. The Prairie-chicken found a wild-cat and killed it. The Prairie-chicken brought the wild-cat to the people and laid it down outside of the camp. The Prairie-chicken then went to Mother-Corn, and said, "Mother, I have killed for the offering." Mother-Corn said, "What kind of an animal is it that you have killed?" The Prairie-chicken said, "It is an animal that is speckled." Mother-Corn said, "You have done right. The animal that is speckled represents the heavens, and the white spots represent the stars. So you will bring it and we will make an offering." The Prairie-chicken went and brought the animal.

When it came time to offer the smoke the people found that they had not the pipe with which to form the smoke. There were three Stars in the heavens, and they saw the pipe was lacking. They said, "Mother-Corn, we will get you the pipe." So the three Stars went and found a stone, and brought it to Mother-Corn. They said, "We are the three Stars that come up in the East. We know the pipe smoked to us." They were Red-Star, Yellow-Star, and the Big-Black-Meteoric-Star. So Mother-Corn had the stone made into a pipe.

When the pipe was made and filled with native tobacco Mother-Corn called the Prairie-chicken, and said, "You must carry this pipe to the God in the Southeast." So the Prairie-chicken took the pipe and flew to the Southeast. It was gone for some time, and when the Prairie-chicken came back it said, "The God in the Southeast received the pipe and smoked." Mother-Corn again filled the pipe with native tobacco and called on the Prairie-chicken again, gave it the pipe, and told it to go to the God in the Southwest with it. The Prairie-chicken flew away again and was gone for some time. When it came back it said to Mother-Corn, "The God in the Southwest has received the pipe and smoked." Then Mother-Corn took the pipe again and filled it with native tobacco, called the Prairie-chicken, and said, "Take this pipe to the God in the Northwest." The Prairie-chicken took the pipe and flew away again to the Northwest. When it came back it told Mother-Corn that the God in the Northwest had received the pipe and smoked. Again Mother-Corn filled the pipe, gave it to the Prairie-chicken, and it flew away to the God in the Northeast. The Prairie-chicken came back, and said, "Mother-Corn, the God in the Northeast has received the pipe and smoked." Then the pipe was filled again and the Prairie-chicken was called to carry it to Nesaru, which it did. The Prairie-chicken flew up into the heavens, and said, "Nesaru has received the pipe and smoked. Other animal gods also smoked with Nesaru." Then Prairie-chicken said, "Mother-Corn, these journeys were very hard. The wind was blowing hard, sand-stones were thick, the little stones struck upon my feathers and made white spots upon them. Flying through these hard winds gave me power to fly through storms. The stones hit upon my feathers and made white spots upon them. I wish to remain as I am now." Mother-Corn said, "It is well. You shall be as you are always." (This is why the Prairie-chicken has white spots upon its feathers.) "As you have carried the pipes yourself to the gods, so it shall be to all people who shall make a sacrifice to the gods that they themselves must go through the smoke ceremony, that the gods may receive the smoke offering from the person himself who makes the offering."

In the smoking Nesaru let the gods know that he had given his consent to Mother-Corn to have people upon the earth; and that the gods were also to give their power to the people and protect them. So it was the place of the gods to help Mother-Corn whenever she called upon them for help.

After they had smoked to the gods there came a Dog running into the camp and telling Mother-Corn that one of the gods, the Whirlwind, who stands a little to the southwest, had been slighted in the smoke ceremony and the Whirlwind was angry. Then the Dog said to Mother-Corn, "That God, the Whirlwind, is coming. Be quick and do something for the people, for the gods in the heavens promised you aid when the people should be in trouble." Mother-Corn stood up and spoke, saying, "Nesaru and the gods, I want help, for the Whirlwind is coming to destroy my people!" A woman stepped in front, and said, "I will be the one to save the people." She stood up and was turned into a Cedar-Tree. Then there was a noise in the heavens and a Rock fell by the Cedar-Tree. A voice spoke from the heavens, and said, "I am the Big-Black-Meteoric-Star. I shall assist the Cedar-Tree to save the people." The people then ran up to the Cedar-Tree and around the rock. The Whirlwind came, and some of the people ran away, some going north, some west, some south and some east, and when the Whirlwind struck these people it changed their language. The people who stood upon the Cedar-Tree and the Rock remained as the Arikara. When the Whirlwind struck Mother-Corn she vomited red water, and after the water there came out a red ear of corn. Again she vomited and threw up yellow water, which was followed by a yellow ear of corn. Again she vomited, and there came up black water and a black ear of corn. Now she vomited and there came up white water and a white ear of corn. The Whirlwind passed the people and it turned back and came to Mother-Corn. It said to her: "You slighted me in your smoke. I became angry. I have left behind me diseases, so that the people will become sick and die. You wanted your people to live forever, but I have left sickness behind, so that it will fall upon the people who are proud and dress fine; but always remember when you offer smoke to the gods to give me smoke towards the last, so that I shall not visit the people very often." The Whirlwind went on. The Cedar-Tree spoke, and said: "Mother-Corn, the Whirlwind twisted my body until, you see, it is bent in many places. Let me remain this way. Let the people know me as the

'Wonderful Grandmother.' They shall place me in front of their medicine-lodge and they shall have a ceremony that I shall give them when they place me in front of their lodge." Then the Big-Black-Meteoric-Star said: "Mother-Corn, I wish to be known as the 'Wonderful Grandfather.' I shall sit by the Wonderful Grandmother, in front of the medicine-lodge, so that the people will always remember that it was I who saved them from the Whirlwind." Then the Dog spoke, and said: "Mother-Corn, I brought the news. I followed up the people from where they came out from the ground. I am always to remain with the people, so that I may guard their camps and villages, and when enemies are approaching their camps or villages I shall let them know by my barking. My spirit is up to all the gods. My flesh is good to eat, and the grease of my body is curative for sores. Let the people in all their ceremonies kill me and offer my flesh to the different gods in the heavens. Let the medicine-men use my fat for their sores." Mother-Corn was satisfied.

Mother-Corn then stood up and said: "My people, this corn is for you. They are seeds. You shall plant them, so that in time you can offer this corn to the gods also. This will be done to remind them that I was once Corn up in the heavens and was sent down to take you from the ground. These people who have scattered out shall be your enemies. The people who have gone to the Southwest you shall call 'Sahe' (Strike-Enemy); the people who have gone to the Northeast you shall call 'Pichia' (People-of-Cold-Country); the people who have gone to the East you shall call 'Wooden-Faces' (Iroquois), for they shall wear wooden-faces in their ceremonies. The people who have gone to the South you shall call 'Witchcraft-People', for they shall understand how to practice witchcraft. They will understand the mysteries of the Owl, Woodpecker, Turkey and the Snakes." (These were the Wichita.) Other people also were named at this time.

Mother-Corn stayed with the people until she had taught them the bundle ceremonies. When she had completed telling them concerning these ceremonies, she told them that she was now to go back to the place where they had come from and that they should sing the bundle songs that she had taught them. She also told them to bring all of the children's little moccasins, and to tie them together and place them upon her back; that it was time now for her to go. She then told them they must take her to the river and throw her in. The people did not understand this, as they kept up the singing in the night. When daylight came they looked behind where Mother-Corn was sitting, and there they found that she had turned into an ear of corn. The buffalo robe that she had about her was tied to the corn. It was told the people through the village, and the people came with their children's moccasins and placed them with Mother-Corn. Then the priests took Mother-Corn and the robe to the river, and threw her into it. For many years she did not return, but one fall, when they were having their bundle ceremonies, a mysterious-looking woman entered the lodge where the bundle ceremony was being given and they finally recognized her as Mother-Corn. She taught them some more bundle ceremony songs and before daylight disappeared, and was never seen again.

FOOTNOTES:

[5] Told by Star.

5.
THE ORIGIN OF THE ARIKARA.[6]

In the forgotten days of old there stood unnumbered people in the dark and gloomy cave down deep in the earth. They were wanderers, not knowing where they came from nor where they were going. In the midst of the blinded multitude there stood the Corn, the Mother of the tribe. For many days they stood in this condition and longed to see if there was any better world. Whereupon, the Mother-Corn called and selected the four fastest birds. She sent one to the east, as she thought, one to the south, one to the north, and one to the west, to look for a better world to live in. The birds went as they were directed and were gone for some days. They all returned, but without any good news to tell to the Mother. Whereupon, they were sad and discouraged, until there came forward from the crowd a tiny animal who thought himself capable to lead the people out of darkness into light. He told the Mother-Corn that he would make an effort to look for a better world. The Mother-Corn was glad to hear it, and consented to let him try to do what he could. Another came and said he would assist him, and still another came to offer his help. The first one was a long-nosed Mouse, or a Mole; the second was a Skunk; and the third was a Badger. The first went and started to dig upwards. He toiled until he was exhausted. Then the second went and worked until he gave out. Then the third came and labored on the same thing, until he was almost exhausted. The Mole made his second attempt and worked very hard. When he was about tired out he ran his nose into a new and better world.

He saw a very faint light, but he could not go further. He returned, and told that he had an idea there was light. The people felt much pleased, and encouraged. The Skunk began to widen the path, and worked hard until he succeeded. He got out; but the sunlight, being too strong, blinded him, and so he turned back and told the people that there was a sun which lighted the world. The people were more pleased, and were very anxious to see it.

The Badger came forward again with his strength and worked on it, widening the path so that the multitude could march out, one by one. After his hard labor he went through, but because he was tired he lay down. He saw the skies, the sun, the mountains and all that there was on the earth.

The sun went down, the stars appeared and the Night came. The Night saw him there and visited him, but the animal was asleep. The Night put forth his hands and held the Badger's hands, touched him on his head and on his neck, then went on his way. Light came again from the east, the stars disappeared and the moon also. The Badger awoke from his sleep and saw the sun rising in the east. He felt satisfied with all he had witnessed. He turned to the people and told all this to the Mother-Corn. Immediately the Mother-Corn marched ahead and stopped at the opening. The opening was somewhat small, but she tried hard to put her head through. The next step she went through as far as her legs. Then she marched out, and all the people followed.

Nesaru from the heavens saw the Mother-Corn and talked to her. He had his mercy on her and he taught her how she should live. He gave her power to use in the times of need. The whole multitude cried for joy. The Mother-Corn started out on a long westward march. All followed, as in a triumphant procession. After many days of marching they came to a wide expanse of water. There they stood on the shore. The Fish came and told the Mother-Corn that he would make way for them. The Mother-Corn gave her consent, because she knew that the Fish had the power to do so. The Fish went into the waters, and thus the water parted. The Mother-Corn led, and they all marched on dry land, but there stood high walls of waters. After a long march they came to the shore, and the waters came together. This was the first obstacle they encountered.

They went on their march again, and here they came to their second obstacle, which was a very thick forest, that no one could go through. The Owl came and volunteered to make a way for the people. So he went and blew down trees, the path was cleared, and the people all went on. They then came to the third and last obstacle, which was a very deep ravine that no man could walk down and up. Then one bird, the Kingfisher, said he would make the way. So he did, and all the people went across. Now they went on. They came to an open prairie. Here they saw a buffalo, a very large animal, whose horns seemed to reach to the sky. The people were amazed, and were very much afraid of him. They could find no way to kill him. But the Mole, the Skunk, and the Badger agreed to work together once more. The Mother-Corn was willing to let them do so. The Fish also said that he would be the one to kill the animal. Where the animal stood there was a very beautiful lake where he had always gone to get his drink. The three went and worked under the surface of the earth. They made many holes all around the animal. The three returned, after they had made all the ground loose about the animal. The animal started, and went toward the lake for water, while the people watched, to see what would happen to him. He came to the shore, and while he was drinking the Fish went up into his mouth and into his throat and into his stomach. Inside, he worked with his fins and cut the animal very badly. The animal ran, then got into the loosened ground. Finally he fell, bled and died. The Fish then came out. All the people came and were very much surprised because of the appearance of the animal. They were afraid of him, so they worshiped him. The hairs on him were grass. The horns on him were trees, with thick bark. The end of his nose was a big, black sunflower. Most of his outside appearance was in the form of Mother-Earth. The blood from the buffalo sank down into the earth, was hardened and became a stone, and from this stone later on they made their pipes. They butchered the buffalo and divided his flesh among the different sacred bundles in different villages. They counted and kept all the joints in the animal, and they are preserved in the bundles.

Then, again, they went on westward, and after many days they stopped, and separation took place. The Mother-Corn called a council, and they all met together. The fowls, fishes, and animals all agreed that they would separate from the people. They gave as much power as they could spare to the Mother-Corn. The Mother-Corn was very thankful, because she was to get her food from any animal that she should like. Besides, she was to get all her clothing from them. At last, the Mother-Corn separated from the animals.

This will give an idea to all how the Arikara originated under the earth. Yet it seems a mystery to us, and it is for us to solve.

FOOTNOTES:

[6] Told by Hand.

6.
THE ORIGIN OF THE ARIKARA.[7]

A long time ago, when I was about thirteen years old, we heard that smallpox was coming from the east, so that we all left our village and went north in order to get away from the smallpox. As we journeyed west we came to many buffalo. My father and I went to kill them. My father killed a buffalo cow. Then he called out, with a loud voice, that he had made a buffalo holy, and called a certain old man who was then the keeper of a bundle.

The old man came and sat down with us. He filled his pipe and smoked to the different gods in the heavens. After smoking he pulled up some wild sage and waved it upon the buffalo. After this he took his knife and cut the skin of the buffalo. Then we all helped skin the buffalo. After we had skinned it, the old man took his knife and took the meat from the back. Then he took the tongue out and carefully cut the meat from the tongue, breast, heart, and lungs. He carefully laid the meat, heart, tongue, and lungs aside, and said, "These things are holy. The rest of the meat I will take home and divide among other old men. You take the meat, tongue, heart, and lungs and jerk it and dry it and when we get to our village we will have the ceremony." The holy meat was jerked and dried. My people took care of it, so that it was very fine. When we returned to the village this meat was put upon my back and some upon the back of my father, and we started for the priest's lodge.

The bundle had been taken down by the woman who had charge of the bundle and placed in the west of the lodge. The women had all left the lodge. We entered the lodge. We were then told to take seats by the priest. The tying of the bundle is peculiar, for it is not a common tie. The man who untied the bundle was told to notice the tie closely so that he could tie the bundle up again in the same way. The bundle was untied and the things inside were spread out, the priest being particular to place the four animals that brought the people out from the earth. They were the bear, badger, mole, and a tiny mouse with a long nose. There were all kinds of birds in the bundle. There were also two pipes in it. One of the pipes was black, the bowl also being black. The bowl of the other pipe was red, the stem was white, and many bird feathers were tied along the pipe stem. The only thing tied upon the pipe was a white shell. The priest took the gourds, and told the errand man to invite four men and four women into the lodge. The women were placed according to the four world quarters. Hoes made of the shoulder-blade of a buffalo were given them. The four men were also placed by the women, and these men were given bow and arrows. The four old men now took up the gourds and the four men and women danced. This was continued until all the songs were sung. The women and men placed their implements at the altar, then went out.

Before the ceremony, many presents were given—such as ponies, blankets, buffalo robes, calicos, guns, etc. Some of these things were given to the old men, who sat on each side of the entrance. Most of the presents were given to the priest, who made offerings of willow sticks to the gods. After this, he told us the origin of the bundle and of our people:

A long time ago, Nesaru made people. They were giants. They displeased Nesaru, and he sent mighty heat upon these people, so that they turned into stones—such as we now find in the earth. This is why we call stones our grandfathers, for stones really are people, who were once wonderful and powerful.

Again, Nesaru made people. This time they were small, but were wonderful. They also displeased Nesaru, so that he sent word to all the animals to hide; that he was going to make the water rise from the earth. The animals held a great council, and it was decided to take most of the people under the ground with the assistance of the Badger, the Mole, and the long-nosed Mouse. The Fox was to act as runner and errand man.

The people lived under the ground for many years. These animals did not like to see the people live under the ground, so the Badger, the Mole, the long-nosed Mouse, and the Fox assembled. This means, not one Bear, one Badger, one Mole, one Mouse, and one Fox, but many of each kind. The animals decided to dig through the earth upwards, and see what kind of land there was above. So the Bears dug, but they all gave out. The Badgers dug and they gave out. The Moles then dug and they gave out. The little Mice then dug until they dug through the earth. Then they went back, for their noses were worn sharp.

When the Mouse came back the other animals saw that his nose was worn sharp. The Mouse said: "From this day on, my people will have long, sharp noses on them, so that people will know that through the long-nosed Mouse they came out from the ground."

The Mole was the first one to stick his head out and see the bright sun. He was blinded. He went back into the ground, and to the animals. He told of the brightness outside of the earth, that he had been blinded. So it was decided by the animals that the Mole should always stay under ground and should never see the sun. The Mole was satisfied, so he always stayed under the ground.

The next to go through was the Fox. The rays of the sun now entered the hole, and the Fox could see, but he could not get through. So the Badger dug away until he dug through. The Fox went again, and crawled out of the ground. He made a loud shout, like a man. The Fox ran around through the country and returned to the people and reported what he had seen outside on the earth.

The animals were all satisfied. They all said, "We will lead these people out, so they can live upon the land, where they can see the sun, moon, stars and heavens." The Bear was told by the long-nosed Mouse to make the hole larger. The Bear went to digging. The people followed. The people did not have any clothing on, neither did they have anything to eat. They did not know how they lived under ground. The Bear made the hole larger, so that there was light where the people were. The long-nosed Mouse went out first, then the other animals followed, then the people followed out.

The people were now standing upon the ground. They did not know which way to go. But there was a woman who seemed to know. She did not speak to the people. She told a man that she was not a real woman, that she was a grain of corn, and that she had understanding of what they were to do. She told the man that they were upon an island in big waters, that they were put there so that they could dig through the earth and could get out.

These people who were taken under the ground by Mice were grains of corn. Now they had turned to people. The long-nosed Mouse now spoke to the woman, and said, "Some of the people will have to remain in this water, for we can not cross this big water unless some do." The Mouse then told a man to get into the water. When the man got into the water he turned into a long gar-pike. It now swam across the big water, but failed to reach the land. So the Mouse commanded one of the women to get into the water and to swim and join the gar-pike in the water. Now, there was a bridge across the big water. The two fish became tired and gave way, so that some of the people fell into the big water, and turned into fish. The others went on.

After they had gone upon the mainland the people began to pick up flint stones and use them to cut with. But another thing happened: There was darkness upon the earth. Some of the people could see plainly in the dark. These people did not know what to do, but the Mouse led the people through the darkness, and led them out from the thick timber. The people who were left in the timber turned to Owls.

The people went out of the timber and again there was trouble, for there was an earthquake. The land opened, and took some people into the ground. It left a deep chasm, so that the people were not able to move on. The Bear went to the chasm and made steps on each side, so that the people went down and climbed up on the other side.

Now they traveled west. Again there was trouble. Thick timber was in the way. The Mouse called on the gods. A Whirlwind came and made a pathway through the timber. The Whirlwind did not hurt the people, although it was mad, for the powers had not called on it for help.

Now they went on until they came to muddy water, in what is known as "Pawnee" country. Here they found many things to wear and to eat. The first bow was then made. The long-nosed Mouse died and the people skinned it, leaving the skull in the skin. The Bear then died, and its skull was also taken from it. So also with the Mole, the Badger, and the Fox. These were wrapped up in a bundle and when the Pawnee invited them to attend the bundle ceremony they went and received their ceremony. Mother-Corn and also a ceremony were given to them. All the bundles received their rituals, each being different from the others.

While they had their village here the Arikara dressed the ear of corn as a woman. They went down to the River and threw it in, the old men singing, "Mother, you are going to the island in the big water, where we came out. Find out for us what we are to do, and how we are to live. Come back to us and tell us how it was that we came here." The corn drifted down the stream and disappeared.

Many years afterwards the Arikara were living on the Muddy (Missouri) River, when, in the fall, there came a strange woman into the lodge where they were having a bundle ceremony. The people took no notice of the woman. The woman left the lodge and went to another lodge and took her seat under the bundle. The people in this lodge fed her, but they did not notice her any more than to feed her, as they would feed any other woman. She left and went to another bundle lodge, always taking her seat under the bundle. She went to all the bundles, but none of the people noticed her. She went to the last bundle, and as she entered, the people noticed her as a strange woman.

She went to the altar and sat down under the bundle. The old man was told that a strange woman had come in. The old man took notice of her and recognized her. The old men were gathered and the ceremony that the people got from Muddy-River country was performed.

This woman was sitting in front of the bundle. When the ceremony was gone through, the woman spoke, and said: "I have returned. I found out that you people came out from the ground. You met obstacles. You came through by the aid of the animals. You went to a strange country. You met difficulties. You overcame them by the power of the animals. It was all done through me, for the four world quarter gods are my father. I prayed to the gods and to Nesaru for help for you, so that your people would live. You threw me into the river and asked me to return. I have come to you again. I shall hereafter come to you in dreams, and tell you about these things that are in this bundle. I will be present with you always. I shall leave you words. Now, before I go to my fathers in the heavens, I want to tell you to tie me upon the bundle and give presents to it by clothing the ear of corn. In all of your ceremonies, always offer it some corn and meat. It will always gladden me to receive anything you people eat. I must go."

The woman disappeared, and there, where she sat, lay an ear of corn. People saw the corn. Other old men were sent for, so that they might also get an ear of corn to tie upon their bundles. But the people all blessed themselves with the corn that the woman had turned into. The people tied ears of corn upon their bundles. Some tied hides upon the corn and hung them up on the walls. This was done for the people who had given buffalo meat to the bundles.

So the old woman disappeared; but the old men in the tribe claimed that the woman came to them in their dreams and taught them songs and how to make sacrifices of dried or fresh buffalo meat, and also the smoke ceremony.

FOOTNOTES:

[7] Told by Bear's-Tail.

7.
THE ORIGIN OF THE ARIKARA.[8]

I sacrificed several buffalo to Mother-Corn. I used to sit and listen to the songs. Finally the old men gave me a seat with them, so I learned to sing the bundle songs. The old men then told us this story:

A long time ago, the Arikara lived under the ground. There were four animals who looked with pity upon the people, and these animals agreed to take the people up on top of the earth. These animals were the long-nosed Mouse, the Mole, the Badger, and the Fox. The Fox was the messenger to the people to tell them of what the animals were doing. The Mole was the first to dig. He ran back, for he was blinded by the brightness of the sun. The animals went out. The people came out of the earth, the Fox being in the lead. As the people were coming out there was an earthquake. The Arikara came out. The other people were again held fast by the earth.

These people who came out from the ground then journeyed west. They came to a place where the earth shook, so that there was a chasm or a steep bank. The people waited and cried. The Badger stepped forward and began digging, so that it made a pathway for the people. The people went across this place, and continued their journey.

All through the journey Mother-Corn was absent, for she had gone into the heavens to ask the gods to let the people live. The obstructions that the people met were wonderful powers. This strange being was known as Sickness (Natogo). After all the people had passed the first obstacle they sat down and gave thanks and made offerings to the gods.

Again they went upon their journey, and it stormed. In front of them was a river. They could not cross it, for it was very deep; but a Loon was sent by the gods. The Loon came to the people, and said: "Your mother is traveling in the heavens to help you. I was sent by the gods to open up this river, so you could cross and go on your journey." The Loon flew across the river, flew back, then dived and came out on the other side of the river. The river was opened; it banked up on each side; the people crossed over and the waters came together again. Some people were left on the other side.

Again they journeyed, and they came to a place where Mother-Corn stopped and said: "The big Black-Wind is angry, for we did not ask it to come with us, neither did we make it one of the gods to receive smoke. But," said Mother-Corn, "the Black-Meteoric-Star understands this storm; it will help us." Mother-Corn went on, and said: "Here we are. We must hurry, for the big Black-Wind is coming, taking everything it meets." "There is a cedar tree. Get under that cedar tree. Get under that cedar tree," said Mother-Corn. "The Black-Meteoric-Star placed it there. The Star stands solid, for its right leg is cedar; its left leg is stone. It can not be blown away. Get under its branches." So the people crawled under its branches. The Black-Wind came and took many people, notwithstanding.

The people came out, and they went on. They came to another difficulty—a steep mountain bank, and they stopped. The Bear came forth, and said, "I will go through this place first." So the Bear went to digging steps for the people. Steps were made on both sides and the people went across.

After they had been gone for some time, a Dog came up, and said: "Why did you people leave me behind? I shall be the one that you shall kill, and my meat shall be offered to the gods. I shall also fix it so that all animals shall make great medicine-men of you. My father is the Sun. He has given me all this power. I will give my power to all animals, then I will stay with the people, so they will not forget my promise to them." The people were thankful to the Dog.

FOOTNOTES:

[8] Told by Four-Horns.

8.
THE ORIGIN OF THE AWAHO-BUNDLE PEOPLE.[9]

We were told by old people that our people came out from the ground. There were some people who came out from the ground, for there was an earthquake. Some of the people were thrown out and put upon the surface of the earth. There were some who were cut off, so there was crying, wailing, and many noises. The heavens heard, saw the people's distress, so the heavens sent Mother-Corn to them. When she came to them, under the earth, she had a robe about her shoulders. This robe was painted red. There were upon the robe five moons and one star.

The people rejoiced when they saw Mother-Corn. She told them that she had come to lead them out from the earth; that on her robe she had had pictured the gods who had sent her and promised her help. She then turned around and spoke to the gods, asking them to make a way for the people to get on the earth. For several days the people waited, but no help came. At last a Badger came out, and said, "Mother, I will make a way for the people." So the Badger began to dig and dug through the earth. The Sun saw the Badger come out, and said, "It is well. I will make your head black; also your fore legs, so that all people and animals will know that you are the one who dug for the people; and you shall also be a great burrower."

The people came out from the ground, led by Mother-Corn. The people were facing west, and then they walked westward. As they went on, they came to thick timber. They stopped. Crying and wailing went up from the people. Mother-Corn lifted up her voice to heaven, but there was no help. Out from the company flew a Screech-Owl, who said, "Mother-Corn, I will make a pathway for your people." The Owl flew through the timber, and made a pathway, so that the people could go through. The Owl and the Whirlwind are enemies. The Whirlwind left sickness, while the Owl gave roots and herbs to cure diseases.

The people went on farther, and a cry was raised,—"He is coming! He is after us!" It was a wonderful animal, known as "Cut-Nose." This was an animal that had been a man, and he had gotten away from the people, but he was now trying to kill these people. His horns were long, and they seemed to touch the heavens. The people ran until they came to a chasm which they could not cross. Mother-Corn called on the heavens for help. The people began to cry and wail. For seven days the people stood. At last a bird came, and said, "I will do my part." The bird flew through the bank, and came out on the other side. The Mole then came and tried, but did not succeed. Now the Badger was again called on, and he it was who made the banks to fall on each side, so that the people crossed.

After the people had crossed, there was rejoicing; but as they went on they came to another obstacle. There was wide, thick ice and deep water. Birds of every description tried to make a way for the people, but their power failed them. The birds faced the ice and water, but with no result. Up in the heavens was seen a bird that circled around until finally it flew downward and struck the waters, and it broke the ice. As it came towards the people, the bird said: "Mother-Corn, I shall make a way for your people. They shall cross this big lake and they shall continue the journey." The Loon then dove, and wherever it went, the ice and the water were thrown far away. There was now dry land, so that the people crossed over.

The Loon spoke to Mother-Corn, and said: "This is your last obstacle. You shall meet no more." Mother-Corn began to teach the people ceremonies and rituals, after they had crossed, even giving the people things to put in bundles. When the things were together the people went through a ceremony. Corn was lacking for Mother-Corn, and Mother-Corn herself said: "Let us wait till to-night. You shall have a Mother-Corn, and you shall wrap her in a bundle. She will hear your prayer, and she will keep you from diseases and give you plenty in your fields." That night Mother-Corn disappeared; but under the bundle was an ear of corn wrapped in a robe that Mother-Corn had had. She had taken and washed it with sweet flowers.

As they went on they found where the other bands had camped. They picked up and ate what meat had been offered as a sacrifice to the gods.

"Awaho" means "left," "deserted," for this band was left, and was the last people to come out from the ground. So they were called "Awaho."

The other bands had gone ahead a long distance. When the Awaho band reached the place where the other bands had camped, they found bits of meat that had been offered to the gods. This is the way the people secured their food.

When the Awaho people made a sacrifice of meat they took a piece off and buried it, eating what remained. The ceremony of burying the piece of meat was to teach the others that this band was at first covered up and was under the earth. These last people, the Awaho, who came out from the earth, knew all the ceremonies and taught them to the others. As they went on, these people were attacked by enemies and they were nearly all killed; but the keeper of the bundle hid it under a bank. The bundle was wrapped up with calfskin. After the people had gone into camp, the women begged that they might get the bundle. So a man went with them, and they got the bundle. A ceremony was performed to purify the contents of the bundle. A wooden bowl of water and a bundle of yellow flowers were used to cleanse the sacred objects. The flowers were dipped into the water; then they shook the flowers over the fire and dropped a few drops; then the flowers were made to touch the contents of the bundle. The people then ran down to the river and bathed. The next day sacrifices of meat were made, for now the people and the bundle were cleansed. These were the first ceremonies given by these people.

We are told by old people that Nesaru made the people; that the people were bad, and that they were destroyed. But Nesaru made some animals to take kernels of corn under the ground. These kernels had been people, and were turned to corn by Nesaru. In this way the people lived under the earth for many years. This is why the animals brought them out from the ground and why they were led, with the consent of the other gods, by Mother-Corn, who was sent by a god in the heavens, who had a field of corn.

FOOTNOTES:

[9] Told by Hawk.

9.
MOTHER-CORN'S VISIT TO THE ARIKARA.[10]

Many, many years ago the Arikara, according to their traditions, were journeying west, when they were told by Mother-Corn, who had led them out of the ground, that in time they must dress her up and put her into the river; and, as they should put her into the river, the priest should say, "Mother, make haste and return to us." For many years the Arikara continued to journey west, until at last they made a permanent village of earth-lodges upon the Missouri River, opposite the city of Washburn.

The old men thought that it was now time to send Mother-Corn down the stream. She was to go to the place from whence the Arikara originally had come, and if there were rituals and ceremonies or medicines that had been left behind, Mother-Corn was taken from the bundle and painted. A dress of tanned buffalo hide was wrapped and tied about the middle of the Mother-Corn.

While the painting and dressing of Mother-Corn was going on, the crier went through the village, telling the people that Mother-Corn was going to leave them for a period of time; and that she was going to the place from whence their forefathers had come; and that the Arikara people must all bring old moccasins for their little children; and that these must be placed with Mother-Corn, so that she might carry the old moccasins to the place whence the people had come, so that the young ones might grow up in life as the Arikara people had grown through their journey, meeting different obstacles, and finally settling down into a village; that the children might grow up; that although difficulties might beset their daily walks, they might overcome them by the power of Mother-Corn, and grow up to be strong men and women.

[Rituals were now recited by Standing-Bull, which were the same as those recited when they were painting the chief.] After the reciting of the rituals the people took up Mother-Corn and took her down to the river. All the people turned out to witness the act. But before the priests threw Mother-Corn into the river, her head upstream and her feet downstream, the children's moccasins were tied about her waist. The people offered their prayers to Mother-Corn, and after praying they all began to cry. But Mother-Corn had disappeared in the Missouri River, and had gone with the current.

Many years afterwards, a woman returned to the village of the Arikara, and as the bundle ceremonies were being given the woman visited these ceremonies. At last, when she visited one ceremony, a man recognized her as Mother-Corn. He placed her under the bundle. She let them know that she was Mother-Corn, and she taught them many ceremonies and songs that night, and she said that she always would be present with them; that she would never forget them; and that the gods in the heavens had promised her and her people length of life. That night Mother-Corn disappeared, and she has never been seen since.

FOOTNOTES:

[10] Told by Standing-Bull.

10.
MOTHER-CORN'S VISIT TO THE ARIKARA.[11]

In olden times during time of need, it was the custom of the Arikara to have a ceremony in which some old man would make offerings to the gods and to the Mother-Corn. It seems that in this ceremony all the old men who were offering smoke wanted the Mother-Corn to come, so that they might have plenty of corn, for it was planting season.

Mother-Corn was pleased to have smoke with the people. She started from the east to visit these people, and came to many other camps, and finally came to these people. She went into the medicine-lodge, and all the people followed her in. She spoke to them and the people cried for joy. The woman was pretty. The people brought her all kinds of food, but she would not eat. She told them the only thing she could eat was a bird, such as a chicken or duck. She stayed with the people many days and taught them many lessons. But the people were now hungry for meat, for the buffalo roamed far away from them. They had plenty of corn, and yet they liked to have meat, but all the animals were now scarce. One wise old man took a sacred pipe and laid it before the Mother-Corn for an aid, because he knew that she had all power from Nesaru.

Mother-Corn was much pleased to smoke with them and to offer smoke offerings to the father. Then she asked certain women to make moccasins for her, and they did so. The people gathered together in the medicine-lodge, while Mother-Corn sat on the altar. She put on one pair of moccasins and arose. She walked very slowly and when she had gone about twenty steps her moccasins were worn out. Then she sat down, put on another pair and walked again. When she had walked about twenty steps her moccasins gave out again and she tried the third pair, but they too wore out. She put on the fourth pair, and that pair brought her back to the altar. Her walk around the fireplace meant that she had walked a long way off in the west, and that the way was very hard. At last she told the people that she had seen some buffalo; that in four days they were to be seen. The men watched every day after that, and early in the morning of the fourth day the buffalo were seen.

The men went out and killed many buffalo on that day and there was plenty of meat. Thus, much respect and honor was paid to Mother-Corn.

After some days another party went on a buffalo hunt, but Mother-Corn stayed with those who stayed in the village. It was not many days until enemies attacked the village. But what few men were there fought very hard, and at last they were driven out of the village. They took Mother-Corn out of the medicine-lodge, but before she escaped she was killed, causing great grief among the people. The Arikara were defeated on that day. They took Mother-Corn and buried her. From the place where she was laid, grass, weeds, bushes, trees, and almost everything sprang up. When the people who had gone out on the buffalo hunt came back they were much grieved and troubled on account of the loss of Mother-Corn.

FOOTNOTES:

[11] Told by Hawk.

11.
HOW THE PEOPLE ESCAPED
THE BUFFALO.[12]

A long time ago, when the people came out through the ground, a woman led them through the country. This woman was known as "Mother." The people were human beings, and they had among them all kinds of animals, except the buffalo. The people traveled over the land, and as they went by a large lake a monster came out from the lake, which looked like a buffalo, for it had horns.

The people ran, crying that this animal was coming. They said this animal was what they called "Cut-Nose". The animal kept coming, and at the same time there seemed to come out from under him buffalo. The buffalo caught up with them and they killed some of the people. The people made canyons behind, so that the buffalo could not cross, and thus they escaped the buffalo at this time.

While they were going on, a Whirlwind came. The people prayed to Mother to help them, and she turned around and told them to give presents and smoke to the Whirlwind. The Whirlwind scattered some of the people over the country. The crowd went on again.

While they were going on, again a noise was heard from behind and the people said, "The buffalo are coming after us again, and Cut-Nose is in the lead." The people ran until they came to a big timber, which was very thick. The Owl came, and tried to make a path for the people through the timber, but he failed. The people cried for help. The Badger worked a little, digging through the ground, but it also failed. The people then looked around for help. The Coyote and the Dog came, and they opened a way through the timber.

These people went on, and again they looked around, and they saw the buffalo coming on again. The buffalo ran after the people, Cut-Nose with them, and they began to kill the people. The people came to deep water. There was no crossing, and the buffalo were killing them. They called on the Mother for help. The Dogs came, and said, "We will try to make a pathway through this water for the people," but the Dogs failed. The Loons came.

They made an opening through the waters, and the people passed through, and the buffalo were left on the other side.

The people after crossing this big water went on, and again they looked, and there was Cut-Nose coming with the buffalo. The people ran. They came to a canyon. The people prayed to Mother to make a pathway. She called on the Kingfisher, who struck the bank on each side, but failed. The Mole came, struck the bank, and failed. The Badger then came and dug on each side of the bank. The banks fell, and thus a pathway was formed for the people. They went across, and by this canyon they made their village.

There Mother held ceremonies for the different bundles. Other people had also received bundles, but no ceremony. The Awaho bundle people were the last to come, and they were the last to receive all the ceremonies from Mother, so that these people understood all the ceremonies. They were known as "Awaho" (Left-Behind), for these people, it seems, had been left behind when the people had come out from the ground. So, as the Awaho people went west, following up the trail, they found, when they reached the camp sites of the other people, meat offerings to the different gods. There was nothing left behind by the other people that the Awaho people were afraid to pick up, for they claimed to be under the protection of the gods, and therefore had a right to all the things that are offered to the gods. So the word "Awaho" means "Left-Behind." Also, it means that they may take and cook again, and eat any meat offering to the gods that has been left behind. Other people who had bundles could not do this. They were afraid to touch meat that had already been offered to the gods.

FOOTNOTES:

[12] Told by Hawk.

12.
WHY THE BUFFALO NO LONGER EAT PEOPLE.[13]

A young man went into a village in the night, and he heard the people talking. He could understand their talking, and by peeping into their tipi, he found out that they were Buffalo people. They were talking about killing the people. So the young man investigated. He climbed up on a high arbor that was in front of the tipi, and there he took hold of a human head. He felt around over the place and he found human meat. He climbed down from this place, and went to one of the large tipis, and here the people said, "We will soon do what we are to do. We will get these people out of the ground, and we will kill them." Now the young man hid.

By the side of the hole where the people were to come out there was a cut in the side of a steep bank, so that, as the people were coming out of the hole, the bulls circled around them and drove the people up into the cut, where they hooked them and killed them. The young man saw the people, men, women, and children running to the cut, and as they went they were singing and crying. The people were coming out from the ground.

The young man felt sorry for the people, so that he went up among the hills. A strange man met him, and told him all about what was going on. He said: "These Buffalo have just started to eating people. I do not like it. Take this bow and these arrows, go to your home, select many young men and tell them to make bows and arrows. Lead them to this place, and kill and scatter the Buffalo so that they will not kill or eat any longer."

The man took the bow and arrows, and the strange man stopped talking. The man found out that the strange man who was talking to him was the bow and arrows themselves. The young man then went to the village. He called many young men together and told them to make bows and arrows.

When the people had many bows and arrows the man led them to the place where the people came out from the ground. There the Buffalo were just trying to make the circle again around the hole, when these men attacked the Buffalo and commenced to kill them. Some of the Buffalo ran on to where the human meat was, and cried: "Get some of the meat and place it under your arm so that we can eat it whenever they let us alone." But the people kept on killing, till they had scattered the Buffalo out. So they became buffalo and never ate the people any more.

The young man saved the people, and these people came out from the ground and made their home close to the village; but finally the last people who came out from the ground went south, away around by the mountains. Later they came back to Dakota, and joined their brothers again, where they have been ever since.

FOOTNOTES:

[13] Told by Star.

13.
WHY THE BUFFALO NO LONGER EAT PEOPLE.[14]

A long time ago, while the Arikara lived together in the village, it was customary to hunt in the spring. The story I am about to tell was told to me by my father; for I was very small when this story was told by the priests:

On one of these hunts, the people failed to find any buffalo. Women and children began to cry from hunger. The men took long journeys hunting buffalo, but they could not find any buffalo. At last the chief was approached by the women and asked to call on the priests for aid.

The chief then took the sacred pipe from his bundle, filled it and took it to the lodge of the priests of the Knot-in-the-Tree (Critatao) bundle. The chief priest took the pipe, smoked it, and offered the smoke to the gods. After smoking, he said: "It is well. We will open the bundle and call on the gods to help us get buffalo. We will make an offering of gifts to the gods, so they will send buffalo." The chief was glad, and went to his own tipi. The chief then called on the crier to tell all the people to be silent. The priest had his tipi cleaned and the bundle was taken down and the other priests were sent for. After the priests were seated and all the chiefs had entered, the priests took up the gourds and began to recite a ritual that had been given to the people by the Buffalo. After the giving of presents—native tobacco, black handkerchiefs, robes, and blankets—the priests stopped singing. The chief priest then went out and cut a long pole, brought it to the lodge and tied gifts upon the pole. The pole was then set in front of the lodge. Gifts were placed upon the pole for the southeast God, the southwest God, the northwest God, and the northeast God.

Again a ritual was recited for the buffalo to come. As they recited the ritual the errand man stood by the pole and would strike at the pole with an ash stick that he had in his hand. "Come, buffalo," he would say, at the same time striking the pole. "You spoke to our people and promised to come when the people were in need of food." After reciting the ritual the priests recited other rituals.

The buffalo came about three days after the ceremony. The chief ordered the crier to go through the village and let the men know that a whole buffalo was needed for the ceremony. The men went out, and a whole buffalo was brought into the ceremonial lodge. All the people were then invited, and the old priest told the people the following story:

There was a village of Buffalo. They were human, but had horns. When the Buffalo wanted meat they met in a tipi where there was the sacred bundle known as Knot-in-the-Tree. In this tipi a ritual was recited. It took them four days and four nights. The third night, the Buffalo gathered about the tipi where the ritual was recited. The fourth day, the four Buffalo who sat singing the ritual arose and went to the side of a hollow cottonwood tree that stood by the side of a steep bank. By the tree was an ash pole. Here the whole village of Buffalo stood around the hollow tree. Another ritual was recited, then the pole was taken up and the tree was struck three times. The fourth time, the people were heard crying, and some were singing. The first to come out was a man by the name of Cut-Nose (Kritstaricuts). This man seemed to be wonderful, for he always escaped his enemies. Next came a multitude of people. They escaped and ran over the prairie, the Buffalo killing them. Cut-Nose ran and returned to the hollow tree and crawled in, when the flood of people stopped coming out. The people were killed, and were taken to the tipis, where they were cut up, and their meat was placed upon the arbor they had built.

In one of these runs there was one boy among the people who was very handsome. A Buffalo cow chased the boy away out among the hills, but finally gave him up. The boy kept on running until he came to a deep ravine. There was a thick bush of dogwood covered with grapevines, in which the boy hid. Now and then the boy would go hunting, killing small birds for his food.

One day, as the boy was crossing a ravine, he saw sitting on the side of a hill a fine-looking woman. The woman's hair was not braided, and she wore a buffalo robe. The robe looked white. There was a peculiar look about her that attracted the young man. The woman arose and started west. The young man followed. Towards evening the young man came to a bottom land, and there he saw a fine tipi. The young man went to the tipi, and there in the tipi sat the same woman. The woman spoke to the young man, and said, "Come in." The young man went into the tipi and sat down. The young man was hungry, and looked at the woman pitifully. The woman put her hand under her robe and pulled out a lump of pemmican. She handed the pemmican to the boy, and the boy ate the pemmican. When he was filled he hid the pemmican under his arm. The woman spoke to the boy, and said, "You may lie with me; cover yourself with part of my robe." So the boy lay down and went to sleep. When he woke up the woman was sitting by him, but there was no tipi. The woman then talked to the boy, and said: "I ran after you, but I did not intend to kill you. My people are Buffalo, and there is a way for them to become real animals. I selected you to be the one to turn them to buffalo, and then my people will not eat your people any more. My father is the chief of the Buffalo, and I learned by listening how your people can be saved. I want you to go with me to where my people are, and you will learn how my people kill your people. We must go and pass between the bulls who are stationed upon high hills. There are four circles of Buffalo bulls. We will have to pass through these stations unobserved."

They began the journey, and they went between the Buffalo bulls who were stationed as sentinels. They went through all the circles of the Buffalo, and now the next thing was to enter the tipi where the ceremonies were held, for this was the place where the woman's father lived. The woman covered the young man with her robe and they entered the tipi. Some of the Buffalo in the tipi, who were awake, said, "I smell human flesh," but others said, "It is because we have just had a killing." So nothing more was said about the smell of human flesh. The next day the boy was covered with buffalo robes, and, as all of the Buffalo went out, the boy felt safe.

In the evening the Buffalo came back to the lodge. They were human, only they had horns and tails. These people brought in fresh meat and it was the human meat. Now they cooked the meat and ate. After eating they lighted the fire. It died out, then the girl said, "Let us go out, I want to show you something." So they went out. The boy saw arbors everywhere in the village. The girl told him to climb upon one of these arbors, and he did so. There he saw fresh meat of human and some bodies not yet cut up. The boy was scared. He told the Buffalo woman that he did not want to go into the tipi any more. The woman said: "Now you have seen bodies of people. These people eat your people, and for this reason I have brought you here to help your people, so they can overcome the Buffalo and kill them. When your people have killed the Buffalo and have driven them far, then they will eat of the grass which Nesaru intended that they should eat." The woman continued, and said: "Then your people will come out of the ground, and you will teach them the ceremony the Buffalo used to sing before they went out to kill you. Come, go with me into the timber. You must make many bows and arrows." So they went into the timber, and the woman said: "Now you remain here. Do not be afraid, for the Buffalo are now going to sit and sing the songs, calling your people together where the tree is. Come, now go with me to where your people come out."

They went, and there stood an old hollow cottonwood tree. Near its base was a knot where there was a hole. Lying by the tree was an ash stick, about six or seven feet long, and about eight inches in diameter. "Now," said the woman, "do you see the stick? That stick is what makes the people come out of that hole. You shall use that stick, only do as I tell you, and you will be successful. Cut-Nose is the one who sits at the entrance, so when the Buffalo gather about the tree, he is the first to come out. He gets away. The Buffalo do not try to kill him, for he helps the Buffalo."

So the young man lay down in the timber, while the woman returned to the camp. When it was daylight he began to make bows and arrows. He made many. Every night the woman would come to visit him. She gave him buffalo meat. Thus the young man stayed in the timber and kept on making bows and arrows. Often the boy went into the village with the woman and listened to the singing of the Buffalo. The woman told the young man to hurry in making the bows, for it was nearly time for the ceremony to be over, then the Buffalo would march out where the tree stood. The young man now hurried to make the bows and arrows. For two days the ceremony was kept up, the singing continuing all night. The third day the boy had many bows and arrows completed. The woman came in the night and gave the boy long sinew strings for the bows. The boy put the strings upon the bows and now the weapons were completed. The woman took the boy into the camp, and there he heard singing. At the end of every tenth song the singing was stopped. In a little while the singing would be resumed. Now the woman told the boy that the next morning they would have to return to the timber and bring the bows and arrows.

The next morning they went and brought the bows and arrows and placed them at the foot of the tree, the bows already strung, and the arrows with the bows. "Now," said the woman, "as soon as you see the Buffalo coming towards the tree, you run up to the tree three times, and you will hear shouting. As soon as you hear shouting, wailing and screaming, pick up the bows and arrows and give them to the men and tell them to shoot at the Buffalo. Do not give any bows and arrows to the first man who comes out, for his name is Cut-Nose, and he it is who helps the Buffalo. Give out the bows and arrows, then pick up your own and go to killing the Buffalo. As soon as the Buffalo see that your people are killing them they will run. Keep right after them, and scatter them as much as possible." The boy placed all the bows around the tree. Then he and the woman hid under the bank.

As the sun was coming up in the east the rattles were laid down. Singing was stopped. There was mourning; everybody seemed to be crying. Then the Buffalo all came to the ceremonial lodge and stood around until the four priests came out, who walked towards the tree. The young man jumped out from his hiding place. The first man, whose name was Cut-Nose, came out with a war-whoop. The people came up next in the hollow tree. There seemed to be a strong current coming out from the hollow tree, blowing the people up and out of the tree. But as the people came out, especially men, this young man picked up bows and arrows, and placed them in the men's hands, and said: "Make haste; shoot the Buffalo. Kill them. Do not be afraid of them." As each of the men came out, the young man handed him bow and arrows, and told him to shoot and kill the Buffalo. It was not long until the young man had a large company of men with bows and arrows killing the Buffalo. As the Buffalo ran towards their village some one shouted and said: "Get some of the meat! Carry it with you, and whenever we stop running we can have something to eat!" So the Buffalo people ran and picked up human meat and each placed the meat they picked up, under the arm, and ran. The human meat that they placed under their arms became a part of their flesh, for the people ran after them so closely that they finally became buffalo. (This is the reason why the Arikara used to cut the meat from under the shoulder and throw it away. This meat the Arikara would not eat.)

The young man and the Buffalo woman now went to the tipi of the bundle and took the bundle. The people came back and burned everything that was in the village. Then they made a new camp and the Buffalo woman, who was now married to the young man, taught the people the songs and ceremony that go with the bundle. So these people became a part of the Arikara.

When this story is told, everybody keeps quiet.

FOOTNOTES:

[14] Told by Snowbird.

14.
THE GIRL WHO MARRIED A STAR.[15]

In olden times, when the people lived upon the Missouri River, there was a village. In this village there were two girls who, in the night, slept outside of their lodge on an arbor. As they lay upon the arbor one night they were talking about the different young men in the tribe whom they liked. One of them spoke of liking a certain young man, while the other girl said she did not like any one of the young men in the tribe. She looked into the sky. She saw a bright, red star in the heavens towards the east. She said, "There stands the star I like, and if that star were here upon the earth I would marry him." The girls then went to sleep.

In the morning they arose and went after water. As they were coming back, they saw a porcupine. The girls ran after it and tried to kill it. One of them said she wanted to get the porcupine, for she did not have enough quills to do some of her work. The porcupine got to a cottonwood tree that was near the river. The girl climbed up after it. The other girl wanted to go home and get an axe, so that they might chop the tree down, but this particular girl who had said she liked the star, said, "No, I can climb." She climbed the tree.

As the girl climbed up the tree the tree grew higher. The girl disappeared, so the girl on the ground went home and told what had happened. The girl kept on climbing for the porcupine until she reached another world. When the girl came into the other world she recognized that she was in a strange country, and she began to cry.

The porcupine had turned into a man. The man spoke to the girl, and said: "Why do you cry? I am the Star that you saw and that you said you liked. I went down after you. I turned myself into a porcupine and you came after me, and now you are here in my home." The girl saw that the man was not young, but middle-aged, though he was very handsome. She stayed with him and liked him, but the man kept going away every night. She cried every night, for she wanted to return to her people.

Many years afterward she gave birth to a male child. When the child was born his mother found the picture of a star upon his forehead. This woman told her husband one time that her son wanted some wild turnips and that she wanted to go and dig some. The man told her that it was very well for her to go and dig these turnips, but that she must not go to the valleys to dig them, but she must go to high places. While she was out digging these turnips she thought about her people and she began to cry. Then she went to the valley and dug into the ground to get a turnip. Her digging-stick ran through the earth. She removed the dirt, looked down, and there saw the people underneath. She then knew that she was far away from her people.

She covered the place and began to cry. While she was crying, she heard the voice of a woman calling her. The voice said, "My daughter, why are you crying?" She said: "I am crying for my people, for they are far away below us. I was brought up by my husband, who is a Star." The woman told the girl not to cry, for she would help her. She took the girl to her cave in the side of a cliff, and there she confronted her. She told her to tell her husband that when he went to kill buffalo he must take all of the sinews from one whole buffalo, and that when she got these sinews she must bring them to her; that she would make a sinew string that would reach to the ground below.

The girl went home. She told her husband that she wanted to do much sewing, and that she needed sinew, and she wanted him to get all the sinew that was in a buffalo, so she could have many sinews and would not have to ask him for any more. The man went hunting. He killed a buffalo. He took all the sinews he could find. He forgot, however, to get the two sinews that are in the shoulder-blade of the buffalo. He brought the sinews to his wife, and gave them to her.

One time when the man was away she took the sinews to the old woman and gave them to her. The old woman was glad. She said: "Now go to your home, and remain there. I am to make a string, and when it is complete I shall let you know, so that you then can go to your people." The girl went home and stayed, but once in a while she visited the old woman's dwelling place, and she saw the piles of string that the woman was making. As soon as the old woman had completed the string she told the girl, and said that the girl must come to her place when her husband was away. The young girl had also made a long string of sinew, but it was separate from the string that the old woman had made. This she carried herself when she went to the old woman's place.

They now went to the valley, and there dug a hole, large enough for her with her boy on her back to go through. After this was done she went to her home, put the child upon her back, covered it with her robe, then tied the robe about her breast. She went to the place. The old woman had brought a large-sized stick, which was laid across the hole, and the sinew was tied to the pole. The girl tied the sinew about her body and covered her hands with a part of her robe. She slipped down, down, down the string and after a time she found herself at the end of the string. The earth was still far away. She took her own string and tied it to the string that she was tied to. She fastened herself to the other string after untying herself from the main string, and slid down upon it. She slid down until she had reached the end of the string, and she was at the height of the highest tree from the ground. She saw that she could not get down, so she made a loop and put her foot in it so that she stood upon the string, and there she hung.

When the woman's husband came home he found her missing. He went out to hunt for her. After a time he came to the place where the hole was, and there he saw the woman hanging on the string. He went and took up a little stone, about the size of his thumb. He took this to the place where the hole was dug. He placed the stone on the string, then said, "Now I want you to slide down on the string and hit the woman upon the head and kill her, but do not harm my boy." As he let go of the stone a sound was heard like that of thunder. The stone slipped down upon the string and struck the woman on the top of the head and killed her. As the woman fell down towards the earth the boy slipped out from the robe upon the back of the woman and fell on the ground, but was not hurt.

The boy stayed around where the woman was lying, for he was now about five or six years old. He would go off from his mother during the day and in the evening he would come back, crawl under the robe, and nurse at his mother's breast. He did this for many days. At last the boy had to leave her, so he went on west from where his mother lay. He came to a patch of squash and also to a cornfield. This he went through, taking corn from the stalks and eating it raw. He returned to his mother and sat there.

In the morning, the owner of the field, who was an old woman, went into her field, and there she saw a child's footprints. She was so glad to see the footprints that she went home and made a small bow and some arrows. She also made a small shinny ball, and a stick. The old woman thought if this child was a girl it would choose the shinny ball and stick, and if it was a boy it would choose the bow and arrows. In this way she thought she could tell whether the child was a boy or a girl. The old woman made these things, and took them into the field and left them there.

The next day, the boy went back into the field. There he saw these things upon the ground. When he saw the bow and arrows he jumped at them and picked them up. When he had picked them up he went through the squash field and began to shoot at the squash. The old woman came upon the boy and caught him. She called him her grandson, and told him that she had been waiting for him for a long time. She took the boy home.

The boy was satisfied to be with his grandmother. His grandmother, before she went into the field, used to roast a lot of corn. Then she scattered this corn in her lodge, then would go out hallooing, and say, "Blackbirds, come and eat of this corn that I have prepared for you." The blackbirds would come in flocks and enter the lodge, and there they would eat the corn that she had scattered over the ground in the lodge. Then the old woman would go into her field and would leave the boy at home. Sometimes the boy went out to hunt rabbits and little birds. In the evening, when the old woman came home from the field, she used to take a lot of corn and put it in her corn mortar and pound it. She made mush out of the pounded corn. There was a curtain of buffalo hide in the lodge. The old woman, after she had made the mush would place a bowl of it behind the buffalo hide curtain. Why she did this the boy did not know.

One day when the old woman had gone out to feed the blackbirds, the boy began to roast some corn. After he had got a big pile roasted he went out and yelled, and said, "Come, blackbirds, I have prepared for you the corn that my grandmother told me to prepare; come and eat!" The blackbirds came in flocks into the lodge. The boy went out and stopped the smokehole with a piece of buffalo hide, then went into the entrance and stopped up the passageway with a dry buffalo hide, so that the birds could not go out. The boy then picked up a club and said: "Blackbirds, I am going to kill you all, for you have been eating my grandmother's corn all this time. You shall not eat my grandmother's corn any more." So the boy began to run around in the lodge after the birds, hitting them with the club and killing them. He killed all of them, and placed them in a pile.

When the grandmother came home the boy said, "Grandmother, I have killed all these blackbirds that have been eating your corn all this time; they shall not eat your corn any more." The old woman appeared glad. She told the boy that he had done right in killing the birds. The boy said, "You may cook the blackbirds, a few at a time." The old woman really was not glad, for these blackbirds guarded her field for her. She owned these blackbirds. She placed them upon her robe and took them out. She brought them to life again, and said: "My blackbirds, fly away." The old woman returned to the lodge.

The old woman then told the boy that he must go into the timber and cut a good-sized ash and some dogwood. The boy went and brought back the ash and the dogwood to the old woman. The old woman scraped on the ash wood, cutting it the right length for the bow and the right length for the arrow sticks. She then told the boy to go west of her lodge and to throw the arrows into a pond that he would come to. The old woman told the boy that when he should throw these sticks into the water he should say, "Grandfather, I want the strongest bow that you can give me, and I want wonderful arrows with it." So the boy took up the sticks and went west from the lodge. He came to the pond. He threw the sticks into the water, and said, "Grandfather, give me the strongest bow that you can give me, and wonderful arrows." Then the boy returned into the lodge. The next morning, the boy went down to the pond, and there he found a black bow and four black arrows. These he picked up, then he went home.

The boy went to hunt every day, for now he had a good bow and good arrows. One day the boy saw the old woman place a bowl of mush behind the buffalo curtain. When she went out to her field, the boy wanted to see what made the old woman place the mush behind the curtain, for each time she pulled out the wooden bowl that had held the mush, the mush was gone. The boy went to the curtain, lifted it up, and there he saw a serpent, with its big eyes looking at him. The boy then said: "Ah! I see now! You are the one that eats all my grandmother's mush." The boy took his bow and arrows and shot the serpent in the head and killed it. The serpent made one great, big noise, fell back, then slipped down into the pond. After the serpent had slipped down into the pond the water spread out and formed a lake.

When the old woman came home, the boy said, "Grandmother, I have killed the big monster that was lying behind the curtain, for he was eating all your mush." The old woman said: "My grandson, you did right. I am glad you killed him. He has gone back into the lake, where he will always remain." The old woman really was not glad, but mad, in her heart, for she now saw that the boy had supernatural powers. She wanted the boy killed. She did not let this be known, for she decided that she would send him to the place where her wild animals were stationed. When the boy was gone the old woman cried and mourned for her husband, who was the serpent. She said (without the boy hearing), "My grandson, you have killed your grandfather."

The next day, when the old woman was ready to go to her cornfield, she told the boy that he must not go to a certain place, for the place was dangerous. After the old woman had gone into the field the boy went to the place where the old woman told him not to go, and there he went around looking for the dangerous place. He finally saw a mountain-lion coming towards him, ready to leap upon him, but he gave a command for the mountain-lion to stop, and the mountain-lion obeyed. The boy went and led the mountain-lion to the old woman's lodge. He told the old woman to come out, that he had an animal for her which she could ride when she went off to her field. She told the boy she was glad he had brought the animal, but she whispered to herself, "Well, you must be a wonderful boy, but you shall be killed." She then took the animal into the brush and told it to go away, for the boy was wonderful and might kill him. As the old woman was going towards the lodge she whispered to herself, "You must be a wonderful boy, but I will send you to a place where you can not kill my animals."

The old woman then told the boy that he must not go to a certain mountainous place, for the place was dangerous. The boy went, notwithstanding. There he found the cinnamon bear coming to attack him. He commanded the bear to stand still and do nothing. The bear obeyed. The boy then caught the bear by the ear and led it into the old woman's lodge. He said: "Grandmother, I have an animal for you that is very tame. You can ride it, and you can have it to help you clear your field." The old woman appeared to be glad, but she was not. She took the bear, led it into the timber, and told it to go away, for the boy was wonderful and might kill it.

The old woman then told the boy that he must not go into the southwest country; that there were four wonderful men there. The boy went, though, and he saw the four wonderful men killing buffalo. These men looked up, and said: "Here comes Old-Woman's-Grandson. He is a wonderful boy." The boy got to where the men were skinning a buffalo cow, and, as the entrails were taken out, the boy saw that the cow had a calf in her and that the men were taking it out. The youngest man picked the calf up, and said, "Old-Woman's-Grandson, take this to your grandmother." The boy jumped away from it, for he was scared. When the youngest of the men found out that the boy was afraid of the calf he kept on trying to get it near him. Old-Woman's-Grandson kept running from the calf, until he came to a tree. He climbed the tree. The young man placed the calf on the forks of the tree, so that the boy could not get down. The men then went home with their meat. The boy stayed in the tree many days, and nearly starved, when one of the men came, and said, "Old-Woman's-Grandson, if you will promise your grandmother to us, I will take this calf down." The boy said, "I promise." So the man took the fœtus down.

The boy came down from the tree and went home. The old woman, when she saw the boy coming back, said that she was glad to see him again, for she thought that he had been killed. She asked the boy where he had been, and what had kept him so long. He told her that the men had tried to kill him by placing the fœtus next to him. He also said that he had had to promise the men that they could have her if they would remove the fœtus from the tree; that he had promised and they had removed the fœtus. The old woman said that it was well, but that she had one thing to ask of them, and that was, that they should give the boy something in return for his grandmother. So the boy went and visited these men in their lodge. He said to the men: "What is it that you are to give me in return for my grandmother? My grandmother has consented to marry you men." The men said, "We are to give you a bow and arrows." The boy went home and told his grandmother that they were to give him a bow and arrows. The old woman said: "That is good. That is what I wanted you to have. Go to the lodge of the wonderful men, and as you enter the lodge, rush around to the south side of the lodge, where there are five bows set up. The middle bow you shall take up, and say, 'This I shall take in return for my grandmother.'" So the boy went into the lodge with the men. He ran to the south side of the lodge, and there the bows were, leaning up against the wall of the lodge. He picked up the middle bow and arrows. The men were all sorry that the boy had picked out the middle bow and arrows. The boy then told the men they could go to the home of his grandmother and be with her. Itaque hi ad anus domicilium venerunt ibique cum ea sicut cum uxore concubuerunt.

After they had left the lodge the old woman called the boy, and said, "Take this flute and play around the lodge of these wonderful men." Her grandson took the flute and went to the lodge of the wonderful men and there he played the flute, circling around the lodge. When the wonderful men heard the flute they were scared. They closed up their lodge with earth. The boy kept on whistling, for he was now taking revenge on them for trying to put the fœtus next to him. The men lived on the meat they had in their lodge, but this soon gave out. These wonderful men died of hunger, and were never to be known again upon the earth.

The young man went home and told the old woman that the men had died; that the earth had closed in on them. The old woman was satisfied. Then she thought, "Now is the time to send my grandson to dangerous places, so that he may be killed, and I shall be freed from him." The grandmother told the boy he must not go upon a certain hill, for the place was very dangerous. The boy went upon the hill, and there he found a den. He entered this den. He found that it was a den of Snakes. Before the boy entered the den he picked up a little rock and took it with him, and when he sat down in the lodge in the den of Snakes he placed the stone upon the ground and sat upon it as upon a stool. The Snakes were glad to see the boy. The boy said: "Well, you people are here in a den, trying to catch eagles. It seems to me that you people ought to welcome a stranger to your den. It seems that I am not welcome." The Snakes all spoke up, and said: "Old-Woman's-Grandson, you have spoken the truth. We will now give you something to eat." So one of the Snakes spread out hot coals and placed a long gut for the boy to eat. This was rolled in the hot coals until it was burned a little, then it was taken off and given to the boy to eat. The boy took up the gut by each end and placed the ends together. He commenced to tell the Snakes that he had come a long way and was very hungry; that he would very much like to eat that, but as he saw that the gut was not well done he could not eat it. He twisted the ends, and the Snakes whispered to one another, "Why, he knows that this is a Snake, for he has twisted the head off." As he twisted the head off he saw plainly that it was a Snake. He threw the head into the fire and placed the gut upon the hot coals again and roasted it some more. He left the Snake burning until it was burned so that he could not eat it. Once in a while he would hear the Snakes say, "What are you waiting for?" Then some Snake would disappear in the ground and would come up and try to get into the boy's rectum, and they would hit the rock and tell the rest of the Snakes that they could do nothing, that the boy was sitting upon a rock.

Soon the boy said: "It is well that we should tell some tales." The Snakes said, "Let Old-Woman's-Grandson tell his story first." But the boy said, "No, you tell the first story." The leader, the chief of the Snakes, who was very large, said that he would tell a story. This Snake began to tell a story of how a girl had said she liked a certain Star, and how the next day, the girl found the porcupine; that the porcupine had climbed the tree and she also had climbed it; that the tree had stretched and went up to the Star that the girl liked; that the Star had married this girl; that a boy had been born to them; that the boy had the image of a star upon his forehead; that the boy's father was a Star; that the woman had requested her husband to get sinews for her; that this woman had given the sinews to an old woman that she might make a sinew string; that the Star had forgotten to get the two sinews under the shoulders of the buffalo, and for that reason the string had proved too short to reach the ground; that the Star had missed his wife and child; that he had hunted and had found a hole in the ground; that the Star had picked up a stone and had sent it down on the string to kill the woman, telling it to save the child; that the child had stayed around its mother until she had decayed; that the child had gone to the old woman's lodge and gone into her field; that the old woman had made bow and arrows and a shinny ball and stick, had placed them in the field, so that she might find out whether the child was a boy or a girl; that the boy had come and picked up the bow and arrows and had gone to shoot at the squash in the field; that the old woman had caught the boy and had taken him home and made him her grandson, when he became known through the country as "Old-Woman's-Grandson;" that through the boy's powers he had scattered the blackbirds through the earth; that the mountain lions were also scattered through the earth; that the bears were scattered through the earth; that even the water-serpent had been killed and sent back to the lake; that the serpent had been the boy's grandfather; that the boy had killed the old woman's husband, who was really his grandfather; that the boy had visited the four wonderful men; that the four wonderful men had found a fœtus in a buffalo cow; that they had tried to put it next to him to scare him; that the boy had climbed the tree and they had placed the fœtus at the forks of the tree, so that he could not climb down; that the boy had offered his grandmother to the four wonderful men to get the men to take away the fœtus and let him down the tree; that the boy had taken the wonderful bow and arrows from the four wonderful men; that these men had married the old woman; that afterwards the boy was given a flute by his grandmother, which was done that he might take revenge upon the four wonderful men; that he had killed the four wonderful men, so they would be no longer on the earth; that now Old-Woman's-Grandson had come to the people who were sitting in a den trying to catch eagles; that he now sat before them, sitting on a rock; that he was given a long gut to eat, but that he had found out that it was a Snake; that he had thrown it in the fire and burned it. "This," said the leader, "ends our story. Old-Woman's-Grandson will now please tell us a story."

The boy then began to tell about himself, just as the Snake had told it, following it up. "Now," said the boy, "as the people in the den were sitting around, listening to Old-Woman's-Grandson, there came a strong wind from the southeast, and blew towards the den." As the wind blew from the southeast the Snakes on that side went to sleep. Then he told about the wind coming from the southwest, and those Snakes in the southwest went to sleep. Then the wind from the northwest came, and those who were there went to sleep. Then the wind from the northeast came, and those Snakes on that side went to sleep. Now the boy waved his hand all around the circle, and all went to sleep as they were listening to Old-Woman's-Grandson.

In the center was the fire. There was a long stick in the form of a circle around the den, and all the Snakes were upon this, in a circle all around. The boy now arose, took his flint knife, and commenced to cut the heads on the stick around the fireplace. When he came to the last one, it opened its eyes and woke up. It ran into a hole, and said, "Old-Woman's-Grandson, watch yourself, for hereafter I am your enemy." The Snake disappeared in the ground.

Now the boy went out and went home, and he told the old woman that he had killed the Snakes. The old woman was then afraid of the boy. She knew that he was wonderful. After that, the boy watched himself in all of his journeys, because of the Snake he had failed to kill. Whenever he wanted to drink he had to go among the rocks, where he would drink from the pools of water. The boy could not drink water from the springs, for the Snake was always ready to jump into his mouth. When the boy wanted to sleep he lay down, placing the arrows he had as follows: One outside of each knee and one outside of each shoulder, sticking them in the ground. The bow the boy used for a pillow. Whenever the Snake approached him sleeping the arrows fell upon him, so that he woke up.

The boy became very sleepy one time, for he had not slept much during all this time. He lay down, and placed the arrows as usual, and went to sleep. The Snake came. One of the arrows fell on the boy, but failed to wake him. Another fell on him, but he did not wake. Then another arrow fell, then the last one fell, but the boy did not wake. The Snake crawled up to the boy, and, as it reached his stomach, the boy, in his sleep, reached for his knife and made motions to cut the Snake, but the Snake kept on going. The boy kept trying to get the Snake, but it went into the boy's mouth. It crawled up into the skull and nestled itself there. The boy lay there as though dead; but the Snake knew that the boy was not dead. The Snake remained there until the boy dried up and became nothing but a skeleton.

The father of the boy studied hard as to how to get the Snake out of the boy's skull. Although the boy was dead, the skull was the living part of the boy. The boy's father then found a plan for getting the Snake out. A storm came from the north. It rolled the skull over and turned it up so that the hole in the skull was upward, and as the rain fell it ran into the skull and filled it with water. This did not drive the Snake out. The father called on the Sun to get nearer to the earth, so as to heat the skull so that the Snake would have to jump out. The Sun moved towards the earth and heated the skull. Soon the water was boiling. It became too hot for the Snake, and finally the Snake crawled out of the skull. No sooner had it got out than the boy stood up and caught the Snake by the neck. He then took up stones and hit the Snake's snout, so that it made its head short. Then the boy sat down upon a rock and began to rub the Snake's teeth upon it, and said, "Now you must promise that you will never bother people again." The snake promised. The Snake, as it was turned loose, said, "Once in a great while I shall bite people, but not often." The boy reached for the Snake and it disappeared, — that is why the people get bitten by snakes once in a great while.

The boy then returned to his grandmother, who was glad to see him. The boy told his grandmother that she was now free to do as she pleased, for he was going off; that the country was now free from wild animals. So the old woman disappeared, and the boy went southeast to the village of the people.

There the boy told his story, and the people knew that he was the son of the girl who had climbed up the cottonwood tree. The boy did many wonderful things for the people, and the people said that it was through the boy that the people could travel through these wild countries, for now all the wild animals had been scattered and were not as fierce as they had been before. The old woman had disappeared and had made her camp in some other place. The boy died after he had cleared the country of all the wild animals.

There is an old cottonwood tree on the south side of the Missouri River, close to the place known as Armstrong, that the people claim is the tree that stretched upward, taking the girl up to the Star. Still south of the cottonwood tree is the place where the people say the stone is that was thrown down by the Star and which killed the woman. To the west is the lake where the monster fell. At the southwest of the cottonwood, it is supposed, was the Snake den. The people say that to-day snakes are very numerous there. South of this place, among the hills, is where the mountain-lion is supposed to have been. Close to the cottonwood, in the timber along the Missouri River, is the place where the bear is supposed to have been.

FOOTNOTES:

[15] Told by Yellow-Bear.

15.
THE GIRL WHO MARRIED A STAR.[16]

One night two pretty young maidens were sleeping on top of a summer arbor. They were ill with monthly sickness. One said, "Kario, I love that little bright star, and I wish it was my husband." That same night, while sleeping, the girl was taken away up in the heavens, to live with her husband, he giving her instructions what to do and what not to do. He could not always stay at home, as he was in the chase. One of the instructions was that the woman should never dig up an Indian turnip at slough-like places. While her husband was away, the woman determined she would discover the mystery connected with her husband's injunction. When she had dug the turnip she saw what the mystery was. She saw the people living on this earth looking like crawling insects.

When she saw this she cried and cried and cried. She went to an old woman for comfort. The old woman saw that the woman had been crying; so she questioned her and found out her trouble. The woman answered that she could easily be relieved of her trouble. So she advised her to collect all the sinew she could find from the meat her husband brought.

The girl told her husband she wanted all the sinew there was in all the game he killed, even the very smallest piece. Her husband did as she asked, not knowing her intention. When a very large number had been made the woman took the sinew and went to the old woman, who began to make what she had promised to make for her. "Come back in a few days," she said, "and I will have the thread ready for you. Remember to come when your husband goes on a long chase."

The husband started on a chase, and the girl went to the old Woman's lodge and told her that her man had gone. The old woman got her sinew rope and fixed it around the woman's waist and began to let her down—down—down. She went with her first child on her back. The place she started down was where she had dug up the forbidden root. The twine was lacking about twenty or more feet. The old woman was an old spider, it was found. Old Spider-Woman did not have enough cobweb and sinew, so the woman hung on the rope, not able to touch the earth.

When her husband returned he found his wife missing. He began to look for her. He thought at once of his order, and so went out where she usually dug. He found a stick in the grass. He discovered the rope tied around the stick, and his wife and child hanging away down near the earth. He picked up a stone and talked to the stone, saying, "Do not harm the boy, but kill the mother." Down—down—went the stone, and struck the young mother on the head; it cut the rope and her body fell; but the boy was safe. The boy stayed by his mother's body and fed himself at her breast for a time. Her body began to decay.

The boy went off and got into a cornfield, not knowing that it was corn. When lonesome he returned to his mother. The owner of the field was an old woman. She saw the footprints in her field. She wondered what it could be. She made a little ball and a crooked stick, also a little bow and arrows. She thought if it was a girl she would take the ball and crooked stick, but if it was a boy he would take the bow and arrows. When the old woman looked she found the little fellow had taken the bow and arrows.

The old woman was very joyful. The little fellow had done much damage to her squash vines with his bow and arrows. She went out and hid in the field, waiting for the little fellow. The boy came as usual with his weapons and the old woman sprang out and caught him, saying, "Oh, atine, atine; you are to come home with me."

She took the boy home and gave him food, such as fresh corn mush, succotash, and squash. The boy seemed quite happy. When the woman went out to work he amused himself with his arrows, shooting little birds in the field, and on his grandmother's return he would bring the birds for her to eat. She was a happy grandmother, proud of her little grandson. The boy grew larger. When he began to make his own bows and arrows to his taste he began to bring home larger game, such as deer and antelope. His grandmother was still happier.

The boy's grandmother was accustomed to place under a curtain which was always closed, a big wooden pan of whatever they had to eat, before she went to her work. The boy, noticing this, made up his mind to find out what it was. While she was gone, he moved the curtain and beheld a huge serpent with large yellow eyes. The boy said within himself: "Ah! here is the one that eats up everything that grandmother puts here." He took his bow and arrows and shot and shot, until he killed it.

The boy's grandmother came in. The boy spoke up, and said: "Grandmother, I have killed the bad one that ate up everything you placed under that curtain." The old woman appeared glad of it, but was hurt at heart. She covered the serpent and placed it in a pool. The serpent said that he could not do anything, because the boy was gifted with a great mysterious power of his father. The dead serpent was the husband of this grandmother.

The grandmother, wounded at heart, planned to have the boy killed in some way. She forbade him to ever go into the timber near by, because there were all sorts of dangers there. In this timber, she said, was a bear that wanted to tear him into small strips. When the old woman had gone he started out to the forbidden place. He found the bear, captured him and thought he was strong and would do to haul corn and wood for his grandmother. On her return she saw the great, big black-bear tied. The boy spoke up, saying, "I have here a strong animal which will work for us." The old woman appeared to be happy, but felt hurt that the boy could have captured the bear. She was the owner of all animals around, both good and bad. She turned the bear loose and explained the case to the boy, saying she could not use the bear in any way.

One day the boy was gone all day and all night. His grandmother now thought him dead. Roaming around, the boy found a tipi. In the tipi were four strong-looking men. Around the fire was the meat of a whole buffalo and an elk. The boy stood on one side looking at the game. The men were playing with plum dice in a basket. The interest of these men was very noticeable. One man's nose got very dirty, but he would not move to clean it. The boy outside did not like it. He took his arrow and shot through the hole he was peeping through. The arrow cleaned the man's nose. The men rushed out and gave the boy a hearty welcome, for they had already heard of his wonderful doings. They took him in and gave him a whole buffalo to eat. He began to eat, and ate as much as usual. The men began to ask why he did not eat more. He said he could not, as he had had his fill. The men ate heartily. They cleared the meat that was before them. The men asked him to stay all night. They invited him to join them on a hunting trip.

Next day they started. They killed an elk. They dressed it and found a fœtus. As courtesy, the hunters took the fœtus and placed it before the boy to take home with him. The boy was affected. He asked them to remove the fœtus. He was standing by a tree. He started up the tree. The men, seeing he was afraid of it, moved it, little by little, toward him. They were afraid of him and were trying to do everything to get rid of him. The boy was afraid of the fœtus. He would not come down while it was in the way. The men came home. By and by a man was sent out to see if the boy was there. Coming to the spot he found the boy still there. The boy asked the man to remove the fœtus. He refused. He went home and reported all he had seen. In about four days the men came around and found the boy still there. They found him very thin, and suffering for food and water. He would not come down while the fœtus was there. The men made a conditional offer,—if he would deliver up to them his grandmother they would remove the fœtus. The boy said he would. They removed the fœtus. The boy started home at once. He told his grandmother what had happened and what he had done. Out of love for his life he had given her up to these men.

The grandmother was happy on his return. She said she would grant his request. About two days after, she and the boy started out where the men were. They stopped at the entrance of the tipi until they heard a voice from within asking them to step in. The boy said, "Nawa, I have done what I agreed to do. Here is my grandmother." "Ah ho! Ah hi!" they replied, "you were honest and have done as you agreed to do. That is the way for noble boys to do. As this is a bargain for your life we will do all we can for you to turn our power and skill over to you." Now they began to teach the boy the ceremony of catching eagles and of hunting. "It was our desire to have your grandmother, and as you have been true to your agreement, we are glad." All were satisfied. The grandmother and son then went home.

The next day the boy started out on the prairie for game. He met a camp of Snakes, mostly deadly Rattlesnakes, and there were all the other kinds of Snakes. They were glad to have him come. They invited him in. They gave him the best seat. He knew what danger there was to meet. So as he sat down he took out a smooth stone which he used for sharpening his knife, and placed it in his anus. The room was clean and there was a ridge around the fire for a pillow. Time and again he noticed a Snake disappear and attack him where he had defended himself. He knew it. They said: "He must be hungry. Give him something." They gave him a spleen. He took it and looked at it. He replied that he could not eat it raw; so he poked up the fire and threw the spleen in. It cracked and made the audience wild. The spleen was the teeth of all these Snakes. The boy knew the secret and could not be fooled so easily.

The Snakes, resting on the square pillow-like structure, demanded of the boy that he relate some happenings or stories, to pass the night pleasantly. He refused to be first. He agreed to take his turn with them. They began. Each Snake had for his subject the life of their guest and that of his grandmother. When all were through with their stories the boy began his story: "Nesaru commanded the winds to blow; at evening they stop, the trees stop rustling, the grass keeps on for a while, but they all fall asleep." This much of the story put a part of them to sleep. "Nesaru sends hurricanes of trials and hardships in our lives; the same to all kinds of trees and to large, deep rivers; they rage and beat against their banks, the water gets dirty, there comes on the gentle night, soft breezes, the trees quiet down, the rivers are calmed, the waters clear up and they are asleep." This was the end of the boy's story. The remainder of them fell asleep.

The boy thought of how he was to have been treated, and he decided to be avenged. He took from his belt his sharp knife and cut along a straight line on the square structure, cutting off the head of every Snake until he came to the last one, which slid away, saying as he went, "Old-Woman's-Boy, I will remember all."

As the boy left he was very particular as to how he should carry himself. Having gone many miles he thought all danger was over. He placed his arrows around him, bidding them to awaken him when danger was near.

While he was sleeping his enemy came. Before the arrow could give the alarm the Snake entered his body. Grasping his knife he cut his stomach open. Up went the snake's head to his breast. He cut his breast open. Up it went to his throat. He cut his throat open. Up it went, into his head, and rested there. His father above knew all of this. He sent a great wind which turned the boy's head over, so that his opened œsophagus turned toward the wind. Then came a hard rain, filling every corner of his head. The Snake's head would peep out of the boy's head, but the boy would say, "Old-Woman's Grandson is still alive." There came a scorching heat, and the water began to make the Snake peep out its head, but the boy would say, "Old-Woman's-Grandson is still alive." It got too hot for the Snake. It fled, and the boy sprang to his feet and caught it. "You will suffer punishment, and you will always be ashamed and crawl on your body in the dirt, your head down, avoiding all decent creatures that Nesaru made." He took the Snake and knocked his head on a flat rock until it was flat and its eyes were close to its mouth.

The reason the boy was afraid of the fœtus was that it was the time of the year when all young animals are as yet unborn, and the cluster of stars to which the boy's father belonged is never seen at this time to come up with the rest. The boy knew that his father could not be present to help him, and so he did not dare to do anything to help himself.

FOOTNOTES:

[16] Told by White-Bear.

16.
NO-TONGUE AND THE SUN
AND THE MOON.[17]

There was a young man in a village who wanted to be great. In olden times the chief thing among the people was to be a great warrior. The young men in those times used to go out among the hills, and then find a place to stand and mourn. They used to stay away from home four or five days without drinking or eating.

Now this particular young man went out alone, upon a high hill, to mourn. In the afternoon a little bird came to him, and said: "This is not the place where you should stand. I will show you where you must stand." So the little bird flew and the boy followed. The bird stopped at a certain place, and the boy stood there. Late in the evening a man came to the boy. The man was all painted red, and he said to him: "I am glad to see you. You are going to be my son, and I am going to take you with me now. All I want from you is your tongue." So the young man pulled his tongue out, cut it off and handed it to the man. As he handed his tongue to the man he fell down and died. It was now dark, and as the young man fell the Moon rose and saw this young man fall down, and the Moon said to himself: "That man who has killed this young man is always trying to do something that is not right. I know who that man is; it is the Sun. I know that he has taken this young man's tongue." So the Moon went to the young man and touched his feet, and the young man waked and sat up.

When No-Tongue saw the strange man he did not know what to do. He was not the same man who had taken his tongue. This man looked white, because he was the Moon. The Moon asked No-Tongue why he had given away his tongue and to whom he had given it. No-Tongue answered, "How can I talk without a tongue?" The Moon said, "Speak, and tell me." So the boy spoke, and he found that he was able to talk. So he began to tell what the man looked like. The Moon said he was sure that the man was the Sun. Then the Moon spoke to No-Tongue, and said: "The Sun was trying to kill you. No-Tongue, hereafter you shall be my son; but let your other father, the Sun, come after you first. I must tell you what to say. You will not be killed by the Sun. The Sun is coming for you to-morrow morning, and when you go up to our dwelling place (the heavens) he is going to show you some things that he has. You must now be careful not to take the new things that he has, but you shall take the old things. Take the old weapons. The Sun thinks a great deal of these old weapons." This is all that the Moon said. The Moon then disappeared.

In the morning, the Sun came to No-Tongue and took him up into the sky to his home, and said, "Now, my son, I want you to choose of these things that I have here." No-Tongue took the oldest things. When the Sun saw that No-Tongue took the best things—the oldest ones—he came out from his lodge crying, because this would give No-Tongue a long life, and would also make him become great, and this was what the Sun did not want of No-Tongue. He had thought that No-Tongue would surely take the new things. But if No-Tongue had taken the new things, that would have shortened his life and made it impossible for No-Tongue to become great. Then the Sun began to think of some way to kill No-Tongue, but he never could take back the things No-Tongue had taken, having promised them to him. As they came out from the Sun's lodge the Sun said: "My son, look. There is your home. Look all around you. You can see everything plainly. When you go home, after two days have passed, you must go on the war-path, and you will conquer old enemies. You will have all you want. You are to be great. But when you, my son, go home, give to me a white buffalo robe." So the Sun went away.

When night came, the Moon came out and spoke to No-Tongue, and asked what the Sun had said to him. No-Tongue told the Moon all that the Sun had told him, and the Moon said, "Do not give him the white buffalo robe, but give that to me, and get a dark-brown robe for the Sun." The Moon then began to tell No-Tongue what to do. He told him to get some white clay and make powder out of it, and then pour the white powder all over the robe, so that it would look white. So No-Tongue did as he was told to do.

When the Sun received the white buffalo robe, which really was not white, he was proud of it; furthermore, he was proud that his son had obtained it for him. One day he hung the robe out, and the wind was blowing hard. The wind shook all the white clay out of the robe, so that the robe turned to a dark-brownish color. Then the Sun saw that it was not a real white buffalo robe, and did not like it.

When the Moon and the Sun got together, the Sun said, "I am sorry for what my son has done to me, and now my dear son is going to kill him." The Sun had a son who belonged to another tribe, and this was the son who was to kill No-Tongue. So the Moon heard all that the Sun had to say.

One night the Moon saw No-Tongue, and told the young man all that the Sun had said. The Moon said that the Sun could not do anything to kill him. The Moon said: "The man that you are to fight with is going to try to shake hands with you, because he is your cousin,—not a real cousin, but because you are the son of the Sun and so is he,—so he is your cousin. He is the one who has been selected to kill you. But do not be afraid; I shall be with you and will help you all I can. Do not shake hands with the young man, your cousin, and if you must shake hands, do not shake with your right hand. Be very careful not to let him strike you first. If you should shake hands with him, strike him. You must not let him strike you first; and when you have killed him, cut his head off and put it under a big stone that shall be near you, so that the Sun will not make him live again. By placing the head under the stone the Sun will be prevented from bringing him to life." The Moon also said, "Be careful to do what I have told you to do." No-Tongue was glad. The Moon also told No-Tongue that the young man he was to fight with was named Little-Sun.

Two days after this some warriors went out on the war-path. Before they had gone far the Sun went to No-Tongue, and said: "My son, I am glad you are going on the war-path; I want you to kill a man for me. He is coming. He thinks he is great, but he is not. So kill him for me." The Sun said all of this, not meaning it, for he was planning that Little-Sun might kill No-Tongue. So the warriors started on the war-path, and in a few days they came to the place which they thought would be a good place to remain for a while. The leaders selected scouts to go out and look over the country. The scouts went up a high hill, and there they met the spies of the enemy coming up from the other side. These did not stop, but turned straight back again, and went and told the enemy, and of course the other scouts turned back and told their leaders that the enemy was coming. So in the morning, the two sets of people came together, and they fought a battle; but before starting the battle there was a man who stood in front of the enemy's line, and said, "No-Tongue, I want you to come and shake hands with me, for you are amongst those people." No-Tongue went to him, and when they were nearly together, everybody saw that the two were dressed so as to look very much alike, but they did not know that they were to fight each other; but the two knew that they were to fight, and that they were both sons of the Sun. No-Tongue did what the Moon had told him to do. He killed Little-Sun. Then No-Tongue's people defeated the enemy. They took many scalps, and returned home.

The Sun became mad at No-Tongue, because he had killed Little-Sun, for the Sun had expected No-Tongue to be killed. The Sun had tried three times to kill No-Tongue; so the fourth time, the Sun himself was going to scalp No-Tongue, so that the people would make fun of him. Then the Sun told his other son, Big-Sun, to try and kill No-Tongue. No-Tongue was the only one living. He was the one who had not treated his father, the Sun, right, for the Sun had not treated No-Tongue right in the first place. But No-Tongue had been assisted by the Moon.

The third time the Sun tried to kill No-Tongue, he changed himself into a Buffalo, so that the Buffalo ran after No-Tongue, but the young man, No-Tongue, ran into a mud-hole, and the Buffalo fell in too. No-Tongue got out of the muddy place, but the Buffalo could not come out, because he was so heavy. No-Tongue told a lot of men to get some dried willows and to place them upon the back of the Buffalo. This they did. They set the wood on fire, so that the Buffalo burned up.

In the evening, when the Sun and Moon were together in the heavens, the Sun said: "I shall do something to No-Tongue, some way." The Moon heard the Sun say this. Then the Sun said to the Moon: "Just see what my son No-Tongue has done; he burned my back. To-morrow morning I am going to scalp him, so the people in the village will be afraid to see him, and so they will make fun of him."

Then the Moon went to No-Tongue in the night, and said: "My son, you always like to be up early in the morning, singing. I want you to get a good scalp to-night—one that has hair, just like this. Then kill a dog and get some of its blood, put the blood inside the scalp, and put the false scalp over your head so your hair will not show."

The boy got the scalp with the hair on it, killed a dog, put some of the blood in the scalp and hung it over his bed. Early in the morning, before the Sun rose, the boy arose, put the scalp over his head, went out, and sang some songs through the village. As the Sun came up in the east the boy heard a noise, and the Sun took the scalp off from the boy, so that the blood ran down. When the Sun saw that he was satisfied. The boy went into the lodge, washed, came out again, and the Sun saw that the boy had hair on, and that he was not really scalped. When the Sun reached the Moon he told him that he was going to let No-Tongue alone until he was old and great, and that he was then going to take him up to his home.

The Moon came to No-Tongue and told him what the Sun, his father, had said. Years went by, and No-Tongue lived peacefully. Finally he became old and blind. At this time the people were about to move away from this place to another place. The Moon came and told old man No-Tongue that it was time his father, the Sun, was coming after him to take him up to his home; and that he himself would come with the Sun to take him up; that he should not be afraid.

While they were breaking camp the old man took his clothes that he used to wear in his early days, and put them on. He also painted himself. He told the people to go on; that he himself would come later. The people went on. The old man went up on the top of a hill, made a circle of red sticks to represent the Sun, and another of white sticks, to represent the Moon, for the west side. While he was doing this the Sun and Moon came. The Sun wanted to know what the Moon was doing there. No-Tongue said, "My father, the Moon is also my father; he has helped me all along." So the Sun was satisfied, and the Sun took the old man up to his home.

Several days afterwards, four young men went to the place where the old man had sat, and he was gone. The sticks were there as he had left them, but No-Tongue was gone. He was never heard from or seen again after that. He was called "No-Tongue," for the Sun had taken his tongue, but after he had failed to kill him, he gave him back his tongue.

FOOTNOTES:

[17] Told by Standing-Bull.

17.
HOW BURNT-HANDS BECAME A CHIEF.[18]

There was a large village in a beautiful valley near a large tract of timber. It was in the winter time. Around the outside of the village and over a knoll lived Stanapaat, or Burnt-Hands, a boy of about eleven or twelve years, and his grandmother. The boys in the village came over the knoll to urinate on the tipi of these poor people. In this village lived one of the chiefs who had four daughters, the youngest of which was very charitable toward these poor people. Her name was Last-Child. She brought food to these folks whenever she could. Red-Bear and Black-Bear were the first chiefs of this village. They ruled their people as though they were slaves.

One day Red-Bear gave notice that the whole village was to turn out on an elk hunt. The next day, the people complied with the chief's orders. The people, as they went through the timber in the deep snow, slaughtered the elk in great numbers. Burnt-Hands with other little fellows followed the chase. He watched the hunters butchering their game. He wished he could kill and take home to his grandmother the nice elk meat. He strode off in another direction, looking around as he went. As he went on he struck a fresh track with drops of fresh blood on clean snow, and there were no footprints of a hunter following. He took up the trail and followed it for a long distance. He found, to his great delight, a dead elk with two arrows through its chest. "Ah ho! Ah ho! The great chief knows I am poor. He has had mercy on me." While he was looking all over the animal he heard a voice. He looked up, and who was there but the two chiefs—Red-Bear and Black-Bear.

Red-Bear gave an angry grunt and struck the boy in the face. "Who are you and how did you find this elk? I never expected to find such a worthless burnt-belly looking fellow as you." Pulling his arrows out of his quiver, he said, "My father will be glad to have you for his meal," and he shot two arrows through the boy. He dragged him out on the ice to a large air-hole and said, as he dropped him, "Father, I have done as you bid me."

In this stream there lived a big White-Bear in a lodge. The young cub heard something drop outside the lodge. He told his father. The old one said, "Go out and see what it is." The cub saw poor Burnt-Hands in his ragged clothing and with wounds. The cub felt pretty bad for the boy and told his father about him. The father told the cub to bring the boy in. "What a poor boy you are!" said White-Bear. "I know who you are, and how you were treated. I never expected to eat a man from Red-Bear's tribe. I commanded him to feed me on an enemy. I will have great mercy on you. From now on you shall be my son. You shall treat Red-Bear just as he has treated you. I will enjoy his flesh. I will endow you with all the power I have. I will teach you all, and you shall go back and do as I say." White-Bear and Burnt-Hands then sat down and began the bear ceremony, Burnt-Hands learning everything and receiving his bundle of medicine and other things. He was then shown the way out by the cub.

Burnt-Hands went on to his grandmother's little home. When he arrived there he called his grandmother to kindle the fire, as he had come. Before this, when the boys found out that Burnt-Hands' grandmother was worrying, they would come in, saying, "Grandmother, I have come home," just to tease her. The old woman thought the boys were teasing her now when Burnt-Hands called. She gave a pitiful cry, saying, "You boys ought to feel satisfied with your teasing now." "Oh, no, Grandmother! I am here! I was lost on the chase. Following up an elk I strayed off to a place I knew nothing about. I could not find my way home, so I stayed all night." His grandmother arose. When she had kindled the fire there sat her boy. She rejoiced, for she was glad her boy was alive.

Nobody in the whole village knew what had happened to Burnt-Hands except Black-Bear, who had witnessed what Red-Bear did. He did not like what Red-Bear had done, but he did not say anything.

One day the scouts, on picket duty, saw a large herd of buffalo. The chiefs were notified. They gave notice that everybody should turn out to the chase, and that Red-Bear wanted the hide of the white buffalo that was in the herd. Burnt-Hands heard the call. He told his grandmother to help him make arrows. He also promised her the white buffalo robe. This was a secret surprise to his grandmother, who did not know that he was anything more than a "burnt-belly."

The next day every one turned out to go on the chase. Burnt-Hands started out on foot with his quiver. A kind young man on horseback caught up with him, and asked him to get on behind him. He did so. While they were riding, the young man told the boy about the white buffalo. The boy asked his friend if he would put the meat and his white hide on his horse for him. They made plans to be together and help each other on the chase. The hunters had all collected on a hill, talking and smoking their pipes. The two arrived and sat around for a long while. Burnt-Hands began to inquire what they were waiting for. They answered they were waiting for the chiefs. "This will not do; if we wait here there may come up a bad storm and we will go home empty handed. Come now, and let us have our chase. Those chiefs will come later, and they will get their share of the meat anyway. I want that white buffalo robe, and when you have taken it off give it to this young man and he will take it home for my grandmother."

The men were all agreed to what Burnt-Hands said. They thought Red-Bear would kill him and not themselves. They got on their ponies and the chase began. The white buffalo was killed and the chase ended. Burnt-Hands was walking along when his friend came and gave him a ride to where they were butchering. He took him where the white buffalo was and the men were standing around looking at the animal. "What are you waiting for now?" said Burnt-Hands. "Get to butchering and give me the hide!" When they had begun, the chiefs came. They gave them a welcome and told Red-Bear that Burnt-Hands had advised them to start the chase and had already spoken for the hide. Red-Bear and Black-Bear said everything would be all right, and that the boy could have the hide and some meat.

The hunters were all on their way home. Red-Bear ordered them to camp at a certain place. This they did. Burnt-Hands and his friend came to the camp and found the meat cooking, and a comfortable place made for the chiefs. "What is this place for? and are you afraid to sit here?" said Burnt-Hands. "That place is for the chiefs," said they, "and that meat." "Come," said Burnt-Hands to his friend, "sit here with me and enjoy the meat with me." The young man, with the rest, thought that Red-Bear would surely kill the boy this time. Burnt-Hands and his friend sat down on the robes and ate the meat prepared for Red-Bear. The chiefs came, and Red-Bear ordered another place and food prepared for him. He did not dare to say or do anything to the boy, suspecting his power as he did. Burnt-Hands' friend and the others thought that Red-Bear had mercy on the poor boy, since he did not hurt him.

Burnt-Hands went home with his friend and pulled off the meat and the white buffalo hide. "Here, grandmother, is what I promised you, and a lot of meat. You now know that I can hunt and bring home game." His grandmother was at once overjoyed. She thought about the pretty girl who always showed them charity. She sent out for Last-Child, who came in. "You have always been kind to us, and I have always been thankful. I want you to have this hide, and to have a robe made for yourself. You are young yet, and it will become you more than me." Burnt-Hands was talked about all over the village, but they did not know that he had been blessed by a Bear.

A long time after this chase the chief gave out an order for everybody to go on an elk chase. Red-Bear had been accustomed to collect all the elk teeth. This was his object for the hunt. Burnt-Hands heard the order and began to make preparations for the hunt. He promised his grandmother an elk-tooth dress. Burnt-Hands told his grandmother that if any trouble arose on his account she must flee into the timber, and on through other timber, and there wait for him. The next day the chase was to come off. The hunters had great luck and were talking happily in the woods. There was a cry here and there for Red-Bear to come and get his teeth. Burnt-Hands and his friend were together. He told his friend to take the teeth out for him, for he did not know how. His friend was a little afraid to do it, but Burnt-Hands said it would be all right. The men, too, rather hesitated to let him have the teeth. They told him that Red-Bear had spoken for all the teeth; but he paid no heed to it, and told his friend to take them. Burnt-Hands had collected a lot of teeth, and so had Red-Bear. The hunters had chased the elk on to a smooth piece of ice and had killed several there. Here, Burnt-Hands and Red-Bear saw each other doing the same work. They met on the last elk, and Burnt-Hands spoke and said: "You have enough teeth. You will keep off and let me have these." Red-Bear gave an angry grunt, and said, "A child like you cannot have much to say." As Red-Bear leaned over to take the teeth Burnt-Hands took his war-club and struck him on the head. He took him by the feet and dragged him to the air-hole. "Father, this is what you asked of me." A great yell was raised, and war was made on the boy.

The boy fled to the village and peeped in, to see if his grandmother had done what he had told her to do. She was gone, and he followed her and found her beyond the second timber as he had directed. "Now," said he, "take one of these bear claws off my wrist and open the little bag of paint." This she did, and he began to sing and perform the ceremony. He adorned his grandmother and himself according to the instruction of his Bear father. The people had all turned out to kill him for what he had done. Still others were calling it wrong to harm the boy, and reminded the people of what bad ruling Red-Bear had done.

Burnt-Hands and his grandmother had turned into Bears, and were making a big noise, growling and grunting. Nearer and nearer the warriors circled around the timber, shouting and yelling. The boy told his grandmother to be first to attack. So she did so. She caught Red-Bear's brother and four or five others of his near relatives. "Now, I will attack," said Burnt-Hands, "for you must be tired." He picked out the leaders and the influential men of the village and scalped them and tore them up. The warriors began to retreat. A cry was raised to end the fight, as many had been killed, but how to stop the boy and the old woman they did not know. They assembled and filled the peace-pipe. They gave it to Last-Child to take to the boy and the old woman. She took the pipe and came toward them, they growling wildly. The boy knew it was the girl. He told his grandmother not to charge at her. The boy accepted the peace-pipe and both smoked it. This ended the fight.

Burnt-Hands asked his grandmother how old she would like to be. She said, "About thirty-eight," and so she was. The boy made himself about twenty-two, and when all was quiet he married Last-Child. Burnt-Hands came to be chief, and had Black-Bear as his slave. The people lived happily under his rule.

FOOTNOTES:

[18] Told by White-Bear.

18.
HOW BURNT-HANDS BECAME A CHIEF.[19]

Once there was an old woman and her grandson. They were very poor; they had nothing. The boy's name was Burnt-Hands. Some warriors got together in the village and planned to go on the war-path. Burnt-Hands heard of it. He told his grandmother that he wanted to join the warriors on the war-path. She told the boy that when he went he must never tell Coyote stories on the war-path. She gave him a round burnt clay ball that had a handle to it. She told Burnt-Hands to go; that the clay ball with the handle was his war-club; that when on the way, when he should become hungry he should place it upon the fire, put kernels of corn upon it, and roast them.

These warriors went out to a camp in the woods. The young man came up with them and lay down by them. The next day they went and in the afternoon they sat down to rest. They made fun of the boy, and said, "Now tell us some Coyote stories." But the boy refused, and said, "My grandmother told me not to tell Coyote stories while on the war-path." They coaxed the boy to sing, but he would not sing.

The boy was hungry. As he saw that the men were not moving on he placed his clay ball upon the fire and put some kernels of corn upon it and began to roast them. While he was doing this he said, "I will tell some Coyote stories." The boy began to tell how the enemy came and attacked a certain war-party. At the same time he kept on roasting his corn.

While he was telling these stories the enemy came, and when the men found out that they were surrounded they became scared. But the boy went on with his roasting of the corn. When he had finished roasting the corn he took a seat and ate his corn, and after he had eaten all, he went out and killed many of the enemy with the clay ball that he had roasted his corn upon, which was really a war-club. The enemy became scared at the boy and ran away.

So the men found out that the boy was a wonderful boy; and as he had killed many of the enemy, when they went home they made Burnt-Hands a big chief, gave him a good tipi and a wife. He moved his grandmother into the new tipi, and there he lived ever after.

FOOTNOTES:

[19] Told by Two-Hawks.

19.
HOW BURNT-HANDS BECAME A CHIEF.[20]

One winter the people went a long distance to hunt. With them was an old woman and her grandson, named Burnt-Hands, who were very poor. One day the people made their village along a stream of water, where the scouts reported seeing many buffalo. The young man told his grandmother to make a bow and arrows; that he was going with the men to kill buffalo; and that he was going to bring back some tongues and hearts. The old woman cried, because she knew that the boy was poor, and that he could not get any tongues and hearts.

The boy started, and when he came up with the hunters some of the people said jeeringly, "Well, Poor-Boy is going to kill the first buffalo." When the hunters stopped it was customary for one of the young men to stand somewhat in front of the rest and make motions for the men to divide up into companies and to go in certain directions, so that they could attack the buffalo on all sides. The boy began to sing about being the one selected to do that. This was announced to the leaders, and they selected him.

The people divided up into companies and circled around where the buffalo were. The command to attack was given and the boy went right among the buffalo, and there he began to kill. After he was through killing, he turned back and pulled out the buffalo beards, and also pulled out a bunch of hair from the side of the shoulder. This he kept. When he went on to find his robe, he found that somebody had taken it. The young man then began to sing about his robe. He wanted some one to return it to him, but they would not return it to him, but made fun of him. Then the boy began to sing about the snowstorm coming. The boy ran into the village where his grandmother lived. He took the hairs that he had taken off from the robe and threw them upon the ground, and there in that place appeared several tongues and hearts. The old woman was very glad that the boy had brought these things. She boiled them, and they ate until they were filled. The cold weather turned into a blizzard, and killed many men who had made fun of the young man, while others came home and said that the young man had done some things that were wonderful.

After the cold weather was over, the village broke up and moved on. Again scouts came and reported that there were buffalo. After this killing the people ceased to make fun of the boy. They called him again to stand in front of the procession and to wave his hand to divide the men into the different companies. They all attacked the buffalo, but the boy was the first to kill, although he was not on a horse. He again simulated the taking of the tongues and hearts by simply pulling out the beard and the hair from the sides of the buffalo. When the boy had taken the hairs and thrown them down in the lodge there at once appeared many tongues and hearts.

People found out that the boy was wonderful, and they finally gave him a pony on which to carry his meat home, and the chief's daughter visited the young man, and finally Poor-Boy married the chief's daughter. Poor-Boy became a great warrior, and at last became a chief.

FOOTNOTES:

[20] Told by Antelope.

20.
THE TWO BOYS AND THE WATER-SERPENT.[21]

Two boys once wandered about the village and they were welcomed to any lodge they entered. One morning they came into one lodge and the people were glad to have them come in, but they claimed that the boys must be the ones who ate up their pot of corn. The boys did not know anything about the pot of corn. They left the lodge and went into another and there they were accused of the same thing. The boys went to another lodge, but were again accused. They were indignant at the accusations that were made against them. They wandered off from the village and returned when the sun set.

Now the two boys said one to the other, "Let us be on our guard to-night and perhaps we may discover who eats the corn." In those times an inclosure surrounded the village, and the two boys sat by the inclosure. They sat there until all the people of the village went to sleep, for they agreed to stay till morning. After all the people had gone to sleep the boys heard much roaring by the river; so they listened. After the noise of the waters ceased, they saw a big black thing going over their heads. It climbed over the inclosure and went on top of a lodge. It was a long serpent. The serpent stuck its head into the smoke hole of the lodge. In a few moments he went to another lodge and did the same thing. Then he went to still another. Now the serpent went back to the river and the boys were glad to find out who ate up the people's corn, beans, and squash that had been prepared in the evening for the next morning.

When morning came the boys went down to the timber and cut many sticks to make arrows with. They sat down and made arrows till evening; but they never mentioned what had happened. Again the boys stayed out, and after all the people had gone to sleep the same thing happened as on the preceding night. Again they saw the serpent climbing over the inclosure and onto the lodges. Then the boys shot at the serpent while it had its head inside a lodge, reaching for food. The boys threw their arrows at the water-monster as fast as they could. They threw so many arrows at the monster that he was almost dead. The serpent came out from the lodge and went down to the river. The waters roared and rose, because the water-monster was dying, but when it was dead the waters were silent. When the waters went down the big serpent was found dead on a small peninsula.

FOOTNOTES:

[21] Told by Antelope.

21.
THE BOY WHO BEFRIENDED THE THUNDERBIRDS, AND THE SERPENT.[22]

Among the Arikara lived a young man who was gifted with powers from the gods in the Heavens—the four-world-quarter gods who give all power. The boy's parents were very poor, so that he would go about and kill so many antelope that people called him "Antelope-Carrier." When he went hunting he killed many deer. It made no difference how far away the animal was, he killed whatever animal he shot at. People wondered where the boy got his power. The boy got his power from the timber. The Wood-Rats had taken the boy and had given him bow and arrows. The arrows were made of dogwood. The feathered parts were wood-rat hide. The boy had for his bow, thick hickory wood. One of the arrows was black, another red, another yellow, and another white. The yellow and the white arrows had flint points, and the boy used them for killing game.

Antelope-Carrier wandered from home and was lost to the people. His friends mourned for him as lost. The boy wandered west, until he came to a lake,—a very large lake. Now the boy thought to himself that he would stay at this place for several days. He killed game, made a big fire, ate meat and slept by the lake, where there were many brushes and reeds. One day Antelope-Carrier killed some birds and roasted them. After eating the birds he lay down and slept. While he slept, two Thunderbirds came and carried him high up and placed him upon a high mountain. When the boy woke up he found himself in a strange place. The mound was high and had steep sides, so that he could not get down. When he found that there was no place to get down he cried. He walked around and found a nest. It contained four young Thunderbirds. The nest was built of sticks and covered with soft, downy feathers. He walked to another place and he found a hollow in the stone and this was full of clear water. He did not drink, but went on crying. After a while he became tired and sat down. He heard above him a noise which sounded like strong wind. He looked up and saw the mother Thunderbird. She lighted close to the boy and the bird spoke and said: "My son, do not cry. I brought you to this place. I watch over you as you go hunting. I see you kill game. You are wonderful. I brought you up here. I want you to help me save your young brothers over there" (pointing to the nest). "Nesaru placed me and my mate upon this high place. I have been here a long time, and every time I place my young upon this place a strange animal that lives in yonder lake comes up and eats my young. I have not raised my young, so I have asked you to help me; and if you save my children I will give you great power. The animal that devours my young is a water-serpent. It has two long heads. It has a very thick covering of flint stones. When I throw my lightning upon it, it does it no harm. I throw the lightning in its mouth and it does not die, for the covering extends beyond its head, so that I do not hurt it. Now, my son, do not cry, but stay here and help me kill this monster, and you shall have lightning in your eyes and your mouth and limbs, and you shall have control of all the birds in the whole world."

The boy wiped away his tears and said: "I will die with my brothers. I will stay here and help you." The Thunderbird flew away, for she was happy. The boy went to the east slope of the mound, which he found very steep, but covered with timber. He clambered down from the crest of the mound and went into the timber, and there he found many birds. This was the home of all birds. He found a deer and killed it. He cut it up and carried the meat to the top of the mound. He carried some wood to the top also, and made a fire with flint stone. He saw the young birds with their mouths open. He took some meat to them and fed them. The parents of the little birds came and saw that the boy was taking care of them and were glad. The male bird spoke to the boy, and said: "We are all glad to have you here. Our young are very young, but as soon as they begin to turn black then it is time for the serpent to come out from the lake and climb this hill, to kill and eat my birds. We will go far away, where we will get more power, for it is nearly time for the serpent to come up. When the serpent comes up we will be here in time to try to kill it. We are gone."

The Thunderbirds flew away and for many days the boy did not see them. He was told that when the serpent was ready to come out from the lake he would see a fog rising from the lake, and by that would know that the serpent was coming.

One fine morning when the boy was sitting down, with his bow and arrows lying in front of him, looking at the sun as it came up in the east, something seemed to move his head towards the lake. He saw a small roll of fog coming up from the middle of the lake and the fog seemed to spread as it went up. After a while the fog seemed to cover the hills around, and to reach up into the heavens. The boy saw something crawling out from the lake. Something came out from another place. These were the two heads of the monster. Gradually it came crawling up the hill. A storm came from the west. The boy saw the rain storm, but no bird. He knew that the storm was brought by the powers of the Thunderbirds. The storm went by the boy. No rain was there where he was. It lightened and thundered under the boy. Presently he saw the two Thunderbirds spreading out their wings, making lightning, and every time the lightning struck the serpent the boy could see a flash of lightning in every direction, but it did not kill the monster. At last the monster came upon the rock where the nest was. The birds flew about, the mother squealed, and as the monster opened its mouth the Thunderbird sent its lightning into the mouth of the monster. The monster was thrown back, but again it crawled up, and the female Thunderbird said: "It is all over. We cannot do any more. We have failed, so we will fly up, and you, my son, will have to die with my children."

The boy now picked up his bow and arrows. He took the black arrow. This he placed upon the bow-string ready to shoot into the mouth of the monster as soon as it should crawl upon the rock. As the monster came up and opened its mouth to swallow the boy he pulled his bow-string and shot into the mouth of the monster. A noise like that of a falling tree was made. The monster fell over and burst open, for the arrow was really a sycamore tree with sharp limbs. The birds flew downward and were glad. Now the other head of the monster came up from another side of the hill. The boy again ran, and as it opened its mouth the boy shot the red arrow into its mouth and another sound was heard. The arrow lifted off the head of the monster and the head fell again upon the rock, breaking it into pieces.

The Thunderbirds now came and flew around the boy, screaming with joy. The two birds flew away to where all kinds of birds dwell. The birds all flew up where the boy and the nest were, and the mother Thunderbird said: "My son, to-day you are chief of all birds. You shall have power as I have. Lightning shall be in your breath and eyes. I give you a stick that shall have lightning, so that you can kill anything you strike. These birds shall follow you wherever you go. They will bring you news of bad animals. They will give you their power. Let us now go down where the serpent is." The boy and the birds all went down to where the serpent was. It was broken in two. The birds all took hold of one side and turned the serpent over. When the serpent fell, the flint rock upon it had fallen off and scattered. The boy cut the serpent open and the birds feasted upon the serpent. As each bird was filled it spoke to the boy and gave him power. The power given to the boy was in the nature of objects, and he swallowed them.

The lake grew smooth after the serpent was taken out. The boy was now chief of all birds, and wherever he went the birds followed him. Wherever there was a bad animal the birds told the boy and the boy went and killed the animal. The boy made it his aim to kill all bad animals. He never went to his people, but roamed over the land as chief of all birds, but still kept the name "Antelope-Carrier."

While this young man was roaming about, two young boys from the village went to shoot birds. They were joined together with rawhide. When they had gone far away from the village they came to a bottom land. Here they found an object that looked like a mushroom. It was white. It was moving up and down. One of the boys said, "Let me shoot at this thing." The other boy said, "No, it is wonderful." But the first boy shot at the object and as soon as the arrow hit the object a strong wind came up and took both boys up, carrying them far away, and they were left on an island out in the great waters near where the sun comes up.

When the boys were landed they cried. All this time they were still joined by the rawhide string. The boy who shot began to make fun of the other, because he cried the most. So the boy who cried the most tried to shoot the other with his bow and arrow, claiming that it was through him that they were now far away from home. The other boy said, "No, do not kill me, for we will go back home. We will first go to the setting of the sun, for that is where our home is. If we do not reach home then we must go east, where the sun rises." So they went west. As they neared the big water they saw a patch of corn and squash. They went on and saw an earth-lodge. They stood outside, and after a while an old woman came out and called them "grandsons" and asked them to enter her lodge.

They went in and she fed them. They stayed with the old woman one moon. Then the old woman said: "My grandchildren, you are far away from home. You were brought here by a strong wind, because one of you shot it with your arrow. I will help you so that you can go back to your people. I will pound much corn and I will make dried mush for you. I will make five large cakes. You must do as I tell you. It takes four days to cross the big water. Four of these cakes will be for your grandfather, who will take you across; one cake will be for you boys." She made the cakes and gave them to the boys, and said: "Go to the bank, and both of you must say, 'Grandfather, my grandmother says that you are to take us across.' A large serpent will come first, and you must say to it, 'My grandmother says you are not the one.' It will go away. Then call for another one. The second one will come. Send it away. The third one will come. Send it away. The fourth one will come. It is your grandfather, for he carries land upon his head, with trees growing upon it. Get on the serpent's head and give the serpent one cake. Your grandfather has lice. Take one off of his head and give it to your grandfather; he likes to eat them." These lice were soft-shell turtles.

The fourth serpent came, and the boys got upon it with their cakes of mush. The boys took one cake and told their grandfather to open his mouth. When he opened it the boys put one of the cakes into it. Their grandmother came and told the boys to get the big serpent a louse and to throw it into its mouth. This the boys did. The boys' grandmother told them not to jump when the serpent was within three or four feet of the bank, but to stay on it until it was up to the bank. One of the boys now said to his grandfather: "Grandmother says that you are to start for the other side of this big water." So the serpent started and went all day. At noon of the next day the serpent stopped, and said, "I want something to eat." So the boys gave it another cake, and also one soft-shell turtle. Then the serpent started again. The next day the serpent stopped and the boys gave it another cake and turtle. The serpent started again, and the third day it stopped and the boys fed it with another cake and turtle. The fourth day, the boys saw land. The wild boy jumped before the serpent came to the bank, and was swallowed by the serpent. The other boy waited until it landed, then got off, and said, "Grandfather, grandmother said you were to stop here and rest." When the boys had got on the serpent they untied themselves, and this is why only one of them was swallowed.

Now the boy on dry land said: "Grandfather, I am about to leave you. Grandmother said that I was to feed you with your own lice" (turtles). The boy took turtles from the monster and gave them to him. "O, grandfather, open your mouth. I must see your teeth. Grandmother said I could see your teeth." So the serpent opened its mouth, and there the other boy was, sitting inside the serpent. The boy asked the serpent to open its mouth wide, so he could see how long his teeth were. He then reached in the serpent's mouth and dragged out the other boy.

The two boys thanked the serpent and went west, hunting their home. They traveled many days, until at last they came to the Missouri River bottom. This river they followed up until they came to some lakes close to the river. Here they wandered until they came to drift wood, and there was a good large-sized log among the drift. Here they made a big fire. The large log was among the burning. The boys noticed drops of grease falling from the log. The wild boy noticed and reached up to the log and he found that the log was a serpent. The foolish boy then took his knife out and cut a chunk of meat and ate it. He tried to get the other boy to eat some of the meat, but the boy would not eat it.

The boys now went on, and in the night lay down. The next morning the boy who ate the serpent woke and saw that his feet had turned red, blue, and white. The wild boy was glad to see the colors upon his feet. The next night, the boy's legs became colored. Another night passed, and the boy's body was colored. The next morning the boy's legs were joined together and were like a serpent. The other boy talked to the part-serpent boy, and said, "I will stay with you." The serpent boy then said: "My brother, carry me to the Wonderful (Missouri) River and put me in the water. I am now wonderful. You must come down to the river, so that I can speak to you, and I will give you powers." The fourth morning the boy was a Serpent. The other boy packed the Serpent boy to the river and turned him loose in the river.

The boy went home. Antelope-Carrier was informed of the Serpent and learned that it was wonderful. Antelope-Carrier came and told all the birds to hunt up and down the river, so that they might find the Serpent. The Serpent knew that Antelope-Carrier was coming, and became scared. The Serpent had his brother dig a hole in the sand for it. He went into the hole and was all hidden but the head, which was covered with willows. Antelope-Carrier with all his birds hunted the Serpent. At last he saw the place where he thought the Serpent was. While examining the place the Serpent used its power and carried Antelope-Carrier into the water and into its den. There Antelope-Carrier was put into the sweat-lodge and was made to vomit up all his powers which he possessed except the lightning in his eyes. "Now," said the Serpent, "your powers are all gone. You are no longer wonderful. Go now to our people and live with them." Antelope-Carrier went home. He had to wear something over his eyes all that time, for they were like lightning. He lived with the people, but never showed to them any powers that he had possessed. The Serpent remained in the river and would sometimes swim around in the waters. It gave its powers to the people and gave them songs and the Medicine-men's ceremony.

FOOTNOTES:

[22] Told by Antelope.

22.
THE BOY WHO TURNED INTO A SNAKE.[23]

A long time ago there was a young man in the village who was an idiot. All the boys plagued him except one whose father was a chief and who took a liking for the boy. This chief's son used to take the boy to his lodge and feed him. One day the poor boy said to his friend: "Let us go on the warpath. Let us go alone, for we can do as well as the warriors." They started out and went south, crossing the Missouri River. After they had crossed the river they went west. For several days they continued their journey, but as they did not have much to eat they became exhausted and turned back.

When they were going over the prairie they saw something in the distance that looked like a log. They came to it and saw that it was a water-serpent. This water-serpent seemed to have no end. The boys walked one way, then another, until they finally gave up trying to find the end, and there was no way to go around it. The foolish boy said: "I know what I will do. I will make a big fire upon the serpent, so that it will burn up and we can cross over." This they did. They gathered many dry limbs and placed them upon the serpent, then set it on fire. The serpent burned in two. Before crossing over, the idiot said, "My brother, that meat looks very nice, let us eat it." "No," said the other boy, "we must not eat it; the serpent is wonderful." But the idiot was hungry and took some meat from the serpent and ate. He tried to get the other boy to do the same, but the boy would not eat of it, although he was very hungry. After the idiot had enough of the meat he went across the serpent. The other boy followed.

The boys now traveled down the Missouri River until night overtook them, when they lay down. The next morning the boys woke up. The idiot looked at his feet and he saw that his feet were colored with red and blue stripes. "Look," said the idiot, "I have colored feet. I will not have to paint my feet when we dance at home. People will like it." But the other boy did not say anything, for he knew there was something wrong. They went on until they reached another stream of water, where they lay down again and slept. This time, when they woke, the idiot looked at his legs and he found his legs also were colored. He was pleased, for he thought that he would not have to paint when dancing. The next night they lay down, and when they arose in the morning the idiot's body also was colored. They kept on journeying. The fourth morning the boy found his legs had grown together and had turned into the tail of a snake. The other young man promised to take care of him as long as he could. He carried the boy upon his back to the nearest lake. The idiot now turned into a Snake.

The next morning, the Snake told the boy to place him in the lake; that if the fishes were satisfied to let him remain with them he would let the boy know. The boy put the Snake into the lake. The Snake swam about the lake and there was a great commotion in the water. The fishes in the lake did not seem to like this Snake which had come among them. The Snake came out again, and the boy took it and put it upon his back and carried it to another lake. There was a great noise again in the lake. The Snake came out again, and said: "Carry me to the Missouri River and put me in. That is where I am to stay." So the boy took the Snake down to the Missouri River and put it into the river. The Snake swam around in the river and came out and said: "My brother, I am to rest in the middle of the Missouri River. Whenever the people cross the Missouri River they must say, 'My brother, let me step over you.' They will then always cross over the river without any danger of drowning. If they do not say anything, there will be danger of their getting drowned. Let them also give me presents, throwing them into the river. Now go home and tell my friends to bring me some presents of pounded corn and dried buffalo meat."

The boy went home and told his friends what had happened. The people brought blankets, tobacco, pounded corn, and dried meat. The boy and some other people went to the river and there they gave presents. The Snake boy received the presents, showing himself, so the people knew that the idiot had turned to a Snake. Every time the men went on the war-path they said: "My brother, we want to step over you. We are upon the war-path. See that none of our young men get lost in the river." To-day these people say to this river: "Brother, I am about to cross over you. See that I do not drown." Presents used to be given to the Snake boy by warriors when upon the war-path.

FOOTNOTES:

[23] Told by Yellow-Bear.

23.
THE BOY WHO RECEIVED THE MOUSE POWER.[24]

A long time ago, when the Arikara were in a village on the Missouri River, the chiefs notified the people that they were going hunting, and that they were all to get ready to go. So all the people went to their caches and placed there all the things that they did not care to carry with them on the journey. Then they packed their ponies and moved on towards the west.

One of the young men stayed behind and went from one lodge to another and finally stayed over night in the village. The next day he went through the village again, and he heard a woman crying. He went to the place where the crying came from. He looked into the lodge, and there was a woman sitting down crying. This woman had a buffalo robe wrapped around her and her hair was hanging loosely over her shoulders. The young man went in to see who it was. He wanted to know what she was crying about. She said: "I know that you are here, and I cried to bring you here. I have been crying for some time, for when the people left this lodge they took my children with them. I would like very much for you to go after my children. If you will bring my children back, I shall call my people together and they will give you some kind of power that will make you a great warrior." The young man wanted to know where her people were. The woman said her children were in the sacred buffalo robe; that all he had to do to get the robe was to go to a man who had the robe and ask him to let him see the robe, and upon opening the robe he would see a nest in the robe, and there her children would be.

It was customary among the Arikara to untie the robe when anybody asked that he might see it, so the young man knew that he would have no trouble in finding the children, and he promised the woman that he would have her children back as soon as he could. The young man ran in the direction where the people had gone, and on the second night he came to the camp which they had made. The young man went to his mother's tipi and told her to give him a little meat; that he was in a hurry; that he could not stop; that he had to go back to the village. The mother gave the young man some meat. He ate and then he went to the tipi of the white buffalo

94 | Traditions Of The Arikara

robe. The young man begged the keeper of the white buffalo robe to let him see it. The keeper of the robe took it down and untied it. While the man was untying it the young man was watching for the nest. When he saw the nest the young man began to cry, as if praying to the white Buffalo, but he put his hands upon the robe, and upon the nest, so that the man would not take any notice of it. The young man stopped crying, took the nest with the young ones, put them in his blanket and left the tipi.

The next day, the young man arrived at the village where the woman was. She was still sitting where he had left her. The young man gave the nest over to her. The woman was thankful, and said: "Now you have returned my children. Go now and return in the night." So the young man left the lodge.

The woman took her nest and went to the edge of the lodge and placed it there. She then turned into a Mouse and nursed her young ones. She went to the different holes of the Mice and Rats, telling them of what the young man had done for her, and asked that they give him power. The largest Rat in the village consented to give the young man power. He told the woman that he would have the Rats and Mice come into the lodge in the night, and that the young man should be there, for they would talk to him. The woman thanked the Rat for what he had said.

In the night the young man went into the lodge, and the woman was there. She told the young man that the priest was to be there that night and that he was to be the one to give him power. So the young man stayed. The woman told him to make a fire, so that he could see what was done. The young man made a fire, and as he took his seat he heard the Rats running around in the lodge. Finally they came, one by one, in the form of human beings, and took their seats around the fireplace. The man who acted as priest stopped, and said: "My son, you have done a kind act to one of my people by bringing her children back. She wants to help you, and I have consented to do this. I am to give you a war-club, and I am to give you power, so that you can turn yourself into a mouse any time that you want to, and when you attack the enemy and when they try to kill you, you shall disappear, so that you will not be afraid of anybody." The young man was given all these powers. At last the priest arose and called the young man up to him. He took hold of him by the shoulders and drew him to himself. Then the Rat-Man blew his breath upon the sides of the man's cheeks, and there were formed pictures of Mice. The war-club was given to him, and he was told that he was now powerful and that he could go home. The young man took the club and a little box of medicine they had given to him, and started to go out. When he heard noises in the lodge he turned around, but the people had all disappeared. The woman was standing outside the lodge, and she told the young man that he was now her son, and that he should tell his mother that when they returned home to their lodge, if they should see any mice they should not kill them, for they were the young man's relatives. The young man started for the camp. He traveled for many days, and at last he reached the camp. He went into the tipi and lay down, and the next morning the people found out that he had come.

This man became a great warrior. He led many parties out to capture ponies, and when he went into the enemy's camp he turned himself into a Mouse, and when he got to the ponies he would cut the ropes, then drive the ponies out of the camp, and if he was found out he again turned into a Mouse, so that the enemy could not find him. In battles, he was a brave man. He killed many enemies with the club that had been given him. He became so bold that he had his own way about everything in the camp. He had some troubles with some of the men, and killed them. The people grew afraid of him and always let him have his own way. At last he found his equal in another young man, who seemed to have the power of a Bear, and he it was who attacked the Mouse-Man. These two fought until both of them fell down dead, one killed by the other.

FOOTNOTES:

[24] Told by Snowbird.

24.
THE BOY AND THE YOUNG HAWKS.[25]

Outside the village there wandered a small boy with his bow and arrows, shooting at small birds and gophers. Day by day he went out looking for game. Once he discovered a hawk's nest with four eggs in it. He went out there every day, fearing that some one might take the eggs away. Finally the eggs hatched and the boy was much pleased to see the young hawks. He brought insects to the young ones for them to eat. He did this every day, and the birds grew and finally began to try to fly. He wanted to take them home, but he thought he would wait two or three days longer.

When he went out to bring the birds home he saw a man in front of him; so he ran, for fear the man would take his nest. But the man reached to the nest first and the boy cried: "Those are my birds. Do not touch them, for they are mine." The man answered and told the boy to come in a hurry, and the boy came. When the boy saw the man he was frightened, for the man was a stranger. The man said: "You have pleased me by taking such good care of my sons, and these birds are your brothers." Furthermore, the man told the boy that he had won much favor and that he would be rewarded, but he told the boy to leave the nest. The boy took some feathers from the young hawks to put on his arrows. He then went home, half believing that he was rewarded.

The boy came to be a good hunter. In the meanwhile he went out on the war-path with some others. When they discovered the enemy, he it was who fought where the arrows were thickest. Thus he became known as a brave.

Some years afterwards he was known far and wide, and even his own people were afraid of him. But finally he turned around and did that which was wrong among his people. Anyone who made any attempt to kill the young man would forget it just as he was ready to. Many a man tried to kill him, but always forgot. He was called "Make-to-Forget." But one man was capable of killing him, and he did so, because he aroused the people so much by doing wrong deeds.

FOOTNOTES:

[25] Told by Strike-Enemy.

25.
THE END OF THE ELK POWER.[26]

There were once four strong young brothers. Only the oldest one was married. He had a wife and child. One day the men went to their traps to lie in wait for eagles. The woman stayed at home, where she was busy preparing a hide for clothing. Toward evening the young men returned home, one by one.

The wife of the eldest brother was missing. They looked all around. There was no sign of the woman. The baby was found on the ground, crying, and the tools which the woman had used were there, but the woman was gone. The men believed that the woman had been taken away captive, and they grieved for her as lost. The baby was hungry and cried so piteously that it brought tears to his father's and uncles' eyes. The father tried to comfort him by feeding him deer brain broth, which would quiet him for only a little time. The oldest of the unmarried brothers was so filled with pity for the young one that he cried from eve till morn, trusting that the chief would hearken to his cry and help him and his brothers. He went out to cry near a strip of timber where he had seen an old dry skull of a buck elk. For two nights the young man cried near the skull. On the second night the Elk heard his cry and before sunrise the young man heard a voice saying: "I am well pleased with your earnest manner of pleading for your loss. I will help you. First, I will say that your brother's wife is alive, but captured by a Bear who has already captured three other women. You may think that the Bear is mightier than I, but that is a mistake, as you will see. Go home with the assurance that I have given you all power that the chief gave me. Tell your brothers to go home at once, and in a day or two come by yourself and I will give you all instructions."

The brother started home. By the time of his arrival at the village the news of the woman's disappearance had spread. It caused great sadness and wailing. Pretty-Voice (this was the name of the eldest unmarried brother) stayed one night, then started to where the Elk had spoken to him. All night Pretty-Voice traveled, and by daylight he reached the place. "I am glad that you have come, and I am prepared to carry out my promise," said the Elk. Sitting down, Pretty-Voice learned the ceremony of the Elks. "Go at once," said the Elk. "Carry out my instructions in full. When the sun has risen full blow your whistle. No matter where the females are, they will be attracted and come to you. At the end of this strip of timber you will see the rough bluff, and at about the middle you will see a little scattering brush. There is the home of the Bear, and there you will find the woman." Pretty-Voice went to the end of the timber as he had been directed. As instructed, he whistled, one—two—three times. The women in the Bear's den heard the whistle and all rushed outside to listen. At the fourth whistle they could not restrain themselves. They rushed toward the sound. They saw a handsome young man standing with his robe wrong side out. Two mid-tail eagle feathers were on his head and a long whistle was in his hand.

Pretty-Voice was surprised to see his brother's wife and three young women who had been missed for a long time. Pretty-Voice said, "Nawa, we will lose no time, but prepare yourselves to run. Understand we are bound for home." They started at a fast pace. When they had gone many miles one turned her head and yelled, "He is coming!" and they began to cry. When the Bear came up too close Pretty-Voice ordered the party to stop. The Bear stopped and sat up on his hind legs, heaving heavily. The Bear was first to speak. He said, "Young man, you will live if you let me have my women." "No, I have captured these women and I claim them. I will not let them go to you. I will defend these women if you are intending to fight," said Pretty-Voice. "Very well," said the Bear, "you will begin the fight if you have any faith in yourself." "That I have," said Pretty-Voice. Throwing off his robe and other things he made his attack with his bow and arrow. The Bear sat up, not minding the arrows. Pretty-Voice had shot all his arrows and the Bear was still looking at him. "Now," said the Bear, "I gave you a chance to live, but you gave no heed to my warning. Now you will die." Pretty-Voice threw himself on the ground and sprang on his feet in the form of a full grown Elk, with antlers like branches of a cottonwood tree. The Bear made a rush and the Elk threw his head down and struck the Bear, picking him up from the earth. The Bear's claws lacked a little of hitting the Elk's head. The women stopped wailing when they saw that Pretty-Voice was their savior. "My friend," said the Bear, "you are true to your faith, and I will admit that you have overcome me and I will say that the women are yours and I beg to be free; but I know that I am going to die." Pretty-Voice pulled up his head with a quick jerk and set the Bear free. After throwing himself on the ground as before, he sprang up a man. He picked up his clothing and started on.

When he arrived at the village the news of his capture of the women spread. There was great rejoicing and the young women were taken to their homes. Pretty-Voice won great honor. He lived among his people, being received in their homes with great respect. He was not yet a warrior, but knew he would have no difficulty in getting a wife.

As he had received all the powers of an Elk, he thought he would use them. One night he painted himself according to the instructions the Elk had given him. Ille, dum summo tumulo terreno stat, pulchram puellam vidit quam habere volebat. Itaque tibia magica canebat, et brevi tempore puellam habebat. Hoc faciebat dum puellas pulcherrimas omnes, quæ eum vicum incolebant, habuisset. Deinde matrones illicere incepit. This caused bad feeling among the majority of the men, but a few paid no attention to his doings, thinking that nothing could be done to stop him. The Indians held a large council, and in this council they, including his three brothers, planned and agreed to make an attack and kill him. One day he prepared to practice his power. He stood on an earth-lodge. The people began to flock into the lodge he was standing on, with their robes around them to hide their weapons. Pretty-Voice knew what was coming and gave no heed to them, trusting in his power. All at once the men rushed out and began to shoot at him. A few who favored Pretty-Voice called out that they were foolish, as Pretty-Voice had caused no one bodily pain. The shooting went on and on, but Pretty-Voice stood still. Once in a while he shook his robe and threw off the bullets and arrows. At last the men gave up, seeing that nothing could harm the young man.

One day the village was attacked by a large party of Sioux. The inhabitants were being defeated on every side. Pretty-Voice was tardy in coming to the fight, and the men made remarks about his not making use of his power to fight. He came in his own time, went into the enemy's field, with nothing to defend himself with but his whistle. The Sioux saw that no arrow or bullet could harm him, and knew that he was powerful. They began to retreat. They were thrown back, scalped and stripped of their weapons and ponies. They attempted a second attack, but were again thrown back. When they had been driven back the second time they knew that nothing could be done to destroy the people while Pretty-Voice was living, for he had made himself famous. They gave up trying to fight, but came there on a friendly visit.

During their visit, Pretty-Voice saw a pretty Sioux girl whom he thought he would take for his wife. So he went through his ceremony and secured the girl. He kept her for his wife. When they had lived together for a long time, loving each other in their lodge, the girl began to question Pretty-Voice about his great power. She said she wanted to know how he could destroy, and she said that if she could be trusted to perform some duty for him she would be glad to do so. Pretty-Voice told all that had happened to him, and said that he could be killed by scraping off a little elk horn and elk hair and making a little incense for arrows and bullets. "When this is done," he said, "the bullets will go through me." The Sioux girl began to get ready to desert her husband and to stir up her people to make another attack and kill Pretty-Voice. When Pretty-Voice had gone off somewhere she started out toward her country.

On her arrival she told her story and stirred up her people to make war and kill Pretty-Voice, saying that she knew his secret. She collected the necessary things and started out at the head of a war-party. The people of Pretty-Voice were moving for their future welfare when they heard that Pretty-Voice's wife was missing. Pretty-Voice knew what was going to happen. He had told his mother long before when in trouble with his own tribe, that if anything should happen to him, even if he should be torn to pieces, she must collect his flesh and throw him into a stream near some timber and then she would see him again.

The girl camped near the village and there prepared the arrows and bullets as she had learned. A fierce battle began. The inhabitants of the village were defeated, and in a short time Pretty-Voice appeared. "There he comes! To-day you are lost!" cried the enemy. Pretty-Voice started after them as usual and drove the enemy a great distance, but his body looked like a porcupine tail with arrows. The bullets and arrows had so loaded him that he fell. The enemy turned around and scalped many of them. They mutilated the body of Pretty-Voice. The battle ended. The people went out to bury their dead, and especially Pretty-Voice. His poor mother, crying for her son, came out with a robe to collect his flesh and do as she had been told. The men noticed what she was intending to do. They asked her what she was going to do. She told all that Pretty-Voice had said, but the men would not hear of his coming again, as he had done enough mischief. The old mother insisted, but the men would not let her. As the brothers disapproved of her plan she gave in, and instead of burying his body they made a big fire and destroyed the body entirely. A number of days after his body had been burned to ashes a pure white fog was seen to arise daily from that place.

FOOTNOTES:

[26] Told by White-Bear.

26.
THE ELK RESCUES A WOMAN
FROM THE BEAR.[27]

There was a young man who fell in love with a certain girl in a village. This girl was the daughter of a chief, and she was very pretty. The young man was poor. He had no ponies, no relatives, but was often looking for them. The young girl fell in love with the young man, and so they planned to run away. The young man took some flint stones, bow and arrows, a knife and some robes, and went to the girl's lodge. He took the girl out, and they rode on ponies. They went off into a wild country by themselves. There they stayed. They made a tipi. The young man went out every day to kill deer, so that now they had plenty of meat all the time. The young man thought a great deal of his wife. The only time he left her was in the daytime. The young man killed so many deer that the woman made buckskin dresses for herself, and also buckskin leggings for the man. The young man killed many elk, and the teeth of the elk were put upon the buckskin dresses. They made a big new tipi. They had much dried meat.

One day the young man said: "I will stop hunting. I will now go to yonder hill, and I will try to catch some eagles." So the young man went up on a hill, and he caught many eagles. He took them to his home. One time while he was in a den, waiting for an eagle to alight so that he could catch it, somebody came to his camping place and took away his wife. This being was a Bear. The Bear had turned into a man and had come to the camp. He had a robe about his shoulders, bear's claws about his neck, and he smelled so fine that the woman could not help but like him. When the man started to go the woman wanted to follow him. She finally left everything that she had and followed the man. This man was a Bear, and he led her into a den where there were a dozen or more women that he had taken from their husbands. In the evening, the young man got out from his cave, went to his camp, and found his wife gone, but everything else was in its place. The eagles that he had killed were there. He knew by this that if the enemy had taken her they would have taken the eagles too. So he hunted and hunted and yelled. At last he gave out. He went along the timber and finally an Elk found him.

The young man told the Elk that he had lost his wife; that he thought a great deal of her; and that now he was about dead from hunting her. The Elk told him that he was going to help him to get his wife back, but that he would have to fight. The Elk taught the man how to transform himself into an Elk. He also gave him a whistle, and told him that he whistled when he wanted female Elk to come to him, and that when he whistled they all rushed to him. The Elk told the young man to remain in the timber; that he would go and watch for the Bear; and that when the Bear should be gone, he would come and let him know, so that the young man might go and blow the whistle, while the Bear was gone. The Bear left his den and went out for a long distance. The Elk knew this. It came and told the young man. The young man went up close to the place where the den was and blew the whistle. As soon as his wife heard the whistle she said, "Women, let us go; that is my husband." Some of the women were afraid to go, for they were afraid of the Bear; but the young man kept on whistling, and when the women heard it again they all rose and walked out of the den. They followed the young man's wife, who was now running to where the young man was standing. The young man saw his wife and was happy. He embraced her, and said, "Go, I will remain behind, for the Bear will surely come after you."

The Elk now came, and said: "The Bear is coming. Watch. Fix your bow and arrows so that you can shoot the Bear, while I put my head down and thus make a kind of barrier so that he can not get through, on account of my horns." The Bear came, and as he attacked the Elk the Elk put his head down so that the Bear could not get through, and as the Elk began to lift its head up it brought its head and the whole weight of its horns upon the Bear, thus sticking its horns into the Bear's body, while the young man shot at the Bear with his arrows. They killed the Bear. The Elk now turned to the young man, and said, "I shall now go to my place." But the young man said, "No, I shall only take my wife; you take the other women." So the Elk took the other women, and they all turned into Elk. For this reason, when a male elk whistles, all the female elk run to him.

FOOTNOTES:

[27] Told by Antelope.

27.
THE BOY AND THE ELK.[28]

There was a young man in the Arikara village who was very handsome. He tried to marry, but the girls all seemed to hate him. He went off to a hilly country where there was a lake. On the west side of the lake was a skull of an animal. He placed himself by the skull and began to cry.

On the second night an Elk came to the boy, but soon disappeared. In a short time the boy heard the clear, beautiful notes of a flute. The sound of the flute came nearer and nearer the boy, until it came to where he stood. There stood before him an Elk. The Elk now spoke to him, and said: "My brother, that is my skull before you. I know what you are crying for. The women do not like you, and you wish to be liked by them. I now take pity upon you. Take the teeth from this skull. Wear the large ones about your neck. Wear the others in your ears. I give you a flute. Go to the village of your people. Blow this flute, and you will see the young girls coming to you." The young man received the flute and also pulled the teeth from the skull. He went home and did as he was told to do.

He tried his flute, and the young girls came to him. This he tried several times, until he was married. Women also came to him. The men did not like this, so they gathered together and agreed to kill him. In the evening the men went out and sat around with their bows and arrows. The man came out from his tipi and walked outside the camp, blowing his flute. The women started to run to him. The war-cry was raised and the men closed in on the boy, killing him. One of the boy's relatives took the teeth from his neck and ears, and also the flute. The relatives of the boy were afraid to bury the boy, so they left him where he was killed. The boy lay there for several days, but one night he came to the tipi of his mother. He woke her up and told her that he had returned. His mother did not believe it. But when she made a fire she saw her son sitting there. The son then said: "Mother, go to the society of Young-Dogs, and tell them to give me some tobacco, so that I may smoke." The mother went to the tipi and they gave her the tobacco. She gave the tobacco to her son, who smoked, and said, "This smoke is good."

The men in the village were afraid. They thought the man would take revenge and kill some of them. The boy did not go out much, and the people doubted that he was back and alive. Some of the men went to the tipi to see if the boy was home and alive. The men saw the boy, and they became afraid. One day the boy sent for all his nearest kin, and said: "My relatives, my heart is poor, for these people killed me. I do not want to live here any more. Will you go with me where I am going?" All said, "Yes." So the boy went and caught his pony. The others did the same. Men, women, and children followed the boy. He went towards the river and told the people to follow him and they obeyed. They went into the water, and as they got into the water they began to disappear. They all turned into some kind of animal that lived in the water. The young man who had the flute and elk's teeth did not go, so he was the only one who lived.

FOOTNOTES:

[28] Told by White-Bear.

28.
THE COYOTE, THE GIRL, AND THE MAGIC WINDPIPE.[29]

A long time ago there lived a beautiful girl who had her lodge in the center of the timber. She loved nobody, but she always had plenty of buffalo meat, and plenty to eat. She had some wonderful bundles hung up in her lodge.

One day as she was eating in her lodge the Coyote visited her. He saw that she had plenty of meat, so he made his home with her. Every day they had meat. The Coyote was now the girl's errand man, and made fires for her and carried water for her. One day the girl was up early in the morning, and she said: "My uncle (Coyote), we are out of meat. I want fresh meat. My brothers will be here to-day, and I want you to stay on the north side of the entrance and cover your head up with your buffalo robe, and not to watch." The girl swept out the lodge, placed some hot coals between the altar and the fireplace, and put some sweet grass upon the coals. As the smoke arose from the coals she went to the sacred bundle, and from it took the windpipe of a buffalo, which was round, and small at one end and large at the other end. She waved this over the smoke, then took it and turned it upside down so that dust came out from it, and as the dust fell out it turned into seven young men, who were her brothers. On the north side, where the sacred bundle hung, were several bows and arrows. These bows and arrows the brothers took down. When the boys took their bows and arrows the girl put her buffalo robe about her. She went up on to the lodge. She gave one yell toward the north, moved toward the west, moved toward the south, and then the buffalo came, from the north and from the west. She went back into the lodge, and her brothers began to kill the buffalo. They killed so many buffalo that the buffalo finally ran off. The brothers went into the lodge and stood in a row on the north side. The girl took some hot coals and placed them west of the fireplace, put some medicine and sweet grass upon them, and each brother, when his turn came, passed his bow and arrows through the smoke and laid them by the coals. Then they let the smoke pass through their bows. Then one stepped to the south of the coals and stopped; he finally disappeared. After that all disappeared. The girl took the windpipe, passed it over the smoke, then put her hand on the ground, got the dust together, and put it back into the windpipe. She passed the windpipe over the smoke, tied it, and hung it up in its place again. She even took the bows and arrows, passed them over the smoke and threw them upon the ground. They became tiny bows and grass arrows. These she hung up by the bundle again.

While all this was going on the Coyote had one eye open. After the girl was through with the performance she told the Coyote to come out. She went out with the Coyote and they skinned the buffalo. They brought the meat into the lodge, and left the hides outside. Every day the girl and the Coyote jerked the meat. The Coyote laid the bones around the fireplace and roasted them. When the Coyote ate the roast meat that was cooked he would think of his hungry children far away. At last he decided to steal the windpipe that contained the young men and to take it far away into his country, so that he could call the buffalo and have the young men to kill them. He said to himself: "If I find the enemy's camp I will attack them. I will turn that windpipe upside down and those brothers will come out, and they will fight for me. The people will think that I am a wonderful man." One day the Coyote asked the girl if her seven brothers in the windpipe were the only ones there. She said, "No, for, if I am attacked, I turn that windpipe upside down and there will be many young men, and my seven brothers will lead them out and they will fight for me." The Coyote said to himself, "That is good; I will steal it." So the Coyote made up his mind to steal the windpipe that night. The girl knew what the Coyote was planning all the time, but she allowed him to steal it. The Coyote went up to the windpipe, took it down and went out of the lodge, to the north. He traveled far. He thought, "I am now far away from the girl; I will lie down by the side of this log and sleep." The girl knew just where the Coyote had lain down, and so she had her brothers bring the Coyote back and place him at the ridge just before the entrance of the lodge, on the north side. In the morning the girl got up, went to the Coyote and waked him. When the Coyote awoke he found himself in the lodge. He said: "My niece, I thought the enemy were coming, so I took this thing down, so that I could put the brothers outside so that they could fight for us. I must have gone to sleep here. Put it back." Again the Coyote thought, "Well, I will stay, and I will yet steal this windpipe." So one night he took the windpipe down again and went off. He went until he came to a place where there were some ashes where timber had been burned. He lay down to rest. The girl told her brothers to bring him back and place him outside of the lodge, where there was a pile of ashes. She went out in the morning, waked him, and the Coyote, when he awoke, found himself by the lodge. "My niece," he said, "I took this thing down, for there was a war-party coming to attack us. I went to meet the war-party and they ran away, and I came back and lay down here, for I was tired." The third time he tried to steal the windpipe, but again he failed. The fourth time, the girl let the Coyote carry the thing off. So the Coyote went off, and the girl did not have him brought back. He became hungry, and as he saw a village he thought to himself, "If I do this wonderful thing to these people they will find out that I am wonderful and they will take me from one lodge to another to feed me." So the Coyote went up on the hill. He commenced to howl at the people in the village to come and kick with him. He thought that if he could get them to kick with him he would turn the windpipe upside down and the young men would run. The young men in the village said: "That fellow is howling for us to come and kick with him. Let us go up and kick with him." So several young men went up on the hill where the Coyote was. The Coyote took the windpipe and turned it upside down, but instead of dust and the boys coming out, a swarm of bumblebees came out, and they commenced to sting the Coyote all over. The boys continued to kick him. The Coyote began to beg them not to kick. The young men ran into the timber and the bees left the Coyote and went up into a hollow tree. There they stayed. The Coyote went off as a coyote. The bees stayed in the timber, as bees.

FOOTNOTES:

[29] Told by Antelope.

29.
THE BUFFALO-WIFE AND THE JAVELIN GAME[30]

A long time ago there was a village upon the Missouri River. In this village was a young man who was well-to-do. He was handsome, but did not care for women. He seemed to be successful in all his undertakings. In hunting he killed many deer and antelope. He dug holes upon high hills and covered them with willows and placed carcasses of rabbits or some fresh meat on them. Magpies would come there and eat of the meat, then eagles would light there, so that he dragged them in. People got to calling him "Man-Who-Kills-Game-Easily."

One day he went hunting, and as he climbed up on a high hill he saw somebody coming. The boy lay down upon the hill and went to sleep. When he awoke the sun had gone down, and it was night. He lay down again and went to sleep. He saw a buffalo cow sitting upon a prairie and two bulls were standing back of her, and each bull was saying, "I will ring her." The boy thought that he was standing by looking on. When the bulls ran to where the buffalo cow was sitting they turned into sticks and the boy also saw that the cow had turned to a ring. The boy, in his dream, picked up each stick and examined it, so that he knew just how they were made. He also thought he picked up the ring and examined it. The next morning he woke up. He looked where he had seen a person the day before and he saw something there. This time it was not a person, but a buffalo cow. The cow came and stopped on a prairie. She sat down. The boy went down from the hill, for the cow was by it. The boy could see no other cow. Bovi appropinquavit quacum, cum benigna videretur, concubuit. When he stood back the cow disappeared. The boy looked into the grass and there was the ring he had dreamed of. He picked up the ring and went home. He wore it upon his wrist. Every night he dreamed about the sticks, so he went out one day and cut ash timber and made the sticks. Every morning the young man used to go outside the village and call out, "I have sticks here to play with!" The young men of the village came out and played the game. Some of them would rather play the game than eat. This particular man was skillful in playing the game. He seemed to be the only one who could catch the ring.

He won many things, such as eagle feathers, wampum, beads and many other things. The game became very popular. Men came from their homes and played all day with the sticks.

One day the boy took his bow and arrows and went hunting for game. The game generally was plentiful, but on this hunt the boy failed to find any game. He kept on going south until he came to a valley where there was a large stream of water. There in the valley he saw a person. He approached and saw that the person was an old woman. The young man spoke to the old woman, and she said: "My grandson, I am weak. Take pity on me. Carry me across the river, that I may go out to the village." The young man told her to walk and that he would hold her while she crossed the river. But the old woman said: "No, my grandson; put me upon your back, take me across, and set me upon that nice grass on the other side." The young man gave in, and he put the old woman upon his back and waded the river. After the boy had crossed the river he said, "Well, you had better get off." The old woman said, "My grandson, take me a little further." So the boy went on. When the boy stopped to put the old woman down she laughed, and said: "No, my grandson; you cannot put me down; I am your wife now." The boy became furious and tried to throw the old woman off, but she was fast to his back. The boy stuck her with his knife and tried hard to get her off, but the old woman stuck on and laughed at the boy. The old woman said: "Grandson, you might as well go home, for I am to stay with you always. Let the young men see you carry an old woman. You are so proud that you do not look at the women." The young man made up his mind to go home. So he went home with the old woman upon his back.

People looked at the young man coming into camp with an old woman upon his back. Children crowded about him and followed the boy through the village. He went into his lodge and told his friends what had happened to him. The people placed the young man in the lodge and medicine-men were sent for. All the medicine-men failed to get the old woman off the young man's back. While the people crowded around, a poor boy came and stood with the people. He spoke out and said, "I can take the old woman from that young man's back." Then he disappeared. The people heard the poor boy speak, and the people told the relatives what the poor boy said. The poor boy was living in a shelter with his grandmother. The boy spoke to his grandmother, and said: "Grandmother, the people are coming after me to take the woman off from the boy. I can take her off." The old woman felt sorry for her grandson, not knowing that the boy had powers to take the old woman off. The relatives of the boy came and brought with them the medicine-men's pipe. The men stood before the boy, holding the pipe before him. The boy reached and took it. The people thanked the boy for taking it.

The boy then took his bow and four arrows of different colors. He put his old robe on, holding his bow and arrows in his left hand. He went into the lodge of the young man with the old woman upon his back.

No sooner had the boy entered the lodge than the old woman on the man's back became scared. She did not talk much. The boy walked up and said: "Woman, you did wrong. You were sent for a purpose, and instead of doing what you were told, you turned into a woman and became fast upon the young man. You came from the Buffalo with a message and now you are an old woman stuck upon the back of this young man. I shall take you off. These arrows are from my father, Lightning. These flint points will be the ones that will take you off." The boy then ran around the lodge. Taking the black arrow, he shot at the woman under the shoulder. The arrow struck the woman and split her in two, taking off a part of the boy's flesh. The boy ran around again. This time he took the red arrow and shot the woman under the chin, taking her entirely off from the boy. The boy then ran around again, taking a white arrow. He placed the arrow upon the back of the boy. Again he ran, and this time the boy took the yellow arrow and placed it upon the sore place of the boy's back. He ran again, and took the arrow off. He also took the other two arrows, and said: "People, take the old woman outside and place her upon a big fire!" The boy went out and went to his grandmother's. They made a big fire, placed the old woman upon it, and burned her.

The people took some gifts to the poor boy. The next morning an old woman went out of the lodge and heard a woman crying at the entrance. It was near where the woman was burned. A voice was also heard to say: "Your father threw you away. He burned you. You must not cry." The young man heard it, and began to think. He would say to himself: "I have never been with any woman. I do not understand this talk." The next night the child was again heard crying, and towards morning the young man again heard the talk. The young man now felt for the ring he had, and it was gone. The next night the boy thought of the woman's voice and lay awake. He did not hear her any more, so he went to sleep. In his dream he saw himself playing with the stick, and every time he hooked the ring he thought he was with a woman.

Some one went out of the lodge, and there, where the ashes were, was a new white tipi, and inside was a woman with a child upon her lap, talking to it. In the evening, the people went out to see the tipi, but there was no tipi. The young man was now well. He made up his mind to go out and see the tipi. When the child began to cry, the young man went out to see the tipi, and as he went out a woman with a new buffalo robe passed by him, leading a child. The young man went into the lodge and gathered up many eagle feathers and made a bundle of them. This he put upon his back, and went out of the lodge, following the woman and the child. The woman had made the young man follow her. By daylight the young man could see footprints of the woman and the child. He now saw the woman and the child walking up the hill. The young man ran to catch up with them, but as he got to the top of the hill he saw the woman and child walking, but this time they were Buffalo. The young man ran after them. Once in a while the young calf would run back, hop around the man, then return to his mother. When the calf would catch up with his mother he would say: "Mother, let us go slow. Father is tired." The Buffalo cow would say: "No, my son, you must not run to that man; he put us into the fire." In the night, the man saw a tipi near a river. He went to it. The calf came out and said, "Father, my mother said you were to lie down outside." The young man lay down outside and went to sleep. When he awoke the next morning the tipi was gone. So he got up and followed the Buffalo. Every time the cow came to a stream of water she would rush in and lay a covering of dust over it, so that the water was hidden. The dust layer would be about two inches deep, so that the man could walk over it. The calf came to the man and said, "Father, do you want to drink?" The man said, "I am dying, for my throat is dry." The calf told the man that he would stick his foot through the crust of dust, so that he could drink when he came to the little hole; that when he was through he must cover up the hole. The man found the hole and drank. He also washed his face and head. He first thought: "What a little hole. Can I get enough to drink?" But he was soon filled, and thought it wonderful that a little hole like that should hold so much water. The man felt refreshed and ran on after the Buffalo. In the night the man again saw the tipi, and he knew that it was the Buffalo tipi. He went to it, and the calf came out, and said, "Father, my mother says you are to come into the tipi and lie down by the entrance." So the man went into the tipi and lay down by the entrance. When he woke up, the tipi was gone. He went on west and saw the Buffalo cow going with the calf. The calf went back and met the man, and said, "My father, are you hungry?" The man said, "Yes, I am starving." The calf said: "Watch me. I will drop something and you are to pick it up and eat it. When you have eaten enough put it away and eat it when you are hungry." The calf ran, and all at once he stopped. His tail went up and he dropped a chip. The man picked up the chip when he came to it, and to his surprise it was pemmican. It was not a very large piece. It seemed to have more fat in it than meat. As the man took a bite he thought the piece was too small to satisfy his hunger, but as he ate, it seemed to grow larger. It was made from a whole buffalo. That evening the man went into the tipi. He was told by the boy Buffalo that his mother had said his father was to sit by her. So the man walked up where the woman sat and sat down by her. In the night they slept together. The boy was very happy. Next morning the boy got up and played with his father. When the woman got up she shook her robe and wrapped herself in it, and there she stood, a Buffalo. The tipi disappeared. The boy was a Buffalo calf. The three now walked on, and the woman spoke to the man, and said, "On yonder hill sits this boy's grandfather, who is waiting for us."

When they arrived at the hill he saw the Buffalo bull sitting upon the hill. When the Buffalo bull saw them coming he stood up, stretched, and said: "So you people have come at last. I have been waiting here for you." The man then took two eagle feathers and tied them upon the horns of the Buffalo bull. He shook his head and jumped around to see the feathers wave. "Go," said the Buffalo bull. "This is what we want. You will see two bulls sitting on yonder hill. Give them presents and they will be glad to get them." So they went on, and when they got to the hill they saw the two bulls. The young man went up to the bulls and put his feathers upon their shaggy heads. They also ran and jumped about, shaking their heads. "Go," they said. "On yonder hill sit three bulls who are waiting for you. Make them glad by giving them presents." So they went on again. They came to the hill and the three bulls sat there. The young man put feathers upon their shaggy heads. They also jumped around and were thankful. "Go," they said. "On yonder hill sit four Buffalo bulls, who are chiefs of the Buffalo camp." The young man took his feathers and put them upon the heads of the Buffalo. The Buffalo jumped around and shook their shaggy heads, each looking at the other's feathers, until they finally locked horns.

The man, the Buffalo cow, and the boy were told to go and enter the village of the Buffalo. They went and entered and drove off Buffalo, but as the man did not have enough feathers to go around, the Buffalo became mad. Some said, "We can not kill him, for he has not enough." But others said, "We must kill him, for he burned our messenger." Some said, "We can not kill him, for the messenger did wrong by turning to an old woman and sticking onto the young man." The Buffalo were angry. They told the woman to tell the man to sit upon the hill until it was decided what should be done with him. The young man went upon the hill, took from his buffalo belt a flint stone knife and stuck it in the ground. As he did so he called upon the gods in the ground to form stone around where he sat. The young man seemed to know what was coming.

The calf soon came and told the man that the Buffalo intended to kill him, for the people had burned his mother. The calf told him that there were Buffalo who took his part, but as they were few in number they could do nothing; that the woman had done wrong by turning into an old woman and causing him trouble, but this story was of no avail, for the Buffalo were determined to kill the young man. The man took his seat upon the hill as he was requested. The calf said: "Father, I am to run a race with three other calves. I have a friend here who says that he will help me." The man looked at Yellow-Calf standing by his son. He knew Yellow-Calf was a wonderful calf, that was liked and loved by all of the Buffalo. So the man knew that the calf was safe. The calves went far away, and ran. The two calves beat the others. The Buffalo were furious, hooking the ground here and there. Again the Buffalo gathered in council and it was decided that the man should hunt his wife. There were four other Buffalo cows placed with the boy's mother, who looked like them all. The boy placed a burr upon his mother's head, so that his father would know her. The man passing the Buffalo knew the woman cow and picked her out.

The Buffalo bulls decided to kill the man by rushing upon him where he sat and stamping him to death. If not, then they were to hook him. The boy went to his father and told him what was to happen. He took a downy feather and placed it in his father's hair. The Buffalo came and stamped about the man, around whose head waved the downy feather. Four times the Buffalo rushed upon the man, but when they scattered he was always found sitting upon the hill. The Buffalo became furious. They ran to hook him, but every time the Buffalo hooked the ground their horns were knocked off. The ground around the boy had spread and formed flint rocks, for the boy had stuck his flint stone into the ground and formed flint rock. Four times the Buffalo attacked the man, but they could not reach him. At last they gave up, and returned to their places in the herd.

The Buffalo now again sat in council. They decided to send the man, Buffalo cow, and calf to the Indian village for presents, such as eagle feathers, and native tobacco. The Buffalo said to the man: "Your people are hungry. You must go home and we will follow you. When the presents have been brought to us, then we will send to your people a bunch of buffalo so that they may kill and have meat to eat." The man was glad, and started on his homeward journey; but a Buffalo bull got in his way. It had also been decided to turn the man into a Buffalo, and the bull was the one to turn him into a Buffalo. The bull attacked the man, but the man stood his ground and met the Buffalo, so that the man was run over by the Buffalo. The next thing he knew he was locking horns with the other Buffalo and to his surprise he found that he was now a Buffalo.

After the man had become a Buffalo he and his wife and the son started for their country, the main herd of Buffalo following. After several nights' travel the man told the Buffalo that he and his wife and child would start for their country at once. The Buffalo were glad. The three, as Buffalo, started on ahead, the rest following slowly. They traveled very fast, until at last they came in sight of the village. The Buffalo rested in a hollow and the next morning turned themselves into human beings and walked on into the village. The man found his lodge. People flocked into the lodge to see them, for they were fine-looking beings. Their robes were all new. The man told the people to keep their distance, for they (the people) smelled very badly. The man told of his errand and the people began to come in with eagle feathers and native tobacco. The man took all the things, and with his wife and son went out. People watched them, and as the three went over a hill they became Buffalo again. The three ran until the Buffalo came up, and the man gave many presents. Those who received presents were willing to go with the first bunch to be slaughtered by the people. So the three ran back to the village, and got there in the night. A big fire was made in the Buffalo man's lodge, chiefs were sent for, and the man told them to be ready to go out the next morning; that the people would find a bunch of Buffalo on the other side of the hills. The people went out and found the Buffalo. They surrounded them and killed all of them. Again the young man told them to go out and kill Buffalo. Four times they killed. The whole drove came to the village.

The leader of the Buffalo now sat upon a high hill, with a Buffalo skull in front of him. The Buffalo man was sent for, and the Buffalo leader said: "I am satisfied. The people are happy. This day I give you sticks to play with. The two sticks are people. The ring is a kind of people—the Buffalo. When you play, the sticks which you ring are the enemy, whom you conquer. The ring is the Buffalo. The people will become very jealous of their hunting-ground. You will be at war with other people in the country." These sticks were placed in the priests' lodge, so that when a bundle ceremony was given the sticks were placed before the people. The sticks were people. Two sets of people who became jealous of the Buffalo then fought. The ones who caught the ring were conquerors. The man went home and lived a long life. The Buffalo calf started the Buffalo ceremony among the people.

FOOTNOTES:

[30] Told by Hawk.

30.
THE ORIGIN OF THE WOLF DANCE[31]

When the Arikara lived on the Missouri River, there was a handsome young man in the village, whose father was a chief. The young man had never been on the war-path. He never played with other young men, but stayed around close to his lodge. Many young girls in the village went to him to be married to him, but he would not have them. There was one place that he went and that was upon a high hill, west of the village. He had a certain way of going to that hill.

Now, there were seven beautiful girls in the tribe, each of whom had tried to marry the young man and had been refused. The seven girls got together and planned to put the young man into a hole, which was about ten feet in depth, and larger at the bottom. They spread some weeds over the hole, and when the time came for the young man to come that way they hid. The young man came, stepped over the hole and fell in.

For some time he stood yelling for help. At last the seven girls went to the hole and they told him that he must give his clothing to them. He took his things off, and the girls each took a little basket, dropped it down, and received in it a piece of clothing. Then each girl dropped her basket, and asked the young man to spit in it, promising that if he did what they asked they would take him out. As each basket received the spittle the girl would pull it out and lick the spittle. After each girl had got the boy's spittle and licked it, they said, "You must give us your loin-cloth." This he gave to them. They tore it in seven pieces, so that each had one piece. Iamque puer nudus erat. Deinde puellæ dixerunt si sibi glandem penis ostenderet eique limum aspergeret, se eum sublaturas. Hoc puer abnuit. Tum dixerunt puellæ, "Si vis nos omnes in matrimonium ducere polliceri, te tollere volumus." Puer pollicitus est. But all the girls spoke out, and said: "You have always been mean; you have had a dislike for us; we will leave you in this hole and let you die; we are not going to take you out." So the girls went away and the boy commenced to cry.

Soon after the girls had gone away a gray Wolf looked down upon the boy, and said, "I am sorry for you, and I will help you." The Wolf went away, and while he was gone a Bear came to the hole. The Wolf came back and a dispute arose over the ownership of the boy. The Bear claimed that the boy belonged to him; but the Wolf said, "He is mine." The Bear said: "He is mine, too. I shall eat him up." So the Bear and the Wolf began to quarrel to see who should have the boy. The Wolf whispered to the boy, and said: "I shall dig with this Bear, and you must dig on this side; for if he digs through first he will eat you; but if I dig through first and reach you before he does I shall save you, and you shall be my son." So it was agreed between the Bear and the Wolf that they each should dig through the earth, and whosoever should first dig through to where the boy was should claim him.

The Bear and the Wolf began to dig. Where the Wolf and the boy were digging there was nothing but sand, while on the side where the Bear was digging it was hard dirt, mixed with stones and gravel; so the Wolf was the first to dig through. When the Bear came through, he found out that the Wolf had already dug through. The Bear stood up, and said, "You have beaten me, but this young man shall be my son, and I shall help him whenever he calls upon me."

The Wolf took the boy among the Wolves. The boy soon ceased to care to walk, and began to crawl upon his hands and knees, and to eat raw meat, just as the Wolves did. He came to act like a Wolf. The skin upon his haunches was now so thick that he could slide on them.

In the village, the boy's father mourned for him for many years. But in a chase for buffalo somebody saw a drove of Wolves with this human being among them. He told other people about it. After the hunt was over, all the men in the camp went out where they had killed the buffalo and there they found the Wolves, and this human being among them. They ran their horses after the Wolves, but this human being ran so fast that he beat all the Wolves and escaped; but they knew that it was the young man. For a whole year they planned to catch the human Wolf, but he was so swift that they could not catch him.

Now, there was a man in the tribe who had medicines for catching the human Wolf and for taking the Wolf feeling out of him. This man agreed to try to catch the human Wolf. So the man went and selected a place in a hilly country. There was a steep bank on the west side, another on the south side, and another on the east side, and there was an opening at the north side. Having selected this place, the man told the people to make their village about three miles east from there. He ordered the women to go to this place, and dig a deep hole on the south side of the banks, so that the Wolves could not climb out. The women also cut long poles and set them on the top of the banks, so that, in case the Wolf did crawl up, these poles would be in his way. At the opening, long poles were set up, so that there was left only a little opening. They also strung a lot of willows, which was to be a doorway to close up the entrance. The man now ordered a certain number of young men to go and kill buffalo. These young men went out, and they killed the buffalo, brought the meat, and placed it inside of this enclosure. The Wolves followed them up, and then the men on horseback circled the Wolves and ran them into this trap, the human Wolf among them. There were four strong men who put on rawhide leggings, and caps with holes in them, so that they could see, and these four men were put into the trap. They ran after the Wolf man. Every time the Wolves ran around by the doorway the door was removed, and the Wolves went out. At last they had the man Wolf by himself. The entrance was stopped. The four men finally succeeded in catching the Wolf man. Then they tied him and took him out. He tried to bite them, but the rawhide was so dry that he could not hurt them. While the four men were catching him the medicine-man had built a sweat-lodge. The hot stones were taken into the lodge quickly and the man was taken in there and tied. The man poured water upon the hot stones, and sweated the Wolf man. The medicine-man kept pouring water on the stones, until the Wolf man begged for some water. Then the medicine-man gave him some medicine that he had prepared, and the Wolf man began to vomit. The Wolf man vomited hairs of Wolves, white clay, also froth and raw meat. All this time the people were rubbing wild sage upon his body, especially upon his knees. The Wolf man became exhausted and finally said, "I feel better now." The medicine-man continued to give him medicine until the Wolf man could vomit no more. They then untied him and took him into his lodge, and he finally recovered.

The Wolf man stayed in bed all night and the next day. Then, in the night, he sent for his father. He told his father that he wanted him to build a tipi, and that towards evening he wanted him to go through the village and invite the bravest men in the tribe to come to his, the father's, tipi—not to the tipi he had built for the boy.

Now, the seven girls who had put the boy into the hole were invited. They were told to dress up in their fine clothes, and as he had promised to marry them he wanted them to come to his tipi that they had put up for him. These girls came to the tipi, and the young man gave them seats. The young man left the lodge, and told his father to place the brave men around the lodge; that he was going out, and as soon as he should come back the guards were to leave their stations. The boy went to the north, and cried, "Father, my father, come and help me!" The Wolves came up, and said: "We will help you. What is it you want?" The boy said: "The girls who were the cause of my being with the Wolves are in my tipi. I want you to devour them." The Wolves promised that they would. Then the boy went to the west, among the cedars, and there he cried: "Father Bear, make haste. I have something for you to eat." The Bear came, and said, "My son, what is it?" The boy said: "The girls who put me into the hole are now in my tipi. I want you to go with your friends and devour them." The Bear said: "We will do this gladly; we will come." The boy went back to the village, and stood a little distance from his tipi. Soon the Wolves came on his left, and the Bears came from behind. He led them up to his tipi. He told the Wolves to stand on the north side, and the Bears to stand on the west and south side. After this was done, the young man went into the tipi, and said: "Girls, you put me into a hole, and you left me there to die. The Wolves took me out, and I was with the Wolves for some time. Those same Wolves are now to eat you up." The girls begged for mercy, but there was no mercy shown them. Each girl tried to crawl out from where she was sitting, but the Wolves ate them.

At the same time the old man, the boy's father, went through the village, telling the people that the seven girls were being devoured by wild animals, because they had dug the hole and placed his son there to die. The old man told the story of the taking off of the young man's clothing, and of the girls' promise to take the boy out of the hole if he would do certain things which he had refused to do, and of their leaving the boy in the hole to die.

When the people heard the story they were angry at the girls, so that the relatives of the girls did not offer to save them, as the girls had done wrong.

The next day the people broke camp and went away from the place. This young man became a great warrior and a brave, and finally became a chief. He married and started a dance among the Arikara that is known as the "Wolf dance." This was a young man's dance, but the people do not dance it any more.

FOOTNOTES:

[31] Told by Snowbird.

31.
THE MEDICINE DANCE OF THE BEAVER, TURTLE, AND WITCH-WOMAN[32]

In olden times the animals met in a lodge to have sleight-of-hand performances. All the medicine-animals and all the birds who had magic power went to this lodge. The animals decided that only the leading animals should perform—the Beaver, the soft-shell Turtle, and the old Witch-Woman.

First, the crowd arose where sat the Medicine-Beaver. The Beaver arose and began to sing, telling his followers to sing. Then the Beaver went to the first post, which was supporting the lodge at the southeast, and began to gnaw it. The post was gnawed until only a small piece of it remained. The Beavers still sang. The Beaver then went to the next post and gnawed away at the base. He gnawed until just a little was left. The Beavers still sang and the Beaver went to the next post and gnawed until he had nearly gnawed through.

The people began to get scared. The animals also became scared, so they called upon the errand man to ask the Beaver not to gnaw the post through, for the lodge was about to fall. The errand man arose and begged the Medicine-Beaver to stop. The Beaver stopped, and then ran around the lodge, repaired all the posts again, and said: "This was only sleight-of-hand. It is not real." The animals and lookers-on rejoiced to see the trick, for now the lodge stood solid as usual.

Now came the Turtle, who was mad because the Beaver fooled the people. So he called for his followers, and they gathered around him and sang:

"Let me stand where my fathers stood.

Let a flood pour forth from my throat!

I am doing something wonderful.

Let all people look!"

So the people looked. The Turtle took his knife and stuck it close to his left collar-bone. Water began to pour forth from the cut, until there was water all over the lodge. Then the people began to get scared. The errand man was requested to beg the Turtle to stop pouring forth water in the lodge. The errand man begged the Turtle and the Turtle inhaled and drew all the water back into himself. The people all took their places again. Stawi, a Witch-Woman, came, and said:

"Gun given me by old medicine-men.

Gun given me by old medicine-men.

Gun given me by old medicine-men."

The old woman had a buffalo robe over her shoulders, and she held in her hands a mysterious-looking thing dotted with spots of white clay and painted in black. At the top of it were red feathers. The object was a gun, a thing to kill with, to shoot medicine. Now, at this time, the old woman wanted to show the power of this mysterious object. She ran around the lodge and then placed the object upon the ground. She ran to it. She wrestled with it. She covered it with her robe. Now she lifted it. She ran around, and all at once she began to groan—as if in pain. At last she called for help, for she was in misery. The people went to her, and there they found the old woman in travail. She was cared for, and she gave birth to a child, who was to become a great medicine-man among the people and a leader in the medicine dance. The medicine-animals rejoiced and sang their songs again with joy.

FOOTNOTES:

[32] Told by White-Bear.

32.
THE VILLAGE-BOY AND THE WOLF POWER[33]

In olden times there was a village, and in this village was a man who had five children—four girls and a boy. In the dances, the girls would go out and take part, although the boy never went on the war-path, and never left the village. For this reason the people called the boy "Village-Boy."

After a time the people began to make fun of the girls for dancing when their brother had never gone out on the war-path nor taken part in the battle, fought near the village. The girls were sorry. The boy saw that the girls were being made fun of for dancing when he had not gone on the war-path. The young man told his father that he was going up on a high mound where there was a graveyard. The father was glad of this. The boy put black soot upon his face, and he stuck some grass arrows in his hair. He went up into the graveyard, and there he stood, mourning.

While he was there, a big white timber Wolf came to him and asked him what he was crying about. The boy told him that he was a poor boy; that he had never been on the war-path, nor taken a scalp; that he had four sisters who danced in the scalp-dance and were ridiculed for dancing when their brother had never been on the war-path. The Wolf told the boy not to cry, for he would take care of him. The Wolf then told the boy that he would look after him; that he should go into the village; and that the first time there was a war-party he should join it and start out with it; that he, the Wolf, would find him and lead him to the enemy's camp.

One day it was noised through the camp that the people were going on the war-path. Village-Boy then told his friend that if after they had been gone for three days the scouts should kill any Buffalo, he should get some of the knee-caps of the Buffalo and keep them for him, as he would follow close after them.

The war-party started out, and after they had been gone three days Village-Boy told his father that he was going to start out to overtake the war-party. He also told his sisters to make him some moccasins. So the young man started out on the journey; but before this happened the Wolf had been coming to visit the young man, and had taught the young man the secret powers of the Wolf. So the young man started out, and when he had come to a ravine he rolled himself upon the ground, and when he got up he was a Wolf.

The Wolf followed the trail of the warriors. Some time in the night he came to their camp. He did not go right into the camp, but stayed behind, and some time in the night he barked like a Wolf. His friend said, "There is my friend, Village-Boy." He took up the burned bones and took them to him. When he got there it was the Village-Boy. He threw the bones at the boy. The boy gnawed at the bones, just like a Wolf. When Village-Boy got through eating, he told his friend to go back to the camp where the others were and to watch out, for the next day he should see him, and that then he should tell the people that it was Village-Boy. The boy went to the camp, while Village-Boy went on ahead.

The next day Village-Boy was seen coming. Village-Boy's friend told the other warriors that he was Village-Boy. So he ran up to Village-Boy. Village-Boy then told his friend that the enemy's camp was a short distance away. The warriors then stopped and sang some songs for Village-Boy. Village-Boy departed. The next day they saw him again, driving many ponies. He brought them to the people. Then he led the warriors into camp. The war-party then attacked the enemy's village. Village-Boy was in the lead. He killed one enemy and took his scalp. He left, and hid out while the battle was going on. After a time the warriors came back where the horses were, and Village-Boy came there. He gave the scalp to the leader of the war-party, also all the ponies, telling him that he was going ahead of them.

Village-Boy now returned to his home. Not a word was spoken by him, nor was anything said by him about the battle. He just lay upon his bed.

A few days afterward the war-party returned home and near the village had a sham battle. The people went out to meet them. It was announced by the leader of the war-party that Village-Boy had done all the killing, and capturing of the ponies. Village-Boy's father thought that the warriors were making fun of his son because he had come back several days before without anything. But when the warriors came into the village and showed the scalp that Village-Boy had taken and given to the leader, and also when the ponies he had captured were brought to the village, then all the old men believed. Village-Boy's father scolded him because he had said nothing. Scalp dances were made throughout the village. The young man's sisters now danced the scalp-dance without fear of ridicule. Whenever the young man went out to dance the women surrounded him. He married and became one of the great men of the village.

One day he took several warriors and went east. He came to a village that was known as the "Village-of-the-Dumb-People." He left the war-party behind and went into the village by himself. He killed their medicine-man, cut his throat, and carried the head away. As he carried the head away it kept mumbling. The people became excited when they found out that their prophet was dead. They began to talk in a peculiar language. These warriors were followed by the Dumb-People, who did not catch up with them.

The head of the medicine-man was placed in the village. When the head dried it turned into a kind of wood. The people used this head for medicinal purposes. When they wanted to give it to a patient they scraped a portion from the head and gave it to the person for certain sicknesses. It cured many people. The same head is still among our people, only it is about the size of a hen's egg now.

FOOTNOTES:

[33] Told by Yellow-Bear.

33.
THE RABBIT-BOY.[34]

In olden times there was a village upon the Missouri River. In this village the young men were all the time going on the war-path, and there were many dances going on. There was a young man who took no part in their dances, nor in their war-parties. The people made fun of him, but he did not care. Each morning he would sleep until after the sun was high. When he ate he would climb up and sit upon the top of the lodge; but the girls did not seem to care for him. His father scolded him, and wanted to know what was the matter with him. So the young man said, "I have never been anywhere, and I have never felt like going anywhere, but to-day I feel like going upon the graveyard hill, to stand and mourn, and to see if the gods will help me." The old man took out his white clay. He put it upon the boy, and told him to go up to the graveyard. He said that he hoped the gods would help him. The boy went up on the hill and stood by the graveyard. In the afternoon it stormed. The boy huddled himself against a grave mound. The boy's father came up and tried to coax him to come down, but the boy was determined to stay there. The old man and the old woman took a piece of buffalo hide and stretched it over the boy, and there he remained during the storm, which lasted several days.

As soon as it cleared up there was a noise overhead that sounded like big wind. The boy did not know what it was, but he could hear whistling coming down from above, then it would come up again. While he was there wondering what it was, there came a Jack-Rabbit. It crawled under his robe. Then an Eagle swooped down and sat by the boy, and it said, "My son, I have run that animal down, and I want you to give it to me, so that I can eat it." The Rabbit said: "My son, do not give me up! Do not listen to the Eagle! Just now he has the best of me. If you save me I will give you powers that I possess." The Eagle said: "Give him to me; I want to eat him! If you give him to me I will give you as many scalps (stretching out his right wing) as there are feathers in this wing." But the young man would not turn the Rabbit loose, for the Rabbit begged him, and said, "I will make you a great warrior." Then the Eagle said: "Turn that thing loose, so I can eat it, and when I am satisfied, I will give you powers that I possess. I will give you as many scalps as I have feathers on both wings." But the Rabbit begged hard, and said: "No, do not turn me loose; he will do nothing of the kind. He will take me and eat me and tell you nothing of his power." The Eagle spread out its wings, and said: "Now see. So many scalps will I give you." Then the Eagle spread out its tail, and said: "As many feathers as are in my tail—as many of the enemy you shall strike, counting coup. Now give me that which you have there and let me eat it." The boy said, "No, the Rabbit came to me, and I will take care of him." The Eagle flew up and away.

The Rabbit now crawled out of the boy's robe and sat down by him. After a while he said: "My son, I am thankful to you for saving my life. I will make you a great warrior. I will give you a war-club. I will give you a rabbit-skin to wear about your neck. I will give you paint, which you shall put upon your body, and with this club you will kill many enemies." So the Rabbit gave the rabbit-skin, the war-club, and the medicine paints to the boy.

The boy went down into the village in the night, hung his club and rabbit-skin over the head of his bed, lay down, and went to sleep. The next morning, when the father woke up, he saw these things hanging up. He awakened his wife and told her to see the things that the son had brought back with him. They were both glad to see that the boy had returned.

At this time there was a war-party starting out. The young man told his sisters to make him several pairs of moccasins, for he was going to follow up the warriors. The warriors had been gone for four days when the boy started to follow them. He overtook them on the same day. He selected himself as a scout to go on ahead and see what he could find in the enemy's country. The young man found the enemy's camp. He came back and told the warriors what he had found. He then sat down among the warriors. The leader took from his bundle a flint knife and stuck it in the ground in front of where the warriors were sitting. The leading warrior also took a spear and stuck it in the ground. He also stuck in the ground an arrow. "Now," said he, "warriors, whosoever is going to do hard fighting will please rise and choose the weapon he wishes to fight with." The young man, who was now known as the "Rabbit-Boy," arose and took the flint knife. He waited to see if somebody else would take the other weapons. None of them did, so the boy took up the spear and arrow.

Among the warriors was a young man who was very poor. Rabbit-Boy took a liking for him and gave him the spear. He told the young man to follow him wherever he should go. Rabbit-Boy then rose, and said: "Leader and warriors! I shall go on ahead. I shall bring all the ponies belonging to the enemy. I shall hide them in a hollow." The leader said, "It is well." So the young man went and brought all the ponies from the village and hid them in a hollow. The young man came and told the leader that the ponies were safe.

The next thing was to attack the enemy in their camp. Rabbit-Boy took his white clay, put it all over his body, put some rabbit-skins around his ankles, also upon his wrists, and then he put a whole skin around his neck, and the two feathers he put on his head to represent rabbit's ears. The only weapon that he had was the war-club that had been given to him by the Rabbit. Rabbit-Boy planned the attack. The warriors all crawled up to the village just before daylight, and as the sun was coming up in the east an old man came out of the village. He went around yelling for the people to wake and go after their ponies. As he passed in front of where the Rabbit-Boy was, Rabbit-Boy ran and struck the old man on the head and killed him. Then Rabbit-Boy went through the village. As he came to the center of the village he was just about to go by a big tipi, when out came a pretty young girl, who carried a hide-scraper and a robe. The girl saw the young man very plainly. She stopped and watched him. She wished that she might in some way assist him to get away. The people tried their best to kill Rabbit-Boy, but he escaped safe. He then went and joined the other warriors, for they had run away. They reached the ponies, which they divided, and then they went home. When they arrived the people told of the wonderful powers of Rabbit-Boy, and there was great rejoicing in his lodge. The people then recognized him as a great warrior.

Three or four days afterwards the same party of warriors went to the same village. The boy went through the same movements, killing the first man that came out from the village, and as soon as the boy had done these things, the warriors became bold and fought the enemy.

The enemy never charged their village for a long time. The young man was never known as Rabbit-Man in the enemy's camp. Every time he attacked the village he went through by way of the girl's tipi. Each time, the girl came out of the tipi. The girl met the boy. At one of these times when the boy had attacked the village and killed a man, he ran by the tipi and saw the girl. The girl cheered him. The boy went on. In another of these attacks, the boy saw the girl. He knew that she must like him. He went on through the village and home.

The people in the boy's village had scalp dances where all the women took part. The young man seldom took part, but his sisters took part. One night when Rabbit-Boy was lying on his bed the women came. They took him out and made him dance. He danced several times. Four or five women became fond of him and tried to marry him, but he would pay no attention to them. While all this dancing was going on, the girl in the enemy's camp was making a pretty pair of moccasins, a pair of beaded bracelets and beaded armlets. She sent for a servant, a woman captive from the Arikara. The girl told the woman that she would help her to get back to her people if she would speak to a young man who was killing her people all the time. This servant woman said that she had no way of traveling. The girl said: "I shall give you two of my best ponies, and I want you to take these moccasins and bracelets to that young man, and tell him that he is a brave man; that I want him very badly; and that when he shall come to my tipi I shall have six tipi pegs drawn up on the north side of the tipi where my bed is; that when he shall reach in his hand I will feel for the bracelet, and if I find it upon his wrist I shall know that it is he." So the girl took the servant woman out of the camp, caught two of her ponies, and they rode many miles. The girl then handed the bracelets, moccasins, and something to eat to the servant woman and told her to go to her people. The woman thanked the girl and went back to her people.

She came to the village of the Arikara. In the night she went to the dances. She asked one woman where Rabbit-Boy was. It happened that on this night the young man was dancing, so the woman went and danced with the young man, then whispered to him and told him that she wanted to see him. The young man thought that she wanted to marry him, but when they were away from the people the woman told Rabbit-Boy how the girl in the enemy's camp had helped her to get away; that it was the girl who had her tipi in the center of the village every time he went through; that the girl wanted him; and that she had given him the moccasins and the bracelets for him to wear when he should go to her village. The young man said, "I will go." So the young man started that night. He traveled all the next day and the next night before he reached the enemy's camp. He went to the north side of the tipi. He felt for the pegs, and there were six of them drawn up. He then knew that the woman had told the truth. He put his hand in, and it was caught. The woman felt for the bracelet, and when she had found it she pulled Rabbit-Boy in. The young man crawled into the tipi and put his robe on top of hers, and crawled under it. There they lay together, although they could not talk. The young man stayed with the girl all night. In the morning, when the girl's father, who was chief of the tribe, woke up, he saw the things that the boy wore in battle hanging down from a tipi pole. He looked down and there he saw Rabbit-Boy in bed with his daughter. He made a big fire and sent for the warriors. The warriors came, preparing to kill the young man. There was one man who did not come with the rest, but when he came he told the people to disperse to their homes; that although the young man had been killing their people, he, for one, was glad that he had come and married one of their girls; that now he would not kill any more, but that he would lead their people out to the enemy's country and help kill the people. So the young man and the girl were told to rise and sit by the fireplace. The young man stayed in this village for several months. Now, the people at Rabbit-Boy's home thought that he had died. But the woman who had returned from captivity told them that he would be coming after a while and that she knew where he was.

The old chief was much pleased to have Rabbit-Boy for a son-in-law, for now he would have scalps hanging on top of his tipi. The people got together one day and said they wanted to go on the war-path. The young man joined them. They went to his own country. The young man put his people at a certain place, while he himself went near to the village and found women who were working in their corn patches. There he found one woman whom the Arikara had captured from the people of his wife's tribe. Rabbit-Boy killed this woman, took her scalp, and took it back to the people of her tribe. Then the people all went back to their camp and had war dances. The scalp was given to the old chief. He had it strung between his tipi poles, so the scalp hung high in the air. Every time a war-party went out this young man would go with it. He would manage to get the people to stay at a distance. He would then go to the fields, and whenever he found a captive from this tribe he would kill it, but he would not kill members of his own tribe. The young man led several war-parties, and always managed to kill captives, but never killed members of his own tribe. Finally the old chief asked that they might go to the young man's home. This they did. The young man's people gave him presents for his wife's people. They then returned to their country. The Arikara visited them, and they made peace. They never made war on one another any more.

FOOTNOTES:

[34] Told by Elk.

34.
THE MAN AND THE WATER-DOGS.[35]

Long ages ago there was a village with so many inhabitants that it had four medicine-lodges. There was one man who was so brave that his fame extended beyond the village. He committed some evil deeds among his own people, but his people were afraid to correct him. Thus he went on, committing more misdemeanors. He became so bad that the people undertook to take his life. They formed a plot to seize him. One family invited the man to a feast. When he entered the lodge many men gathered about the lodge and waited till he came out. The man came out and walked very slowly toward the river. He never paid no attention to the men nor even tried to fight back, but went on his way. Finally he stepped into the river, and some one cried out to the men to catch him, but it was too late. He sank down in the water and the people shouted for joy, because they thought he was drowned.

The man walked on down on the bottom of the river and he saw there a tipi. From its door came a Dog, and the Dog called to the man to come in. He went in, and he saw many Dogs. The leader of the Dogs raised his head and said that he was not hurt and that they never would injure him. The leader showed much mercy toward the man and told him not to be afraid of any man; and that if he should ever get hurt he was to come right to the water and the Dogs would be glad to receive him. So the man went out of the tipi and came up out of the water. When it was night he went to the village.

He entered his house and saw his wife. He sat down and told her that he regarded as nothing all the wounds he had received from the men who tried to kill him. The woman was surprised, and was much afraid of him. The man ordered his wife to go after some tobacco from one of the councils that was being held in the village. She went at once and entered one of the councils. She asked the head men for some tobacco for her husband. The men were much agitated and afraid, so they gave her some tobacco. The woman returned and the man was much pleased. The men in the council decided to send a messenger to see if the man had returned. One young man went and peeped in and saw the man, all naked, sitting in his tipi. He returned to the council and told what he had seen. The men were more afraid. From that time on, the man committed worse crimes than before, yet the people were afraid to make another attempt to kill him. The man's relatives gathered with the woman's relatives and they separated from the village, to return no more. They went in the night, and before morning they camped. Some young men and the famous one came to the village and killed a man and a woman. The people knew who it was and yet they did not dare to fight them. This was a separation where the people never meet again, which happened because the man did the bad deeds.

FOOTNOTES:

[35] Told by Strike-Enemy.

35.
THE FIVE TURTLES AND THE BUFFALO DANCE[36]

In olden times, while the people had their village upon the Missouri River, five soft-shell Turtles came out from the river and went into the village. The two on each side of the middle one received a bunch of eagle feathers on the head. They were placed with the fifth, which had black feathers. When this Turtle saw that its feathers were black, it was mad. It told the people that it was going away, and it marched back into the river. The people gave it smoke from their sacred pipes. The Turtle paid no attention to it, but went into the river, so there were but four left. These four Turtles were to remain with the people.

These Turtles died. The people made them into drums. Some years afterwards they changed these drums into rawhide drums, making them in imitation of the Turtle drums. They organized a dance known as the "Buffalo dance." These Turtles were drums. They danced four days and four nights, and although this was a Buffalo dance, there was one mysterious being in the crowd who had a bunch of feathers of the magpie growing up all over his head. Pieces of skins of animals were strapped over his back, and he had a buffalo beard about his ankles, also about his waist. His face was painted with all colors. Sub eius inguinibus palus erat qui penem simulabat. Ex illo autem, dum saliebat et quasi equus acer huc et illuc currebat, palus semper pandebat. Ubicumque mulierem videbat, eam circumibat motusque dabat quasi cum ea concumberet.

Now, in this village there was a young girl who was never permitted to be out of the lodge while this Buffalo dance was going on and this being was dancing around. The girl asked her parents to place a buffalo rawhide in front of the lodge, over the entrance, that she might be permitted to peep out and look at the being. She became bold, and went out from behind the hide. She was seen by this being. Ille motus dedit quasi cum ea concumberet. Puella in domicilium rediit; posteaque per menses magis atque magis gravida fiebat. Iam tandem puerum parit. Anum comitem habet, quæ autem reperire non potest. The mother told them that the child had been born, so the people looked around with lights, trying to find the child. They looked everywhere, but could not find the child. After a while they found the child standing under the altar, grinning. The child looked to be about two years old, and had teeth. It walked about constantly, just as its father did, and was like him in appearance. Finitimi repperunt eam numquam virum cognovisse, sed ab eo monstro per eius motus gravidam factam esse. The people caught the child and killed it. They put it into a bag and threw the bag into the river.

The father of the child heard about this. He went to another wonderful man who could see better in the night than in the day and asked him to help him find the child. The man consented. He took his medicines, put them upon himself and led the man to the very spot where he had danced and where he had made the motions. Then the medicine-man led the mysterious being into the lodge of the girl who had given birth to the child. He showed where the boy had been born, where he had run, where he had stood under the sacred bundle, how the people caught him and killed him, and how the people had taken him to the river and thrown him in. They went down to the river. The medicine-man took a big rock and told the strange being that when he should throw the rock into the waters, the waters would part, and that he must be quick to jump in and get the boy. The man threw the stone up into the air, and as it fell into the water, the waters parted, and they could see the boy lying there. The man jumped in and pulled him out. When the boy was pulled out the father cried, and said that he wanted this wonderful man to select a place to bury him, for he was a strange child. The man led this mysterious being about the hill on the Missouri River, and there the man took his club, and striking the largest stone that the people knew of, he split it in two. They buried the child between the two stones, and then went home. The mysterious being then married the girl who had given birth to the mysterious little boy who, immediately after his birth, got to dancing and running around as his father had always done in dances.

FOOTNOTES:

[36] Told by Yellow-Bear.

36.
THE NOTCHED STICK AND THE OLD WOMAN OF THE ISLAND[37]

When my people held the medicine-men's ceremonies, the leading medicine-man, who sat in the west of the lodge, had a roll of dried buffalo hide and a long stick with notches upon it. The leaders of the medicine-men's lodge had sticks that they rubbed on this notched stick so that the dried buffalo hide made a noise sounding something like that of a drum. When this noise was begun they began to rattle the gourds. At the end of the ceremony of the medicine-men the lodges inside of the big lodge were taken down to the river, and the notched stick and the dried buffalo hide were taken and placed upon an island. We were told not to go to the island; but knowing the place, one man went, and he saw in place of the hide and stick an old woman sitting there. He saw her plainly. Her ears hung down with great, big cuts in them. She had a very long face. When he took a look at her she turned her nose up. He was scared and ran away towards the village. He met some other boys and told them about the old woman. They would not believe him, so they went back, and when they came to the island, sure enough, it was no longer the old woman, but the hide and stick.

When the man went home he told his father all about it, and he said: "True, my son; that is the reason that they put the objects upon the island, because really they are an old woman." Other boys also visited the island, and they saw the same old woman. When several went to the island another time, it was again a stick.

FOOTNOTES:

[37] Told by White-Owl.

37.
THE MAN WHO MARRIED A COYOTE[38]

A long time ago there was a war-party that started out from the Arikara country toward the south. They were found by the enemy and attacked. One man was killed and the others all returned home. After many years this man who was killed rose from where he was lying, for he had not really been killed, but was simply stunned by falling onto hard ground. He had not been scalped. After this man came to, he wandered over the prairies and fell in with the Coyotes. He finally married a Coyote, and lived with her for several years.

One day some men went hunting, and they saw a mysterious being crossing the Missouri River. The warriors went down and surrounded this mysterious being and caught him. He was not scalped, nor wounded, but he had changed his ways so that he could live with the Coyotes, and he was almost like an animal. The people begged him to go home, saying that his wife and children were well and that his wife was not married again. But he said: "I know; but I cannot, for I am married." They took him notwithstanding, and they gave him medicines. He became well, and he entered the medicine-lodge. The man asked permission to do some sleight-of-hand, and the medicine-men gave him the privilege to do so. He took a man, went around the lodge and vomited up a lot of hair, white clay, and other things. After all this had come out of him he was cleansed from being a Coyote. He continued with the sleight-of-hand, and he told the people that he was going to call his wife; that his wife was the one that he was afraid of, and this was the reason he had not returned home. So he went up onto the top of the lodge and shouted and shouted; then he went around to the west and shouted; then to the north and to the east; then he came into the lodge, and said, "My wife is far away." He went out again and shouted to the northwest, and after a while the people heard the Coyotes away off. They kept coming nearer and nearer, and the people ran away. The Coyotes kept on coming, and the people ran into the lodge. The Coyote whom the man had married came into the lodge. When she entered the lodge she went around to the northeast of the fireplace, by way of the south, west, and north, and then to the northeast, and there she took her place. "This," said the man, "is my wife." The men called her names, saying: "You long-

Traditions Of The Arikara | 135

nosed thing! Why did you not come? Why do you run off so far away?" The leading medicine-man now arose. A pipe was given to him filled with native tobacco. He made some smoke to the Coyote woman. After the smoke the Coyote woman left the lodge and went off to join the other Coyotes. The people saw this female Coyote, and now knew that this man did have a Coyote woman.

Many years afterwards this same man was roaming over the prairies, when a blizzard blew up. Just a little before sunset he came to a bank of snow, and there lay one of his baby Coyotes. He went to pick up the baby, but as he was so cold, he let the baby Coyote stay in the snow, and he went home. After he had warmed himself he went out to see if the baby was still in the snow, but when he got there, there was no baby at all.

FOOTNOTES:

[38] Told by Many-Fox.

38.
THE MAN WHO TURNED INTO A STONE[39]

Once upon a time there was a big village on a prairie. In the village there was an old man who was respected by all. Because he was well-known as a medicine-man he had one of the sacred bundles, and he used to call councils and many other meetings. If there was sacrifice to be offered to some of the gods it was brought before this old man, because the gods seemed always to make returns for all his offerings. For this reason, he was above all other medicine-men in the village.

At one time a very large party went out from the village on a buffalo hunt. A few were left in the village. For many days one young man kept coming and reporting that the people were coming not very far away. The next day they saw them coming, but away in the distance. It was the custom for these people to go out to meet them before they reached the village, so many, including the old medicine-man, went out to meet them. The old man came to a hill, and there he sat down. The people traveled on foot in those days. As the party came to the old man they only saluted him. There was another custom of bringing some dried meat to some medicine-men, especially to this famous old man, and offering up sacrifices to the gods. This was the old man's reason for going up there. Finally most of them passed toward the village, but none of the young men had any dried meat to present to the old man for him to give thanks to his sacred bundle. They all passed, save one young man who came last. When he saw the old man sitting there he saluted him and gave him a dried buffalo tongue. The old man did not seem thankful for it, but sat there with his head down.

When they all reached the village they made many feasts, and councils were held in many places. The next day it was noticed that the old medicine-man was missing. They looked for him, but could not find him. One young man told that he had seen him sitting on the hill. So they went to the hill and asked the old man to come down, but he would not. One medicine-man took a sacred pipe from his bundle and offered it to the old man to smoke, so that he might forget his sorrows. The old man would not accept it, because, he said, it was too late. The people begged him to come, but still he sat there with his head cast downward. After a while he raised his head and said to all, that it was too late to get up, that he was to sit there always. He removed his blanket, and the people saw that his legs had already turned to stone. The people all wept and went away. They came the next day, and they saw a rock in the form of a man, and they all cried again for the loss of the old medicine-man, because there had been no one to give him any dry meat to offer up as sacrifice to the gods.

FOOTNOTES:

[39] Told by Hawk.

39.
THE WOMAN WHO TURNED INTO A STONE.[40]

In the village there was a nice-looking young woman, daughter of one of the chiefs. They all liked her and had much admiration for her. Many young men made great efforts to get the young girl to marry, but she would not consent. After many failures on the men's side the young woman's father tried to persuade her to marry some young man. After all their advice the young woman refused to marry. Again the old mother related to her daughter that it was most enjoyable to live with a man, to have a man to support her, to cherish her, and to protect her from all troubles. The young woman accepted the mother's advice at last, and she said she would marry.

One young man, a very good hunter, came to the young girl, and after a long conversation persuaded her to promise that she would marry him. The young woman told her mother, and she was glad, and willing that her daughter should marry him; for the young man was capable and qualified to support a family. Finally the young man was called, and came to their lodge. Puellam in matrimonium duxit. Cum nox esset, ad lectum genialem venerunt. Iuvenis gavisus est quod tandem puellæ amore potiturus esset. Cum autem cum uxore sua concumbere conaretur, non poterat. Per noctem totam frustra conabatur. Postridie puella ad matrem venit, eique ostendit cur virum habere noluisset. Deinde tunicam sustulit ostenditque se helianthes pro volva habere. Mater autem vidit quo iuvenis helianthi nocuisset dum cum uxore concumbere conabatur. So the young woman took her bundle on her back, journeyed to a certain place, sat down and turned to stone, because she was ashamed.

FOOTNOTES:

[40] Told by Hawk.

40.
THE POWER OF THE BLOODY
SCALPED-MAN[41]

There was a young man in the Arikara village who wanted to have some mysterious power. He went through the different places, over high mountains, and steep banks. He had heard of a place to the west of the village where young men had been scared away. He went to the place and stood upon a hill which was close to the Missouri River. He stood there for three days and nights, and during the third night he heard a mysterious noise from the Missouri River. He looked, and saw a man coming. The man approached, and said, "You will please leave at once, for you make too much noise around this place." The man had a war-club in his right hand. His body was daubed all over with white clay; his head was red with blood and the blood was dripping from his forehead. The boy became scared, and he ran home. He told one of his friends what had happened to him and his friend laughed at him for running away from the place where he had gone to get some power.

The young man's friend made up his mind that he would go to the hill. He went to the hill, and there he stood and cried for three days and three nights. On the fourth night a being came up, and sure enough, it was the very same being that the first young man had seen. The boy became scared, but he closed his eyes and thought, "Well, I came here to see this being, and if he wants to kill me he can do so." The young man made up his mind not to run. He looked at the man as he approached. Drops of fresh blood were dripping from his head, so that he looked as if he had just been scalped. The young man closed his eyes and the man came up to him, and said, "If you do not run, I will hit you with this club!" The boy did not move, but the man did not strike him with his club. At last the man said: "Come with me. I am the errand man of the men who live under this hill." So the man took the boy down towards the Missouri River, and there, under the bank, was an entrance. They went into this entrance, and there they found a long passageway along which they traveled, and finally they came to a cave. There the men were seated around in a circle; but not one of them was scalped. The man who took the young man into this place now took off the headdress that he had on, and his hair fell over his shoulders. He placed his war-club and the bloody headdress that he had had on his head, before the leading man. The man took his seat at the entrance, and the young man was given a seat in the lodge. The leader of the men in the lodge said: "You are the first young man who has not run from our errand man, and now we will give you the power that we possess. When you want to perform the same thing that you saw that man do, take wild sage, put it on hot coals, and smoke yourself over your body. Then take this sweet grass and spread it all over yourself. Then take this paint and put it in the water and after putting this skin over your head, place this paint, mixed in water, on your head, so that you will look like a scalped-man. This war-club you shall take. This root you shall put into your mouth, so that you can run swiftly. When you have killed an enemy and taken his scalp, bring that scalp to us." The young man took the things and went home. The next morning, the people found a war-club hanging over the young man's head, and the young man was lying upon his bed.

Many days after this there was a cry in the camp, "The enemy is coming to take the village!" The young man sent all the people out of his lodge, and told them to tell the people not to be in a certain pathway that he had to go through, for he wanted to go that way. The young man took up some coals from the fireplace and placed them west of the fireplace. On these he placed the sage, and let the smoke pass over his body. He took the white clay and put it all over his body. Then he twisted his hair, put the skin over his head, then took the red paint and put it in water. He dipped his hands into the water and put it on top of his head. He took the war-club and ran out of the lodge, and some of the people were scared when they saw him, for he looked like a man that had just been scalped. He ran to where the battle was going on, and the people saw him on the west side of the battlefield. He ran towards the enemy and killed one. He went around his own people, and went on the west side again and attacked the enemy, killing another one with his war-club. He scattered the enemy, because he looked so fierce on account of the blood which was dripping from his head. As soon as the enemy retreated and his people ran after them, he went back to his lodge, took the skin off from his head, put some medicine upon the fire and smoked all over his body. He then went to a creek and washed. He came back into his own lodge, and by this time the people had returned. The scalp which he had taken he put upon a long pole and placed it outside of the lodge. In the night he disappeared, for he went to the place where he had received his power.

The people did not know who he was, but after several battles they found out. They also learned that he had great powers. He became a great man through attacking the enemy, for he had power to go out on the war-path and bring home many scalps. They were not really scalps, but were pieces of scalps which he had made himself. He would not be a chief, but became a great medicine-man.

FOOTNOTES:

[41] Told by Antelope.

41.
THE BOY WHO CARRIED A SCALPED-MAN INTO CAMP[42]

In olden times the Arikara went on the war-path. They came to a lake where they made their camp. In the night the enemy attacked them, and ran them into the lake, killing all the warriors and taking their scalps.

Another party of brave warriors started out from the same village, and went on the war-path. As they journeyed towards the east they came near to the lake. There they made their camp. Among these last warriors was a very poor young man who had joined them. In the night the leader asked the young men to go after some water; but all the young men refused. The poor boy took up the vessels and went down to the lake. As he tried to dip the vessel into the water, some one spoke close by him, and said, "Go a little beyond and dip up water." The young man waded into the water, and as he was about to dip the water, again some one else spoke to him, and said: "Go beyond. Go further into the lake and get your water." The young man went on into the lake, and just as he was about to take up the water, again some one else spoke to him, and said, "Do not dip up the water there, but go further into the lake to dip it." The young man turned around, and said, "Who are you that speaks to me?" The man said: "I am the leader who took the young men out on the war-path. We ran into this lake and were killed, and we were all scalped. All around the edge of the lake the water is colored with our blood, and that is why I am telling you to go further into the lake to dip your water." About this time the moon appeared. The night was windy and cloudy, so that every once in a while the clouds passed over the moon and hid it. The boy looked around, and he saw sitting near him a man whose head was all bloody, and whose hands and feet had been cut off. He had been stabbed in several places.

So the boy dipped his water, and said to the Scalped-Man: "I want to carry you upon my back to where we are camped, for the people will not believe me when I tell them that you were killed." The Scalped-Man said, "Very well." So the poor boy sat down and put the dead man upon his back. The poor boy carried the dead man to where the other men were. The poor

Traditions Of The Arikara | 143

boy placed the Scalped-Man outside of the tipi. He went into the tipi with the water.

After they had drunk the water, the poor boy told the story. He said that all the other warriors had been killed; that every one of them was scalped and was lying in the lake; that he had waded waist-deep into the water to get clean water. Some of the boys made fun of the poor boy and said that he had imagined all this. But the poor boy said, "If you do not believe me I am going to get one of them and bring him in here, and you will see that all I have said is true." They said, "All right." They did not believe the poor boy would go. But he did go out, and dragged the Scalped-Man to the entrance of the tipi. Old and young men crawled out and ran away. The poor boy laughed at them for being afraid of a dead man. The leader was the only one who stayed. The Scalped-Man told the leader not to be afraid; that they would give them success, so that they might take revenge on the people who had killed them. So the men came into the tipi, but not till the poor boy had taken the dead man out. Then they all wanted to go home at once. They left the tipi and went on. The next day they found a hunter, an enemy. They lay low, and when he was within reach of them they shot him and killed him. Now the other young men wanted to go home, but the poor boy said, "Let us go on." They kept on. Each day they killed one or two of the enemy. When they had killed a number equal to the number in the lake the boy was satisfied. Then they returned home. The chiefs heard of the poor boy's bravery. They sent for him through their council, and they made of him a brave. So the poor boy became a brave man, and executed the orders of the chiefs.

FOOTNOTES:

[42] Told by Standing-Bull.

42.
THE GIRL WHO WAS BLEST BY THE BUFFALO AND CORN[43]

In one of the lodges in a village there stood a mother, and in her arms was a baby girl. It was about to rain and the mother wanted to bring in her corn and other things to keep them dry, but she did not know where to put the baby. In her excitement she forgot that there was a bed, and she laid the baby up on the buffalo skull at the altar, then went about her duties. The buffalo skull was thankful, because he thought the baby was given to him. He cried out, saying, "Hi ni, hi ni—you have pleased me, you have pleased me, giving me the baby." But Mother-Corn, who stood over the buffalo skull, told him that the baby girl had not been given to him, but had been placed there for the buffalo skull and herself to watch while the mother was busy. The buffalo skull and Mother-Corn blessed and poured their mercy on the baby girl. After a while the mother came in and took the baby. The child grew, and showed some signs of having power from some of the gods. She would eat no corn, squash, or anything, except chicken or duck. The girl grew to womanhood, and all the people respected and honored her.

One time famine prevailed, and the people were in much distress. The medicine-men did all they could, but all in vain. Some came and talked to the woman, and she told them that it was an easy matter to give them aid. She advised all the people to open and clean their cellars. They did so. The people took out the little corn they were saving for seed and gave it to the woman. Again she advised them to stand by their cellars until she had relieved them. So she went with a little corn, beans, and squash, and when she came to the first one she asked what things were usually kept in that cellar. The owner of the cellar gave his or her answer—such as, "Corn and beans were kept in this." The woman then would throw down the seeds in the cellar and tell them to cover them up. She did this to all the people's cellars, and they were all covered. She advised them not to open the cellars until at the end of four days. So the people waited, and after the fourth day they all opened their cellars and beheld the corn, beans, squash, and other things, which filled their cellars. The people were pleased and showed more respect and honor to Mother-Corn. Later, the woman did many other things for them.

FOOTNOTES:

[43] Told by Hawk.

43.
THE FIGHT BETWEEN THE ARIKARA AND THE SNAKES[44]

One summer the Arikara went out to hunt buffalo, deer, and antelope. On their way they saw by the path a pretty little snake. Some of the old people told the others to give presents to the snake, such as deer meat and moccasins. There were two foolish boys in the rear of the crowd, coming along on foot. When the foolish boys saw the pile of presents they wondered what it was for. They looked all around the pile, but could see nothing; but after a while they saw the little snake on top of the presents. The boys were mad, and said: "We are poor. We are living with these people and they do not give us anything, although they know that we need help, and here they have given these things to this little snake." "Let us kill it," said one of the boys. The other one said, "All right." So they killed the snake. The boys told the people that they had killed the snake. The people turned back from their hunt and went to their village, and they began to climb upon high arbors for refuge. From the top of the arbors they saw something coming down both sides of the Missouri River. Soon they discovered that what they saw were all kinds of snakes. They were ready to meet the snakes, for they knew what they had done, and they were ready to die. They took their clubs and killed the snakes, although the snakes killed many of the Arikara. By and by the snakes killed one of the foolish boys. They bit the other boy all over, but he killed many of them. After a while they went away, but they had killed many people, and all because the foolish boys had killed the young snake.

FOOTNOTES:

[44] Told by Two-Hawks.

44.
THE FIGHT BETWEEN THE ARIKARA AND THE BEARS[45]

There was a young man who had a beautiful wife, whom he loved. She had a garden in the woods where she went every day in the spring to hoe. Each morning, before starting to the garden, she prepared pemmican and dried meat to take with her. She took enough for two or three persons. Her husband noticed this. One day while she was preparing the meat he asked her why she was preparing so much, for he thought that she must have some of her relatives to help her in her garden. The woman made no reply. One day, as she went out to the garden, her husband secretly followed her. When her husband came to her garden he hid near by. He saw that the garden was well cared for, and he knew by this that some one had been helping her to clean it. The man waited a little while, and there came forth from the woods a man, who walked right over to the woman. The woman seemed glad to see this man who met her, and the man was glad to meet the woman. This strange man was painted, and upon his head were feathers, and a set of bear's claws were about his neck. The man went to work in the garden, helping the woman. The woman's husband lay upon the top of the hill, watching them. When the sun was high, the strange man and the woman stopped working. They went over in the shade of some trees, and they ate the meat that the woman had prepared. After eating, the strange man lay with the woman. The woman's husband saw all that went on. He slowly made his way toward the camp and went home. When he got home he took down his bow and arrows and began to fix the arrow-points and bow-string. In the meantime, the woman returned. She asked her husband where he was going, and he made reply that he was fixing up his bow and arrows to go hunting the next day. The man then asked his wife how she was getting along with the work in her garden, and she said she was nearly through.

The next morning the woman got her meat and things ready to go to her garden again, and the man got ready to go hunting. The woman went first to her garden. The man went afterwards, in a different direction. After a while he circled around to his wife's garden. He got to the garden and lay down. He waited for the strange man to come. The woman sat around near her garden, doing nothing, for there was nothing to do; she had already got through with her field. The man looked up and again he saw the strange man come from the timber and begin to talk to his wife. They sat around until the sun was high. They again ate meat together, and after they had eaten, the strange man again lay with the woman. While they were lying together, the woman's husband came up from behind them, took an arrow, put it in the bow-string and pulled it. He shot the man. The man made a big groan, got on his feet, and ran through the timber.

When the woman got up, her husband got a stick and clubbed her. The woman said: "My husband, you should first have found out who that man was who was with me, before you shot him." Her husband said that he did not care who he was. The woman said that he was a Bear, and that was the reason she let him lie with her, for she was afraid of him. She said that the Bear told her that if anybody did anything to him while he was with her he would get all his people together and kill everybody in the Arikara camp. The man said he did not care.

About three days afterwards the people saw what seemed to be buffalo in large droves, coming from the hills. When they came near the village the people found out that they were Bears instead of buffalo. The young man who had shot the Bear in the garden said to the people, "The Bears are coming to kill us, for I shot the Bear." The Bears soon reached the camp and tore the people to pieces, as many as they got hold of; but some of the people, who hid in their cellars, were saved. The Bears did not stop until they had killed the man who had shot the Bear.

FOOTNOTES:

[45] Told by Two-Hawks.

45.
THE WIFE WHO MARRIED AN ELK[46]

There was a man who went hunting with his wife. They were alone. Whenever the man was out hunting the woman would stay at the lodge and take care of all the things that the man had brought in, and she would also jerk meat. There she stayed, while her husband went out day after day. One time when her husband was gone a man came to see her, but she did not know who he was. One day five men came, and the fifth one she liked best. He was fine-looking, and young. This fifth man asked her to go home with him. She liked him so much that she did not feel like refusing him, so she went with him.

When the husband returned he found that his wife was gone. He looked all around until at last he found their tracks. He ran along, following the tracks. The poor man was getting tired, but the more he thought of his wife the more he felt like following her, for he thought a great deal of her. He caught up with her, and to his great surprise he saw his wife walking beside an animal. The man ran and shot at the animal, but could not kill it. This animal was an Elk. Not far away was a lake, toward which the Elk and the woman were headed. The Elk and the woman went right into this lake. The man shot at the animal, but the arrows did not seem to harm the Elk. When the man came to the lake he remained there. He would think of going away, but when he thought of his wife he would stay. He cried and cried. He neither ate nor drank.

At last the woman came out from the lake, for she felt sorry for her husband. She said: "You must go home, and whenever you start upon the war-path come to this place before you go and I will see you, and I will do anything to get out of this place so that I can tell you where to go, and if I can go with you I will do so." So the man went home, and when he got there, the people asked him what had become of his wife. He told the people what had happened to her. After many days, the man thought he would go on the war-path. He invited several young men, and they went out. When they were near the lake, the man told his companions to stay at a distance from the lake, while he went on by himself. The man had a dress for the woman. When he got to the lake she told him to go west; that in a few days he would find three tipis; that there were three men living in the tipis, and that he should kill them; and that he would capture all their ponies. The woman then disappeared. The man threw the dress into the lake and went back. The man then led the war-party to the west. In a few days they found the three tipis. They attacked them and killed the people in them. Their ponies they captured, so that it all came true, as the woman had said. Then they went home and had a great time dancing the scalp-dance.

The next time the man went on the war-path he took several young men with him, and he again visited the lake. This time the woman came out, and said: "My husband, I can never leave this lake any more. You must go to the west, and there you will find the enemy. In the fight you will see a woman who looks like me. Go to this woman and catch her. She will become your wife and be good to you." In a few days they found the enemy's camp. They attacked the village, and they fought. While they were fighting, this man saw the woman who looked just like his wife. He stopped fighting and went after the woman. He captured her and took her home with him.

The man never went to the lake any more, but was happy with his new wife, for she looked very much like the woman who had gone into the lake with the Elk.

FOOTNOTES:

[46] Told by Standing-Bull.

46.
THE FOUR GIRLS AND THE MOUNTAIN-LION[47]

There were four girls who went to gather wood. While they were gathering wood they heard a Mountain-Lion coming, who said, "I want you girls for my wives." The girls ran to different wonderful beings for protection. Each wonderful being said, "I can not do anything for you, for the Mountain-Lion is more powerful than I." At last the girls came to a place where there was a man whose name was "Hair-Cut-in-Notches." (His hair was so notched that one could see through the notches by looking at the side of his head.) The girls ran to this man, and said: "A Mountain-Lion is after us! Save us!" Hair-Cut-in-Notches said, "What shall I get if I save you?" The girls said, "We will live with you as your wives if you will save us." Hair-Cut-in-Notches said, "You will go into my lodge and stay there." Then he sang about his head and hair, for his hair was his arrows. When the Mountain-Lion came up Hair-Cut-in-Notches would make a motion toward his head, then to his bow, then shoot at the Mountain-Lion. Finally the Mountain-Lion dropped down, for he had killed it. Hair-Cut-in-Notches went into the lodge, and said: "You will now come out. Go to your homes. I shall not keep you here, for I am not a human being, but I am glad to have saved you from being killed by that animal." The four girls thanked the man and returned to their homes.

FOOTNOTES:

[47] Told by Little-Crow.

47.
THE DEEDS OF YOUNG-EAGLE[48]

Many years ago the Arikara separated into two bands, one band going south, the other going north. But still the young men visited from one camp to the other. In the north village the leading chief had a daughter who had grown up to be a beautiful young woman. In the other village the leading chief had a son who was handsome. The young man's name was Young-Eagle. The young girl's name was Yellow-Calf.

When the north village visited the south village the north people told the south people about the chief's daughter, who was very pretty. When the south people visited the north village they told of the chief's son, who was very handsome, but who had never looked upon women with favor, for he had always kept himself in the lodge, not even having been on the war-path. When he came out of his lodge everybody looked at him.

Young-Eagle made up his mind to visit the north village to see the beautiful daughter of the chief. He told his sisters to make him several pairs of moccasins; for he intended to go to the north village. Now, Yellow-Calf, in the north village, also made moccasins for herself, for she had made up her mind that she would visit the south village and see the young man who was so handsome.

One day Young-Eagle started for the north village. On the same day Yellow-Calf started for the south village. Now, between the two villages there was a high hill, and as Young-Eagle was climbing the hill on the south side Yellow-Calf was climbing the hill on the north side. They both saw each other as they reached the top of the hill and were greatly surprised to see each other.

Young-Eagle asked Yellow-Calf where she was going, but she answered by asking where he was going. Finally the girl told him that she was going to the south village to see the man who was so handsome. Young-Eagle said, "I am that young man, and I am going to see the young girl who is so beautiful, down here at the south village." They now knew that they were speaking of each other.

They sat down and talked, and here they found out each other's mind. Young-Eagle wanted to know how many days it had taken Yellow-Calf to come there. She told how many days it had taken, and Young-Eagle told Yellow-Calf how many days it had taken him. They knew by this that the hill was just half-way between the two villages. This hill is known at the present time as "Lovers' Hill," because these two people met here. They agreed to place a pile of rocks upon the hill, and each was to place on the pile a number of stones equal to the number of days it had taken to come to the place. First, Young-Eagle placed a stone, then Yellow-Calf placed one, then Young-Eagle placed another, and so on, until they had a pile of stones. Yellow-Calf told Young-Eagle that she wanted to go with him to his home. But Young-Eagle said, "No, I would rather go with you to your home." Yellow-Calf finally consented; so they went on. Yellow-Calf was satisfied and happy, for this young man was handsome and had a quiver filled with arrows, and a bow.

In the evening they came to a lake, and Young-Eagle told Yellow-Calf that they must take a swim and wash themselves; that it was not right that they should go to the village without being washed. So Yellow-Calf went into the lake first and washed. When she came out, Young-Eagle, with his leggings and all his things on, waded into the water for some distance. He told Yellow-Calf to watch for him. He dived, and stayed a long time under the water. Towards evening, at dusk, Young-Eagle came out of the water, having all his clothes on. He came upon the bank, and Yellow-Calf saw that he was not the same young man who had left her a little while before. This young man now was not so tall, nor was he handsome. His hair was unkempt, his nose was all covered with sores, and he seemed to have vermin. The robe he had on was a little piece of buffalo robe. His leggings were made of deer skin, but were very dry. His belly looked so large and plump that people would take him for a "burnt-belly" boy or a "burnt-fingered" boy. Yellow-Calf became scared, but she thought Young-Eagle was only making fun, so she took him home that night.

Young-Eagle lay down by the side of Yellow-Calf, and the next morning, when the parents arose to prepare the meal, they went to the girl and found a young man lying by her. The old people, knowing that Yellow-Calf had been away for some time, thought, of course, that she had got married, and had brought her husband home. They waked the young man. He did not attempt to wash, but jumped at the pot with the food in it, and he licked the mush off from the spoon. The old folks looked at him, and were sorry that Yellow-Calf had brought him. Yellow-Calf, too, was ashamed of him. She prayed hard in her heart that the young man might turn into the young man that she had first been with. But the young man remained the same and the people made fun of him. They called him the "Big-Belly-Boy." The boy acted childishly all the time. When there was a battle going on the boy never went out, but stayed around the lodge.

One time the boy heard that a war-party was going out. He told the girl to tell her youngest brother that when the party should be out three days he should get some long intestines from the buffalo that the warriors would kill, and also some bones; these he should put in the fire; and that in the night he would hear the whistling of a young eagle, and he must know that it was his brother-in-law coming. The girl told her youngest brother all that Young-Eagle had said, and the boy said that he would do so, only he was afraid that what she had told him would not come true; he did not believe that his brother-in-law would come. But the girl said, "Brother, watch out, and when he comes, do as he tells you, for he is wonderful." But the brother felt like making fun of his brother-in-law, Young-Eagle. It was announced through the camp that the Big-Belly-Boy was going on the war-path with the rest. They all laughed at him and made fun of him because he was going on the war-path for the first time.

The warriors started out, and after they had been gone three days Young-Eagle took his wife out to the lake where he had dived once before, and there he told her to take a swim. The girl went in and washed. After she came up, Young-Eagle went in, just the same as he had done before, with leggings, moccasins, etc., and he waded into the lake, then he dived, and stayed a long time. At dusk, Yellow-Calf heard a noise in the water, and Young-Eagle came out, the same man that she had first met. Young-Eagle told her not to touch him, but to go home; that he would come home soon; and that she should watch for him. He sat down and covered himself with his robe. All at once the robe rattled, and there flew up a young Eagle. It flew towards the southwest, where the warriors had gone, and in the night, the brother-in-law heard the cry of an Eagle. He rose, and said, "That is my brother-in-law; he has come." The other warriors who heard it made fun of him, and said, "Do you think that that Big-Belly-Boy brother would come this far?" But the boy did not say anything. He went out, and sure enough, there was his brother-in-law.

The boy gave Young-Eagle the intestine to eat, and also some bones to gnaw. Young-Eagle told his brother-in-law that the enemy were within a short distance, and that he was going out to bring all the ponies that they had in the village; and that he was to turn all the ponies over to him; and that his brother-in-law should divide the ponies among the warriors.

The leader of the war-party had sent out different scouts, but they had seen no enemy's village, nor any ponies. But every once in a while Young-

154 | Traditions Of The Arikara

Eagle would appear, and this brother-in-law of his would go to meet him. The warriors still doubted that they were brothers-in-law.

The next day, when they saw a drove of ponies coming towards them and Young-Eagle driving them afoot, they knew him. Young-Eagle's brother-in-law went out to meet him. Young-Eagle gave him all the ponies and told him to divide them among the people. Young-Eagle went back into the enemy's camp. He killed one man, took his scalp, and gave it to his brother-in-law, who in turn gave it to the leader of the war-party.

Young-Eagle went back to the village, and about this time the enemy were coming after him. Young-Eagle killed several more, taking their scalps. He gave the scalps to his brother-in-law, who in turn gave them to the leader. They knew that the young man was brave. After the battle he went home as Young-Eagle. The others drove ponies.

Young-Eagle went into his lodge where his wife was. He did not tell her what had happened. Two days afterward, the war-party came, singing scalp songs and telling all that Young-Eagle had done. Yellow-Calf's father sat upon the lodge, listening, and thought that they were making fun of his son-in-law.

The warriors entered the lodge of the priests, and there they told the story, from the time they had left and from the time Young-Eagle overtook them, and the capturing of the ponies and the killing of the enemy. This was all true. Scalps were brought to Young-Eagle's lodge, and the old man put them upon a long pole, and stuck the pole in the ground outside of the entrance of his lodge. The ponies that were left over after dividing them up between the warriors were given to Yellow-Calf's father, who took only so many. Then Young-Eagle went out and gave the remainder of the ponies to the poor people.

Some people went to the other village, and reported all that Young-Eagle had done, and the father of Young-Eagle was ashamed, for he thought they were making fun of him, for when Young-Eagle had been at home he would never go out on the war-path. He did not believe the story; he believed the boy to be dead, for he had been away for some time. So all the sisters of Young-Eagle had cut their hair and mourned, as had also his father and mother.

Every time a war-party came to attack the village Young-Eagle was there to save the village. Once in a while, when a war-party went out, Young-Eagle followed. He did the same as he had done before. On one of these occasions he made up his mind that he would go and get his own likeness; for, although he had changed once, when first he had gone on the war-path, he still retained his big belly. One evening he went with his wife to the lake. He went into the lake. When he came out he had on his fine leggings, a fine robe and a mountain-lion quiver, and he was fine-looking, with long hair. The girl was proud of him now. They went home.

In a few days, Young-Eagle told Yellow-Calf to take all the scalps that he had taken, and saddle the ponies; for they were going to visit his father's village. His father's name was "Black-Sun." They went south to Black-Sun's village. One evening they came to the village. Young-Eagle left his wife outside of the village, and went to his father's lodge. He told his father that he had come back. His father got up and made a fire. He told his woman to get up, for their son had come back. The four sisters got up from their beds and hugged their brother, for they had been mourning for him as dead. Young-Eagle told his sisters to go out and to bring their sister-in-law. They went out, and they found Yellow-Calf sitting outside of the lodge, holding three ponies. The girls embraced their sister-in-law and led her into the camp, took in the things that belonged to Young-Eagle and his wife, but led the ponies away. The stick with the scalps was fastened upon a long pole and stood up in front of the lodge.

Early on the next morning, Black-Sun got up and went through the village singing scalp songs, thus letting the people know that his son had returned with many scalps. The people heard it. They went out, and they saw the pole that had the scalps upon it. The people rushed into the lodge, and that very same day the braves and warriors decided that this Young-Eagle should lead the people to the girl's village.

So the people of the other village went north, and the north and south tribes of the Arikara came together and became one tribe again.

FOOTNOTES:

[48] Told by Yellow-Bull.

48.
THE GIRL WHO BECAME A WHIRLWIND[49]

Many, many years ago the Arikara left their village and went west on a buffalo hunt. They left behind a family, the woman of which was leading a pony that dragged a travois with two children on it—a girl seven years old and a boy of five. As these people were crossing a little stream of water the pony jumped across the stream, and the children fell off. The woman, supposing the children still to be on the travois, never looked behind, and did not miss the children until she came into camp.

The men were then sent back to try to find the children, but they could not be found; for when they fell off, instead of following their parents they had gone back in the direction of their village, but instead of going into the village they had gone into the timber west of the village. There they wandered through the timber, and at last they came to a cave, where they stopped. The girl left the boy there while she went about trying to find something for him to eat. While the girl was gone, a Whirlwind came and took her far away. It was not long before the girl returned; but often after that she would go away for days. When she returned she was always very happy. Now, the boy told his sister that he wanted a bow and arrows; that he was all the time going around through the timber seeing rabbits and smaller game. The girl disappeared, and when she came back she had a bow and four blunt arrows. For many days the girl would disappear and then would return. One day the boy said: "My sister, I wander through the woods, and I am getting older; I think I ought to have a larger bow and many arrows." So the girl said, "All right." She went away, and when she came back she brought the bow and quiver filled with arrows for the boy. The boy was thankful for this. The girl disappeared very often. Every time she came home the boy would hear the storm coming, then, all at once, the girl would appear.

One day when the boy was out hunting, an Owl came to him, and said: "We have taken pity upon you. We have an animals' lodge close by. We have taken pity upon you because your sister is now a wonderful being—a Whirlwind. She goes from one place to another, killing people. She has planned to kill you, that she may be the Whirlwind always. She thinks that you are in her way, for she has to look after you. Now, the girl travels far over the land. She visits places where people have food, and there she finds bows and arrows, knives, axes, and hoes, and she brings them here to your place. Testes autem moribus excidit, domumque adfert; eos frictos, dum dormis, dentibus frangit et mandit. To-night when she comes home, stay awake, for she intends to kill you soon. You will find out what she eats." That night, when the boy lay down, he watched and waited for his sister. She came at last. She looked down and saw that her brother was sleeping, then she took some of her special meat and placed it upon hot coals, took it off and began to eat. When she got through eating, the boy arose and said, "Sister, I am glad you are back." She said, "Well, I am going away, far away from here to-morrow, and I want you to stay here until I come back." The next day the girl was gone. The Owl came to the boy, and said: "Make haste! Come!" So the boy followed the Owl, and as they traveled along the Owl said: "Do you see that cloud coming? That is the Whirlwind coming to destroy you. Make haste and come with me!" They ran, and as the Whirlwind was near, the boy was taken into the den of the Owls.

The Owls told the boy that when the Whirlwind should come it would make threats, but that they had taken pity upon him and would keep him there; but that there was something that this girl wanted, and they were going to tell him what it was. They said: "Your sister wants a woman. You tell her that the first woman you marry you will give her." So the Whirlwind came to the side of the hill where the Owl's den was. The wind blew and the girl spoke, and said: "You big Owl, turn that boy loose! He is mine! I must kill him!" But the Owls would not turn the boy loose. They said, "He is here under our protection." The girl kept on demanding the boy. At last, the boy said, "My sister, if you will let me go, the first woman I marry I shall give to you." The girl said: "That is what I want; I shall let you go." So the boy was turned loose, and traveled towards his people.

When the boy came to his people, he saw that they were very poor. He entered his father's lodge and told his father that he had come back. His father arose and built a big fire. He saw the boy sitting there and recognized him. The father asked about the sister. The boy said that his sister was well, but that she was far away. Then the boy told his father to tell the chief to come to their lodge. The boy told the chief that he had come to tell them that the buffalo were not very far away and that the people must go and kill these buffalo. The people sent hunters out and they found the buffalo as the boy had said they would. In a few days the enemy attacked this village, and they saw that the boy was a wonderful boy, for he made a way for his people to kill the enemy. The people cried through the village, and said that they should give him a nice young woman to marry. The chief's daughter was the one to be given to him.

That night the boy went out and called for his sister. The sister came that night into the tipi and sat down by her brother, and said, "I have been far away." The boy said: "My sister, I am now to marry. Here is the girl that I promised you." The boy's sister said, "That is what I want." She went to the girl, and the sister and the boy's wife were together. The boy went out. The next day the brother came into the lodge, and his sister said: "My brother, I give you this club and this medicine, and I give you the power that I possess—that of the Whirlwind. You will have power to kill the enemy. They will try to shoot you, but they can do you no harm. For many days I shall now go towards the southwest, where I shall always stay. When the wind comes you must know that I am the Whirlwind. I will listen to the prayers of our people. When I am coming do not let my people be afraid of me, for I shall always hear their prayers and shall always heed them. I shall not destroy them, but will always comfort them." The young man became a famous warrior, and finally became a chief.

FOOTNOTES:

[49] Told by Many-Fox.

49.
THE COYOTE AND THE MICE SUN DANCE[50]

While the Coyote was wandering in the evening he heard dancing, but he could not see the dance anywhere. He went on walking around and hunting for the dance. He was about to give up, when he found that the noise of the dancing came from an elk skull in the bushes.

The Mice ran away as soon as the Coyote came up, but the Coyote begged to see them dance. He addressed them thus, "Uncles, I want to see you dance." The Mice said: "We are afraid of you, for you may eat us. We would like to see you, but you are very tricky, and you might eat us." The Coyote begged so hard, saying he had not seen his uncles for many months, and he wanted to see them; so the Mice agreed to let him into the dance. They let the Coyote peep into the back part of the skull, so that he could see the dance. As soon as the Coyote had run his head through the skull the Mice ran away, and the Coyote was held fast with his head in the skull. The Coyote begged the Mice to take the skull off, but the Mice would not listen to him. They told him to go away. So the Coyote went on his way, with the skull on his head.

The Coyote could not see very well, on account of the skull being over his eyes. He heard some noises at a distance. He went straight to a camp. He came to the edge of some water. The people saw the animal coming on the other side of the water, and some of them hallooed, "A wonderful animal coming on the other side of the water!" When the Coyote saw that the people were scared he commenced to make funny noises. Some of the people said, "Make way, so that we may be spared and live." The Coyote said, "Give me the chief's daughter and you shall all live." The people gave him the chief's daughter. The Coyote swam across the water and the people made a tipi for him. The girl took the Coyote by the horns and led him to the tipi. The Coyote stayed with the girl all night. In the morning the Coyote and the girl were sent for to come and eat. The Coyote was still close to the girl, and some boy saw that it was a Coyote. The boy yelled, "This being that is in the tipi with the girl is nothing but a Coyote!" The people rushed there and the Coyote was forced out beyond the tipi. As he could not see very well he ran into people and dogs. The people struck the skull until they broke it to pieces. They caught the Coyote and brought him home. They tied his legs with strings, drove some pegs into the ground, and tied him fast to the pegs. As the people went out they would go to the Coyote and urinate and defecate on him. One old woman went out to defecate on the Coyote, and as she lifted her dress she wanted to know how she was to do it. The Coyote told the woman that the first thing to be done was to pull the pegs, then pull up her dress, then defecate on him. The Coyote took a long stick, and as the woman lifted her dress and tried to defecate on him he ran the stick into her rectum, then stuck the stick in the ground. He then ran away and defecated as he went. For this reason the Coyote defecates easily and is always running from the people.

FOOTNOTES:

[50] Told by Joe Reed.

50.
THE COYOTE BECOMES A BUFFALO[51]

The Coyote was going along when he saw an old bull sitting down on the side of a hill. The Coyote went up to him, and said, "Well, my grandfather, are you sitting here sunning yourself?" The bull said, "Yes." The Coyote said that he was hungry; that he would like the Buffalo to give him something to eat. The Buffalo said, "Why are you not like myself, a big Buffalo, eating grass." The Coyote said, "Well, grandfather, I wish that you would make a Buffalo out of me." So the Buffalo said: "All right. You will then have to break up your bow and arrows, for you will need them no more." So the Buffalo placed the Coyote, and said, "Now you must keep a strong heart; do not get scared." The Buffalo rushed at the Coyote, and just as he was about to hook the Coyote, the Coyote jumped sidewise. Then the Buffalo said: "Why did you get scared? Now stay right at this place, and I will come and make a Buffalo out of you." But every time the Buffalo ran toward him the Coyote would jump away. The last time the Coyote stayed, and as the Buffalo went up against him there were two Buffalo bulls. They locked horns, then the Buffalo told the Coyote-Buffalo to eat grass. The Coyote-Buffalo obeyed and ate until he was filled. Then the Buffalo said, "We must go to the Buffalo herd, for there is one bull there who has control of all the female Buffalo, and we will fight him, and when we have killed him we can have all the female Buffalo." So they went to the Buffalo herd. The Buffalo bull was going around among the Buffalo. They were waiting to fight him when it should come time. They fought, and they killed the Buffalo bull.

Now each bull took many cows to look after. When they all came together they lay down in a hollow for the night. The next night the Buffalo all jumped and traveled toward the western country. When the Coyote-Buffalo got up he saw that he had been left behind, all alone. He arose, but did not follow the other people. The Coyote-Buffalo came across a Coyote, and said: "Why are you not as I am? I was a Coyote once, but now I am a Buffalo." The Coyote-Buffalo told the Coyote to throw his bow and arrows away, for he was going to make him into a Buffalo. He set the Coyote in a certain place and made a rush at him. The Coyote jumped sidewise. Three times did the Coyote-Buffalo try to run into the Coyote, but every time the Coyote jumped sidewise. The last time, the Coyote-Buffalo said, "Now you must close your eyes and let me run over you." The Coyote obeyed and the Coyote-Buffalo ran into him, and there were two Coyotes instead of the Coyote-Buffalo and the Coyote. So the Coyote-Buffalo turned back into a Coyote.

FOOTNOTES:

[51] Told by Antelope.

51.
THE COYOTE AND THE ARTICHOKE[52]

The Coyote was going along through thick timber. He saw an Artichoke plant, which he dug up. He asked it its name. The Artichoke said, "Cososit," meaning artichoke. The Coyote wanted to know if he had any other name. The Artichoke said, "Take-a-Bite." When it said that, the Coyote took a bite. The Artichoke repeated this name four times, and every time it repeated it the Coyote took a bite of the Artichoke. Finally, the Coyote had eaten the Artichoke.

The Coyote went on, and again and again he expelled flatus, moving his feet each time. Every time he expelled flatus he seemed to grow worse. Once it threw him up in the air. Now, before expelling flatus, he got hold of a tree, and he said, "Now let me expel flatus." The flatus threw him up in the air, tree and all. Again he went on, and he came to a stone, and when he knew he was to expel flatus, he said, "Now let me expel flatus." This he did, and the stone went up with the Coyote. The stone fell on the Coyote and killed him. This is the reason we find coyotes lying beside stones.

FOOTNOTES:

[52] Told by Cut-Arm.

52.
THE COYOTE RIDES THE BEAR[53]

The Coyote was going along through the timber, and he met a Bear. The Coyote made all kinds of threats against the Bear, and finally got on his back and rode him. All at once the Coyote jumped off and said, "You can go your way, and I will go mine!" The Coyote went up on the top of a hill, to see if the Bear was still going, but he did not see him. Then the Coyote yelled, and said, "You Bear, you claim to be a fierce animal, and here I have ridden upon your back!" The Bear, hearing this, became mad. He turned around, and said: "I will kill that being, whoever he is. No matter where he goes, I will follow him." So the Bear ran up the hill, and when the Coyote saw the Bear coming he ran. The Bear caught up with the Coyote on the next hill, and killed the Coyote and tore him up.

FOOTNOTES:

[53] Told by Antelope.

53.
THE COYOTE RIDES THE BUFFALO[54]

There was a village, and in the village lived one young girl who was very pretty. All the young men courted her, but she did not care to marry. A Buffalo came who wanted to marry her. Once in a while he would turn into a young man, nicely dressed and smelling very fine. The girl became very much attached to the Buffalo.

The Coyote came to visit the girl, and he talked to her. The girl said she did not care to talk to anybody now, because she had a young man, and that young man was the Buffalo. The Coyote said: "Why, that Buffalo is my horse. I ride him." The girl said, "If you will ride that Buffalo here I will marry you." The Coyote went home, took a club and hit himself very hard on the knee, so as to make it sore. The Buffalo came to the girl to talk with her. The girl told the Buffalo what the Coyote had said. The Buffalo was mad, and said, "I am going to bring the Coyote here and kill him." The Buffalo pawed the ground and threw up the dirt. The Coyote saw the Buffalo coming. The Buffalo called to the Coyote to come out. He said: "I want you to go with me to the girl's tipi; I am to kill you." The Coyote said, "I am a cripple, I can not go." "It is not true," said the Buffalo. "Come out, uncle, can't you? Come on." Said the Coyote, "If you want me to go, and can carry me to the girl's tipi, I will go." The Buffalo agreed to carry the Coyote. The Buffalo got down on his knees and the Coyote got on top of him and sat upon him. The Coyote had a cane that he was to hit the Buffalo with.

The Coyote jumped up and ran back to the village and married the girl. The Buffalo was so ashamed that he never came back to the village. For this reason, the descendants of the Coyote are bad and tricky. By foul means, they marry.

FOOTNOTES:

[54] Told by Cut-Arm.

54.
THE COYOTE AND THE BUFFALO RUN A RACE[55]

Once when a Coyote was sauntering along he looked up and saw a Buffalo a long distance off. The Coyote ran, and nearly caught up with the Buffalo. The Coyote saw the Buffalo drop chips. He went and ate some of them. The Buffalo looked around and saw the Coyote eating the chips. The Buffalo turned back and asked the Coyote what he was doing. The Coyote said: "O, you shaggy-looking thing; why do you not go on your way and not bother a poor fellow like me? I am eating some pemmican that some fellow must have dropped." After a while, the Coyote said, "Say, grandfather, can you run?" "Yes," said the Buffalo, "I can run fast." "But," said the Coyote, "I do not see how you can run with such big feet. Then there is danger of your breaking your legs. Ah, grandfather," said the Coyote, "I think I can beat you. I am a man who has fought in battles, and have killed many people on account of my swiftness. If you are willing to run with me, do not stand there and laugh at me. I can beat you." So the Buffalo said, "If you want to run a race, I will run with you, and I will show you that my legs can carry me a long way and beat you." "All right," said the Coyote, "I will go and measure the ground, and we will run." So the Coyote went away and selected a place. The place selected was a tableland, and there was a steep bank at the other end. The Coyote set landmarks near the steep bank and winked to himself, and said, "Now I will have a whole buffalo to eat," for at the bottom of this steep place there was a rock. The Coyote went where the Buffalo stood, and said: "Now we will run. As soon as we get to the two landmarks I have made we will run fast. At this place we will close our eyes. When we have gone a short distance we will open our eyes and see who is in the lead." The Buffalo agreed. They began the race, and as they came to the landmarks, the Coyote said, "Now run your best and close your eyes." The Coyote, being on the right side of the Buffalo, closed his left eye. The Buffalo ran with his eyes closed and jumped over the steep bank. The Coyote stopped, looked, and saw the Buffalo lying dead at the bottom of the steep bank.

The Coyote went down and skinned the Buffalo and cut him up. He then took the meat to a place where there was a creek, and there he put up a small lodge for himself. He made a fire and roasted some meat. Then he went out to see if he could see any one. He saw a Fox coming along. He waited for the Fox. When the Fox came up, the Coyote said, "My friend, I want you to come to my lodge and pack water for me." The Fox said, "I will go with you and pack water for you." So they went together and entered the lodge. The Coyote fixed the buffalo pouch for a bucket, and said, "Fox, you go after water with this pouch." The Fox obeyed. Before he got to the creek he had eaten up the pouch. Four times the Coyote gave the Fox a pouch to bring water, and every time the Fox would say, "Coyote, as I dipped water, something came and took away my pouch." The Coyote was mad, and he took some coals and threw them into the Fox's face, so that the Fox cried and ran off. The Fox told his story to every animal he met. All the living animals got together, and when the Coyote was fast asleep they went in and ate all he had in his lodge. When he woke up he found all his meat gone, and he went away crying.

When you have plenty, do not trust your friends, or they will get all you have.

FOOTNOTES:

[55] Told by New-Man.

55.
THE COYOTE AND THE DANCING CORN[56]

Two Coyotes were going along, and as they became hungry one of them said: "Let us go where the people have left their village. We will find some pounded corn." As they came to the village they separated, one going through many lodges, while the other went another way. The leader came to a lodge, and there he saw pounded corn, in lumps, running into the mortar. The Coyote ran into the lodge and begged the lumps of pounded corn to come out, saying that he was an old man who sang for people in their sacred ceremonies. The Coyote walked around the fireplace and began to sing. The lumps of pounded corn came out and danced. The lumps began to dance with the Coyote. "Close your eyes," said the Coyote. The lumps had danced so hard that they had raised a dust, and the Coyote thought it was time to act. So he ran to the mortar, stuck his head into the bowl, and became fast. After a time the brother of the Coyote came, and said, "Wa, what are you doing?" The captive Coyote said: "I am fast, but I have lots to eat in this bowl. Take an axe and cut the bowl open." The other Coyote took the axe and chopped the mortar open, cutting the other Coyote on the head so that he died. There was nothing in the mortar. The Coyote went away crying, for he had killed his brother.

FOOTNOTES:

[56] Told by Little-Crow.

56.
THE COYOTE AND THE TURTLE
RUN A RACE[57]

One time a Coyote met a Turtle. The Coyote began to boast of his swiftness, and the Turtle said, "Why, I can beat you running!" So the Coyote said, "We will run a race to-morrow." That night they parted, and went to their homes, so that they could get ready for the race the next morning. After the Turtle reached home he began to worry, and he could not get to sleep, for he knew that the Coyote could run fast. But the Turtle said to himself: "I will take him up there and go to the other Turtles, and ask them to assist me." So the Turtle went to the other Turtles, and said: "I am about to run a race with the Coyote. I want you to help me." He told them the place where they were to run, and the distance they were to run. So several Turtles volunteered to go and help the Turtle to beat the Coyote.

All the Turtles went to the place. They placed one Turtle at the end of the course; then they placed another one at a certain distance back of him; then another back of this one, and so on, and finally the Turtle himself took his stand. Each Turtle carried a long pole, and hid in the ground.

The next morning the Turtle met the Coyote. The Coyote began to run around and was happy, for he thought that he was going to beat the Turtle. The Turtle and the Coyote got ready to start. The Turtle gave the command to start. The Coyote ran and the Turtle crawled into his hole. When he got over a little ridge the Coyote saw the Turtle going ahead of him. Coyote ran and caught up with the Turtle. The Turtle threw his pole away and crawled into the ground. When the Coyote got to another knoll, there was the Turtle ahead of him again. The Coyote caught up with him. The Turtle crawled into the ground. The Coyote ran, and when he got up to another hill, there was the Turtle going ahead. The Coyote caught up with and passed him. At the end, the Turtle was at the goal, and the Coyote got up, and said, "You have beaten me." This fine stretch of running killed the Coyote.

FOOTNOTES:

[57] Told by Standing-Bull.

57.
THE COYOTE AND THE STONE RUN A RACE[58]

The Coyote went up on a high hill, and there he saw a stone. The Coyote asked of the stone its name. The Stone said, "Run-Fast." "A good name," said the Coyote, "but I can beat you running." The stone said, "You will spoil my rest, but if you want to race I will run with you." The Coyote said, "All right, I want to race with you." So the Stone told the Coyote to carry him to the top of the hill. The Coyote placed the Stone upon the hill and started him rolling down the hill. For a time the Coyote ran along side of him, then passed him. The Stone ran down the hill and caught up with the Coyote, and rolled upon his back. The Coyote then tried to shake off the Stone, telling him that he had beaten him and begging him to get off his back. But the Stone stayed upon the Coyote's back. As the Coyote walked along the Stone grew heavier. It was now towards evening, and as the Coyote walked along he saw the Bull-Bats fly overhead. He told them to fly lower; that he had something to tell them. The Bull-Bats flew down. The Coyote told them that the Stone had been calling them names. He said: "When I told the Stone that I would tell you he jumped up on my back so that I could not tell you." The Bull-Bats said, "We will take the Stone off." So the Bull-Bats flew up high in the air, then came down with a swoop, making a peculiar noise upon the stone and cracking the Stone. The Bull-Bats kept on flying towards the Stone, until the Stone split in two.

After the Stone had fallen from the Coyote, the Coyote ran along making fun of the Bull-Bats, calling them names. He said, "You spoiled my hair by scattering some of these stones upon my back." The Bull-Bats told the Coyote to go his way and they would go theirs. They separated.

FOOTNOTES:

[58] Told by Cut-Arm.

58.
THE COYOTE AND THE ROLLING STONE[59]

The Coyote was once going along, and he became hungry. He heard a noise in the distance which sounded like dancing. He went to the place from where the noise came and there were some men dancing around the fire. When he came close to the place he saw that these men were Jack-Rabbits and that they had taken out intestines from the fire. One took them out, and they began to eat them. The Coyote asked them where they got the intestines. The Rabbit men told the Coyote that they would not tell him. The Coyote was very hungry, and he wanted very much to find out. He made all kinds of promises to the Rabbits, if they would only tell him, and if they demanded pay he promised that he would pay them. The leader of the Rabbit men said, "If you will pay us a good price we will teach you how the big intestines are made." The Coyote was willing to pay them. He stood up, and said: "Grandchildren, I have been very far away, on the war-path. You can see that I am a warrior by this headdress that I have on; but, to know the secret of making these intestines I am willing to part with this eagle war-bonnet." The Rabbits told the Coyote to go and get some red willows. The Coyote went and brought a few red willows, and these the Rabbits threw into the fire. Then they began to sing a song, and all the Rabbits stood up and danced around the fire. As the willows burned they turned slowly into large buffalo intestines. When these were roasted on the coals the Rabbits told the Coyote to take the intestines off from the coals and eat them. The Coyote took the long intestines, and they were so good that he asked the Rabbits to do the same thing again, for he was still hungry. The Rabbits told the Coyote to get a good armful of willows. When they were brought and placed upon the fire all the Rabbits stood up, and the Coyote was among them. They danced around, and as the willows burned they turned into large intestines. As each intestine was roasted the Coyote went and pulled it off the fire. The Rabbits had been eating these things, so they did not care for any. The Coyote ate them all, and was filled.

The Coyote then began to look around to see how he might get back his war-bonnet; for he thought he now knew the secret of making these long intestines on the coals. He said to the Rabbits: "Let me take this war-bonnet, and let me show you how it must set upon the head; let me show you how I wear it." The leader of the Rabbits said: "We are afraid of you; you are tricky, and you might get away with it." The Coyote said: "I will not get away with it. All that I want is to show you the way it must be worn." "Well," said the leader, "you may have it, and show us how you wear the bonnet." As the Coyote put the war-bonnet upon his head he made a long jump sidewise, and got away from the Rabbits. The Rabbits got after the Coyote, but he was too swift for them. The Rabbits said: "You can go; you will not be able to do the trick four times." The Coyote turned around and laughed at the Rabbits.

The Coyote ran far away, and as he was becoming hungry he made a fire, gathered some red willows, threw them into the fire, and danced around the fire all alone. He succeeded in making the buffalo intestines. He did it again, but the third time it began to fail. The fourth time the red willows burned up into ashes. They did not turn into intestines for him. The Coyote began to cry, for he knew that now he must go hungry. He went along, and after a while he began to have the stomach ache. Deinde ventrem facere volebat, et, loco idoneo reperto, insedit. Dum defæcabat leporem circumcursantem vidit, undeque esset miratus est. Quo magis defæcavit, eo plures lepores vidit. Tum se lepores emittere repperit. Paulum cunctatus, dixit: "Cogitem quo modo hos lepores prehendere possim." Nam lepores occidere volebat. Itaque pulchrum pallium quod armis trahebat sibi humi sedenti circumposuit. Hoc saxis gravibus onerato, iterum defæcare incipit. Usque ad vesperum defæcabat; tandemque exortus locum pallio operuit, eique saxum imposuit. Deinde ingentem stipitem nactus, lepores quos sub pallio esse putabat occidit. Pallio autem remoto, nihil nisi excrementum repperit. Quod cum vidisset, se dixit stultissimum esse.

The Coyote did not know what to do with the robe. He got hold of the robe and dragged it along until he came to a big Stone. He said to the Stone: "I am going to make you a present of this robe." The Stone was pleased with the robe. The Coyote went away. When the Coyote was a little way off he saw a big hail-storm coming. He had nothing to cover himself with. He turned and went back to the place where the robe was. When he got to the robe it was clean, and it smelled good. The Coyote said to the Stone: "O, you have made the robe nice and clean. I came after it." The Stone never said a word, and the Coyote stepped over and took his robe again. He went on. The storm never came near the Coyote. Soon he heard something coming behind him. He did not pay any attention to what he heard. By and by he looked back and saw the great, big Stone coming toward him. The Stone spoke to him, and said, "You, Coyote, stop!" This scared the Coyote very badly, for he knew that he would be killed for taking the robe back. The Stone chased the Coyote all the evening, and the Coyote became very tired and was about to give out, when he saw two Bull-Bats flying around in the air. He called to them, and said, "My brothers, this big Stone is after me and wants to kill me." The Bull-Bats asked the Coyote why the Stone was chasing him. The Stone then spoke up and told the Bull-Bats not to believe anything that the Coyote might tell them. The Coyote begged the Bull-Bats, and said that the Stone had said something bad about the Bull-Bats; that the Stone was afraid that he would tell the Bull-Bats about it; and that was why the Stone was mad and ran after him and was trying to kill him; that he wanted them to help him by destroying the Stone. He said: "If you will stop the Stone I will change the color on your wings and tail." The Bull-Bats said: "We will destroy the Stone, but you must first tell us what the Stone said about us, and what names he called us." The Coyote said: "The Stone said that you were the ugliest-looking birds that he ever saw, because you have short beaks and big mouths, short legs, and are very dirty." The Bull-Bats and the Coyote were talking on the top of a hill, and the Stone was trying to climb the hill, but could not get to the top.

After the Bull-Bats had accepted the Coyote's word, one flew up, and when he came down, he expelled flatus upon the Stone and it burst in two. Another Bull-Bat split the Stone again, and soon they had it all broken up. (It is claimed by the people that there was no stone in the world except this big stone; and when the Bull-Bats broke the stone it scattered all over the world.) The Coyote was saved. He got some white clay and put it on the top of the Bull-Bats' heads and bodies. The Coyote went on his way, happy.

FOOTNOTES:

[59] Told by Two-Hawks.

59.
THE COYOTE AND THE ROLLING STONE[60]

One time when the Coyote was going along he met a Rabbit. The Coyote said to the Rabbit: "Let us gamble to-night. Let us gather dry limbs and make a big fire, that we may look at one another, and the one who goes to sleep first is to be covered by the other." The Rabbit agreed to this. So the Coyote and the Rabbit gathered a lot of dried limbs and made a big fire. The Coyote sat on one side and the Rabbit on the other side of the fire, so that they both looked at one another. The Rabbit went to sleep, but he had his eyes wide open. Every time the Coyote looked at the Rabbit he saw that his eyes were wide open, but all this time the Rabbit was asleep. By morning the Coyote went to sleep. The Rabbit went over and covered him and then went his way.

The Coyote woke up and was very mad. Profectus, ventrem facere volebat. Dum defæcavit, multos lepores parvos emisit, qui autem extemplo evanuerunt. Idcirco viatus est. Itaque pallium suum deposuit, ut, cum defæcavisset, eo lepores prehendere posset. Cum igitur in pallio defæcavisset, se lepores eo prehendisse arbitratus, pallium stipite iterum atque iterum feriebat. Cum autem pallium aperuisset, nihil nisi excrementum repperit. He dragged the robe along and gave it to a Stone that was lying near by. When the Coyote turned around to look at the robe that he had given to the Stone, he saw that it was clean and white. So he went and took the robe, and as he dragged it away from the Stone he found that it was as before. Again he gave the robe to the Stone, and said: "It is yours; I did not mean to take it." The Coyote started off again, but he looked back and he saw that the robe was all painted in colors and was very beautiful. He went and pulled on it to take it away, and again it was as at first. Four times the Coyote gave the robe back to the Stone, and four times he took it away from the Stone.

At last the Stone moved, for it was angry, and the Stone ran after the Coyote. The Coyote ran down a hill, crying: "Father and mother Bull-Bats, this Stone that is running after me called you names! I told him that I would tell you Bull-Bats, and now he is trying to kill me!" The Bull-Bats told the Coyote to climb up a tree, where the young Bull-Bats were. The Bull-Bats expelled flatus on the Stone and broke it all to pieces. The Bull-Bats, as soon as the Stone was broken to pieces, flew up high in the sky, and when they were gone the Coyote saw the young ones in their nest and ate them up; then he came down from the tree. The Bull-Bats missed their young ones and they knew that it must have been the Coyote who had eaten them, for they heard the young ones crying in the Coyote's belly. They were mad, and they expelled flatus on the Coyote and killed him.

Because the Coyote is up to all kinds of mischief he is often killed, and this is why we so often find a dead Coyote on the prairies.

FOOTNOTES:

[60] Told by Cut-Arm.

60.
HOW THE SCALPED-MAN
LOST HIS WIFE[61]

One time the women went into the timber to gather some grapes. One of the girls went far. She saw some grapes away up in a tree, so she climbed the tree to get them. While she was up there, a Scalped-Man found her. The woman cried for help, but the other women had already gone home. The woman came down from the tree and went with the Scalped-Man to his den. But before getting to the den, they had to cross a creek. Before they crossed the creek, the girl said, "Now, if you will just go in and swim and wash your head, then I will be your wife and will not be afraid of you." The girl made the Scalped-Man dive many times, and while he was diving she ran away and came to a grapevine, and crawled under it.

When the Scalped-Man came out from the water the girl was missing. He followed her tracks to the grapevine, and he said, "You are to come out from there!" But the girl said nothing. After a while he went on. He kept going through the timber back and forth, until at last he gave up. The woman got out from the place, and ran home. She told her people about the Scalped-Man.

FOOTNOTES:

[61] Told by Many-Fox.

61.
THE GENEROUS SCALPED-MAN
AND HIS BETRAYER[62]

There was a man from an Arikara village who went hunting, going west from the village. He saw some antelope in a valley. He crawled up to them, and just as he was about to shoot he saw one antelope hold its head up, so that the man knew that it must have seen something. A mysterious being jumped up by the antelope, and before the antelope had time to jump the being had struck it and killed it. This being, who was a Scalped-Man, walked around the antelope, then took it by the legs, swung it upon his back and carried it off towards the Bad Lands. The hunter followed. The Scalped-Man came to a steep bank. He entered the bank and disappeared. The man kept his eye on the place where the Scalped-Man had disappeared. He came to the bank, looked in, and saw that there was a door, made of willows sewed together with sinew. Mud had been put over it and there was a root sticking out for a handle. By catching hold of the root the door was opened. The man went in and closed the door. Then he went in further, where the cave was, and there he saw the Scalped-Man sitting down by the fireplace. The antelope was lying by the entrance and the Scalped-Man was sitting down waiting, for he knew that the man was coming. The man spoke to the Scalped-Man, and said: "Why do you hold your head down? Speak! I am here. I am not afraid of you." The man kept talking to the Scalped-Man until the Scalped-Man became friendly, then the man sat down. The Scalped-Man began to cut the meat. The man stayed with the Scalped-Man four days and nights.

The Scalped-Man told the man that he knew the country all around, and that he took long journeys into the enemy's country and had killed many enemies; that if he would keep his secret of his living in the Bad Lands he would help him to become a great man like himself. The man promised, so the Scalped-Man told the man to remain in his cave while he should go off to the enemy's country. The Scalped-Man went off, and was gone for several days. When he came back he took the man out of his den and told him that he had brought several ponies for him. The ponies were in a valley. The man thanked the Scalped-Man. He took the ponies home. The people were surprised to see the man coming with the ponies, for he had not been on the war-path, but had been out hunting, as they thought. The man stayed in the village several days, then he went out again.

The man went to the Scalped-Man's cave. The Scalped-Man asked him what he wanted. The man told him that he wanted many ponies. The Scalped-Man told him to remain in his cave; that he himself was going out into the enemy's country. The Scalped-Man disappeared and in a few days returned. He gave the man all the ponies he had brought from the enemy's country. The man now thanked the Scalped-Man and drove the ponies to the village. The people knew that the man had gone off alone on the war-path, and now they were glad to see him bring many ponies. The people did not know that the Scalped-Man had helped this man.

When the man had been home with the ponies for several days he again started on the war-path. He went to the home of the Scalped-Man and told him that he wanted scalps. The man stayed right in the Scalped-Man's cave when he received the scalps. He fixed them on sticks. The man now returned to his village, singing war songs. The people heard the songs and knew that he must have killed the enemy. When they went out to meet him, sure enough, he had several scalps hung upon poles. There were dances all through the village on account of the scalps.

In a few days the man went out again. He told the Scalped-Man that he wanted some more scalps. The man remained in the cave while the Scalped-Man went off into the enemy's country. In a few days the Scalped-Man came back with the scalps. The man received the scalps. He stayed in the cave while he fixed them on poles. At this time the man told the Scalped-Man that several men wanted to join him on the war-path. The Scalped-Man said: "Very well, come with them and stop near this place. Leave them in a hollow and come into my cave, and we will go together. I shall be glad to scout for your people." When the man went home there was again rejoicing in the village and scalp dances were had in the village.

In a few days the man made it known to the people that he was about to go on the war-path. The old men flocked to him, for they knew that he was very lucky capturing ponies and bringing scalps. When the war-party started out the man who was in the lead led them to the cave of the Scalped-Man. He told the warriors to remain in a valley, while he went a short distance to look for some deer. The man went to the Bad Lands to the cave of the Scalped-Man. He entered the cave. He found the Scalped-Man sitting there. They started on their journey, but the Scalped-Man would not join their party, but he went on ahead. The Scalped-Man led them to the village, helped to kill the enemy and capture ponies. The war-party returned with scalps and many ponies.

The friend of the Scalped-Man was afraid that the people would find out about the Scalped-Man, so he thought it was about time that the Scalped-Man should be caught; for the Scalped-Man had not been really scalped, but had been wounded a little on the top of his head, and so he had stayed away from the people and had become accustomed to stay by himself. The friend of the Scalped-Man was afraid that if the people found out that the Scalped-Man had done all the killing and capturing of the ponies he would be looked upon as a coward, for he was now a chief for having done all his great acts. So this man invited a lot of men in the night and told them that it was his intention that morning to go out and capture a Scalped-Man who dwelt in the Bad Lands; that this Scalped-Man was the one who was assisting him to get the ponies and kill people. The men in the village thought this very wrong and did not want to do it. But the man was determined.

The next morning the people went out. They surrounded the bank where the Scalped-Man lived and the man went into his cave; but the Scalped-Man was gone, for as they were holding their meeting in the night the Scalped-Man had come to the man's lodge to listen to the council that they were having, for each night when the man was home, the Scalped-Man watched around his lodge to see if he would betray him. At this particular council the Scalped-Man had listened to all their plans about catching him. So when the Scalped-Man returned into his cave that night he picked up his things, moved them away from that country to some other place, so that after that, when the men went out to capture this Scalped-Man he was gone. The Scalped-Man was never seen any more.

FOOTNOTES:

[62] Told by Elk.

62.
THE SCALPED-MAN[63]

In olden times there were certain men who went upon the war-path. Scouts were sent ahead, and when the scouts came back they brought word that they had seen a mysterious being. The thing was dressed in coyote hide and had crawled around, but finally had stood up and walked away. The scouts said that they had watched the man and that he had disappeared in the side of a steep bank. The leading warrior said: "If that being is a Scalped-Man we will go and find him. If he has any power we want to receive it. If he can tell us where the enemy are we want him to tell it." So the party went to the bank and hunted and hunted. They could find no place; but one man saw a dry root hanging on the side of the bank. This root he pulled and a mud door fell; and there was the entrance to the place where the strange being lived.

The men were afraid to enter the place. Among them was one young man who cared for nothing. He was dared to go into the den. The young man stepped forward and said: "Men, follow me. If he kills me you will get to see what the thing is." So the boy led the way into the cave and there sat in the cave a man, who was crying. He was dressed in coyote skins. His head was tied with a piece of white sheeting. The cave smelt very good, for there was wild sage spread all over the cave. There was also sitting in the lodge a buffalo skull. The men now agreed to talk to the Scalped-Man and to ask him to help their war-party to be successful.

FOOTNOTES:

[63] Told by Antelope.

63.
THE DEAD MAN'S COUNTRY[64]

Six or seven years ago I was out upon the hills after my ponies. On my way back towards the camp I fainted, and lay upon the ground for a long time. Finally I felt better. I rose and walked towards home. I entered my tipi and lay down, and when I lay down I died.

As soon as I had died I saw a path leading east. There seemed to be a kind of inclosure. There was a little hole. I looked in that hole and saw lots of people in the village. I wanted to see the people and get acquainted with them. I went through this little hole. When I had gone through the hole I was in the dead man's country. Before I entered the village a man with a robe and anointed with red ointment came in, and said: "Young man, you must not go into this village. Go on, and at the south side of the entrance you will see a lodge where you will stop. You must not enter that lodge, for it is the lodge of the dead people." I went to the lodge, and I saw many people looking in. I stood on the south side of the entrance to the lodge. I saw that whenever a person who had died came, he entered inside the lodge and took his seat among the people in the lodge. The ground all over the lodge was covered with white clay, and it looked like ashes. There were many people in the lodge. I looked, and there the drums were resting in the east. The drums were black. The men were painted red. As they began to sing one old man came and stood out; then another man, younger than the first; then another, younger than the second; then another, until there were seven who came in this fashion. The last one to come was a little boy, whom they were about to paint. Now the drummers began to sing in a low voice. The dancers had dried willow sticks, which were representatives of their relatives who were still living upon earth. Each of the men was calling his people to the dead, so that they could come and be with them. The dry willows were used because the dead people wanted their living relatives in the world to become sick—as, for example, with consumption—and to dry up like the dry willows. When one of these dancers had to leave this place and go up to their village in the west, another man of his age would go out and take his place, and so on around. They wanted me to go into the lodge, but the man behind me said, "Do not go into the lodge." Every time they got to a certain part of the songs they would take the willow sticks, then move them towards themselves. Then the man that was watching me said, "Come, you must not stay here; you must be going to your country."

Now I woke up, but I remember the story well.

FOOTNOTES:

[64] Told by White-Owl.

64.
THE COYOTE WHO SPOKE TO THE EAGLE HUNTERS[65]

One time there was a prominent warrior who made up his mind that he would take a company of boys up into the hills to catch eagles. He led them out into the hills, and there he had many holes dug for the young men. They dug a big cave in the bank of the Missouri River, and this they made their permanent home.

One night, while they were sitting around in a circle telling Coyote stories, telling things a little bit in excess of what the Coyote had done, they were startled by the bark of a Coyote just outside of their den. Presently the Coyote walked into their den and said: "You people tell things about me that are not true, but then, it is all right." He jumped out of the den and went off. All the young men, and even the leader, were scattered, on account of this Coyote's coming into the den. They left their den and returned to their village. They thought that it was a bad sign for the Coyote to talk, but the other people thought that it was wrong for them to be scared. They thought that the Coyote had brought a good message to them, and they should have stayed and should have caught many eagles.

FOOTNOTES:

[65] Told by Many-Fox.

65.
THE GIRL AND THE ELK[66]

One time the Arikara went hunting on the Missouri River. They made their camp in the timber. Every evening the men used to go across the river and kill Elk. One evening, after the men had come home from their hunt, they heard the Elk whistling across the river. There was a fine-looking young woman in the camp, and as soon as she heard the Elk whistling she jumped up as if something had struck her, and she said: "Oh! I like that whistling; I must go and find out what it is." The people got hold of this woman. Every time the Elk whistled it was hard for the girl to stay away from him. For many days the Elk walked on the other side of the river, and the husband of the girl began to get jealous of the animal, for every time the Elk whistled the girl would jump up as if to run after it.

One day as they heard the Whistling of the Elk they all agreed that it was time to kill it. As they were getting ready to go across the river to kill the Elk they heard the whistling on their side of the river. There was the Elk going slowly through the timber. The men shot and shot and shot at it, but they could not kill it. The girl had to be tied up, because she wanted to go to the Elk. Finally one of the men took one of his cartridges and put in it some medicine, and said, "Now I will see if we can kill you." This man shot at the Elk, and his bullet was effective. While the Elk was whistling through the timber the girl was being held down. She had almost gotten away from three or four strong men. After the Elk was dead they had to give the girl some medicine to keep her from running away. She was put in a sweat-lodge many times, until she got over this crazy spell.

FOOTNOTES:

[66] Told by Many-Fox.

66.
HOW THE RABBIT SAVED A WARRIOR[67]

One time the Ojibwa stole many ponies from the Arikara. The Arikara followed the Ojibwa, and they overtook the horse thieves, but a different band of Ojibwa. There were several wagon-loads of them. The Arikara attacked them and fought hard. Several Arikara were wounded, including one of their brave men, who was shot through his neck by a bullet, which passed clear through his neck. The Arikara expected that he would die from loss of blood. As the man seemed about to die he saw a Jack-Rabbit, who spoke to him, and said: "You are not to die; you are to live." When the battle was over the man was brought to the village of the Arikara. He was taken into the medicine-lodge, and there was attended by the Rabbit medicine-man. In less than four days the man was up and around. He told the Arikara that the Rabbit had spoken to him, and told him that he was not to die from his wound. The man became well, and was one of the leading medicine-men of the Rabbit band. He lived to old age. He died only a few years ago from the bursting of a blood-vessel in the old wound.

FOOTNOTES:

[67] Told by Elk.

67.
THE WOMAN WHOSE BREASTS WERE CUT OFF[68]

In olden times when the Arikara lived in a village, there was a man who had a beautiful woman. This woman gave birth to a baby boy. One time when the child was about five years old the father went off on a hunt. While he was gone another young man, who was very handsome came and courted the woman. She liked the young man and did as he wanted her to do. They loved one another so much that they finally agreed that they would find a plan whereby either they could get rid of the husband or the woman would feign sickness and death. If she pretended to be dead she was to be placed upon an arbor instead of being buried; so the woman feigned sickness when her husband came home. She pretended to die, and they placed her upon an arbor. Her lover killed three dogs, skinned them, took the dogs up to the arbor and untied the girl. The dogs were placed upon the arbor, so that when the dog meat decayed it would smell. The young man brought leggings, moccasins, blankets, and beads, and in these the girl dressed as a boy. Her breast was tied with wide strings, so that not much of it appeared. They went off to another village, which was about four miles from the original village, where they lived happily. The young woman passed herself for a young man from the other village.

After they had stayed a long time in the village the woman grew anxious to see her child, so they painted up as men, and went and sat upon a rock that was by a spring. There they watched for the child to come to get water. One day the woman's boy came to get water from the spring, and she recognized him. After she had seen the boy she wanted to take him up in her arms, but the young man said, "No!" The woman insisted, and said, "He will not find me out." They went closer, and when the boy came where they were standing by the tree the woman spoke to her boy, and said, "Boy, will you let me drink out of your bucket." The boy looked at the woman for a long time. He went into his lodge and told his father that he had seen his mother. The father would not believe it, but the boy said, "There are two people standing yonder, and one of them is my mother."

The father thought, to make sure that it was true, that he would send for them. He had some dried buffalo meat boiled, and sent an invitation for the two young men to come and eat in his lodge. In the meantime he had sharpened a long knife and placed it under the meat. "Now," he said, "if it is true that that woman is not a man, but my wife, I will find out. There are two things she is to do when she enters the lodge. First, when she enters and steps over the ridge inside of the lodge, he will step forward as he steps; and if she is a female she will step over the ridge with her foot sidewise. The second thing is, when they have eaten and when I offer them the pipe to smoke, I shall know she is a female if the person refuses to smoke."

The two young men were sent for. They came, and the real young man entered the lodge, and stepped over the ridge straight forward, while the next young man, instead of walking straight forward like the first, moved her leg over sidewise. By this the husband knew that the person was not a man. He let them eat, and after they had eaten, the man filled the pipe and gave it to them. When the female took the pipe, instead of trying to smoke she put the pipe up to her mouth, and instead of drawing the smoke she blew into the pipe. The husband now took out his knife, and said: "I wanted to find you out. You are my wife." The woman screamed, and asked him to forgive her, saying she would live with him and try to be a good woman. The young man ran away. But the husband was angry, and said: "You are dead to me any way, but rather than that your breasts be tied down to make you look like a man I will cut them off, so that your breasts will be smooth." The husband took his knife out and cut her breasts off. The woman ran and fell at the entrance and died. She was taken up by her people and buried. The man went to the place where he supposed he had laid his wife, and there were three dead dogs. He knew by this that the two had played a trick on him. The girl's parents never said anything, but they were glad that the woman was dead. Nothing more was said about it.

FOOTNOTES:

[68] Told by Young-Hawk.

68.
THE WATER-DOGS[69]

Once there was a young man who slept outside of the lodge. He heard dogs bark at night, and as it was moonlight he saw a dog coming out of the river carrying her little ones in her mouth, one at a time, into the hills, to a spring. This young man saw the water-dog carrying its young ones. His name was Poor-Bear. He died shortly after he saw the dogs. At another time an old woman went to get some water out of the river, at or about the same place the water-dogs were seen. As she stooped to dip the water up she heard the dogs chattering in the water. She became frightened. She went home with the water and told the story. She became sick and died shortly afterward.

These water-dogs are supposed to be very powerful in killing people. They are hardly ever seen by people, and when they are seen the person who sees them generally dies.

FOOTNOTES:

[69] Told by Two-Hawks.

69.
TWO-WOLVES, THE PROPHET[70]

On what we call "Stevenson Flat" is a good piece of timber. There the Arikara were camped a long time ago. One day everybody turned out on the hills some few miles away on a buffalo chase. While they were making preparations to go home there came up a very bad storm. The hunters were scattered in small groups, some fleeing with the wind, others heading toward their camp. Two-Wolves, a rather quiet but good-hearted fellow, was rather slow about getting away. He was left all by himself in the storm. He stayed out all night and was missed the next night. They thought that he was a victim of the bad storm. His relatives mourned for him, and when the storm was over they set out to look around for him and to bring home their meat. Two-Wolves had been pitied by a Prairie-Chicken that had saved his life. The ruling power, Waruhti, had given him power to understand the speech of Thunder. The hunters met Two-Wolves coming home, and as they rushed up to greet him and inquire of his troubles he answered that he was all right.

A long time after this had happened Two-Wolves began to practice his power. The men began to be interested in him. He always had his lodge full. A few of the wonderful things that he did are these: Once a man named Two-Bears had a herd of ponies. They were badly disturbed by a horse owned by a man named Roving-Coyote. One day as Two-Bears was driving his herd to water, this horse acted very badly, cutting out the mares and chasing the horses. Two-Bears grew tired of the horse's behavior and took a strong, sharp-pointed ash stake and threw it at him. The horse was badly injured by the pin and died. Roving-Coyote, wondering who could have killed his horse, made up his mind to find out. He took the matter to Two-Wolves. "Aye! I want to find out who shot my pony. I do not want to make any trouble, but I want to know who did it." "Yes," said Two-Wolves, "my father will be the one to decide, but I will perform the ceremony to him." He called all the men together that belonged to his fire. He then asked the crier to call all over the village: "O! people of this village! Two-Wolves wants the man who killed the horse belonging to Roving-Coyote to report to his lodge." The crier repeated this over and over. When all had heard he went into the lodge again. While the ceremony had been going on black clouds rose in the west, and "Ah ho! Ah ho!" was repeatedly said by Two-Wolves. "Now my father is coming." He called again for the man to hurry, saying there was no use of secrecy and that he should know. Another call was given, and the Thunder was heard in the distance. Two-Bears did not believe that Two-Wolves could learn anything from Thunder, and so would not come. Thunder told Two-Wolves that Two-Bears was the man who had killed the horse. When Two-Bears did not come, Two-Wolves sent his servant to tell him to come right away. When he had come he was greeted heartily by Two-Wolves and placed beside him. "I am glad you have come. Now I want to say that my father says you are the man that killed Roving-Coyote's horse." "Yes," said Two-Bears, "I know now that you are a wonderful man. I did what you have accused me of. Ah! my friend," said he to Roving-Coyote, "you know how trying your horses are sometimes, and we lose our temper and are sorry for it afterwards. I did kill your horse with a picket pin, but I did not think you would find it out. I have nice ponies, and you may have your choice for my deed."

Another time an old brave named Wolf-Chief could not believe that such a thing as to understand the speech of Thunder was possible. Whenever he heard a call from Two-Wolves he would remark: "Now, what has that young rascal heard from the Big-One. We are gifted with power from different sources and we do not send out criers to make it public. Oh! grandson, if you will show us that you are something more than a man to go on the war-path and bring home scalps and ponies, then we will believe your doings." Two-Wolves heard all of these things, but never said anything. One day as it was raining and thundering Two-Wolves heard his father speaking, telling him to get Wolf-Chief and speak to him about his making fun of him, and to have him kill a black dog that he had and perform the ceremony with the feast. Two-Wolves sent out a crier to call for the man that would not believe Two-Wolves' prophecies. The caller passed by Wolf-Chief's lodge and Wolf-Chief remarked, "Well, that young rascal has something up again." Again the crier was out saying that the man who ridiculed Two-Wolves was wanted at Two-Wolves' lodge, right away. At the third call he did not come, but Wolf-Chief knew he was the man wanted. Two-Wolves then sent a servant to tell Wolf-Chief that he was wanted. When the servant arrived at Wolf-Chief's he found the old brave making arrows. "Nawa, you look as though you had something to say," said Wolf-Chief. "Yes," said the servant, "you are wanted at Two-Wolves'." "I will come," said he. He laid his work aside and went on to answer the call. He was greeted cheerfully and seated beside Two-Wolves. "I called you here to remind you that I have heard all the ridicule you have made, but I did not mind it until my father himself spoke to me of it, and that is why I have you here. You are to stop your jesting and make a feast for my father's ceremony with the black dog my father said that you have." "Ah, my grandson! You are wonderful. I know now, and I will do as you have asked me, and the servant will go with me and bring the dog you speak of."

Two-Wolves sent out only one war-party, and it was a failure. He gave out notice that he was to be a leader of a war-party. The party was held back on account of the rain, and he prophesied that there was a party of five enemies near on foot, and if they did not hurry they would miss them. On their way they saw the footprints of five men that had already passed. Two-Wolves was disappointed by the slowness of the party, and on their way he gave notice that no bird of any kind should be killed. This same day, the picket men found a bunch of buffalo. They gave chase and killed several. Strike-Enemy sacrificed one buffalo to his sacred bundle. The men got together around the meat. An eagle flew around them. It came nearer and nearer. They knew that the prophet had forbidden any birds to be killed. The temptation was so great that finally one took his musket and shot the eagle. Two-Wolves on hearing this was displeased. He warned the party to remain together, for they were to meet a party of seven. Sure enough, the scouts saw seven men in a party, but the men saw the scouts and they escaped. Two-Wolves called the party together and told them that he was discouraged by their errors and would not go further. They returned home. Two-Wolves lived a long time, doing good work, discovering thieves, and prophesying many wonderful things. At last he was taken sick and died.

FOOTNOTES:

[70] Told by Strike-Enemy.

70.
HOW THE MEDICINE-ROBE
SAVED THE ARIKARA[71]

A long time ago I joined a war-party. We went south, into the western part of the Sioux country, known as Nebraska. We came to an old village site. At this village site we found four large mounds where there had stood the four lodges of the bundle lodges. On the east side was a mound. The old men sat down by this mound and smoked. The oldest of the men told us that once the Arikara lived here; that while they were having their medicine ceremonies in one of these lodges a Sioux or one of some other tribe came and went through the village.

Now, there was one lodge where all the people, except one young woman who had just married, had gone to see the medicine-men's ceremony. While she was keeping the fire up and had the entrance fast, she saw at the top of the opening a man, an enemy, peeping down and looking at her. She sat and watched the enemy. He crawled from the lodge, then dug in the side of the lodge. She kept running around, until she went to the fire and poured water over it, so that the fire went out. After a while her husband came. She told him about the enemy. The young man accused his wife of having her lover around. The next day the young man went to the timber and gathered a lot of dried willows and some dry grass. This he took to his lodge. He placed the dry wood by the entrance. That evening the young man hid in the lodge, and allowed his wife to remain in the lodge as before. When it became dark, the enemy came and looked through the opening he had made the night before. The enemy then walked to the entrance and found the entrance open. So he walked in. The husband then arose from his hiding place. He caught the enemy from behind, so that he held his arms. The woman took the grass and willow limbs and threw them upon the hot coals, so that there was a big blaze. She then went out and screamed, "My man has an enemy in our lodge!" The men ran into the lodge, and there was the young man, holding on to the enemy. The enemy was overpowered, and a seat was given him.

The man had long hair. His face was painted. Bunches of medicine were tied upon his head. On his right arm was tied a rattlesnake skin. On his left arm was tied the shell of a turtle. The tail was upon it. The man made signs and said: "Next month, all of you people will be killed by the southern tribe of Indians. You make fun of me, but it is true. I came to capture a woman." The man was then taken to the Awaho-bundle's lodge. There they had singing. In a few days the man was placed upon a scaffold of four ash timbers, and his hands and feet were tied with strong buffalo strings. He was left upon the scaffold to die, but the man was a wonderful man, for he shook his arms and the strings became loose. The people saw it, and they tied him again. Every time the man shook his arms he broke loose. One of the old priests was selected to stab the man to death. The man was left upon the scaffold, and his body dried.

One night as the medicine-men were having their ceremony this man who had been put upon the scaffold came into the lodge. All the medicine-men ran out of the lodge. Word was sent to the man who was the keeper of the wonderful robe.[72] He went into the lodge and found the dead man lying upon a buffalo robe. The man wrapped the dead man in the robe and packed him to the river. He threw him into the river, saying, "You wonderful man, I throw you into the river, and your bones shall stay here." The man went to the lodge. Sweet grass and wild sage were burned in the lodge. The medicine-men then resumed their performances. In about a month the medicine-men's ceremony was over. Each medicine-man took his medicine things to his lodge and wrapped them up.

The month came to an end and the Indians looked for the enemy. One fine day the Indians saw the Sioux coming from over the hills. There were so many that the people became scared. The keeper of the holy robe sat down in his lodge. The men were going out to meet and fight the enemy. The enemy were so numerous that the medicine-man with the holy robe and the robe's belongings made medicine-smoke, then laid down the gourd [rattle]. He took the robe and wrapped it about his body, the hair side turned out. The inside had the sun, moon, and stars upon it. He then took an eagle wing in his left hand, the gourd in his right hand, went out and climbed upon the top of his lodge. By this time the enemy were close to the village. This man upon the lodge then shook himself, and shook the robe towards the sun, then he closed the robe. While he was doing this the enemy noticed some of their men fall off from their horses, bleeding from their lungs and seeming to be out of their heads. The enemy saw the man upon the lodge. They became scared. A shout was heard. The enemy gave way and ran; for the power of the man was so great that whoever came under his power ran into the village, powerless to defend himself. The enemy gave way, and there was great slaughtering. The village was saved.

The wonderful man went into his lodge and made sweet-smelling smoke, passed his robe over the smoke several times, then wrapped it and hung it up. The gourd was then passed over the smoke and hung up by the robe. The medicines were then passed over the smoke and put away. The man had red clay all over his body while going through this performance. He also passed smoke all over his body, and said: "I am satisfied. Our village is saved. The enemy are killed. Scalps will be brought in, so we can have great rejoicing." Scalps were brought, and there was great rejoicing. There were three different kinds of scalp dances given by the women. One was a dance learned from the Cheyenne, another from the Grosventre, and another from the Pawnee. Of course, they had their own scalp-dance, but these three were the best dances.

Some years after, some of the Sioux visited the Arikara, and they told of the strange man, and that he was a Wichita. The Sioux also said that at that time many tribes had got together to annihilate the Arikara.

FOOTNOTES:

[71] Told by Sitting-Bear.

[72] The tribal medicine of the Arikara.

71.
THE MEDICINE BEAR SHIELD.[73]

I was fourteen winters old when my father died. I did not go to see him buried, for I was feeling very bad. After the people had come away from where my father was buried I went to the place. There was the grave. The people had stuck two forks in the ground and placed a pole across the forks. Then some poles were placed on the sides, and instead of piling stones and dirt over the grave a buffalo robe was spread over it, so that there was no dirt. Stones were placed on the robe where it touched the ground. I cried and cried, and in the evening I fell asleep. I dreamed I had seen a Bear standing by my father's grave, and I was scared. The Bear spoke, and I always believed that it was my father who spoke to me, and said: "My son, the shield was upon the grave; some one has removed it. Find it; it is yours." I slept a long time, for when I woke it was nearly daylight. I stood up and cried again, and stood by the grave all day. I was young. There were many enemies in the country, but I did not care. In the evening I saw clouds coming from the west. Soon a rain storm came, but I did not go home. When it began to pour I ran to a steep bank. There was a crevice. I crawled in there and lay down. It was now dark. I did not go to sleep, for I kept my eyes upon the grave. There was a lightning flash. The flash struck near the grave. I saw standing by the grave a Bear, its paws upward toward the sky. It became dark again. I kept my eyes upon the grave. Again the lightning flashed and again the lightning struck by the grave, where I saw the lightning come together and form a circle with a black mark upon the center. On each side of the black mark were black spots, as if the circle had eyes and nose. I watched the circle, and I was satisfied that the black center mark was a Bear. The two marks I saw were Bear's ears. On each ear I saw branches of cedar and pine. As it was dark the circle gradually disappeared, and I saw in its place a rainbow. Then it disappeared. The rain storm passed, and I crawled out from the place and went to the grave and began to cry. I cried all night, and also the next day. In the evening I fell asleep. In my dream I saw my father, who told me that a shield was placed upon his grave, and that Howling-Wolf had taken the shield from the grave. My father further told me that the shield belonged to me and that I must get it and make another one such as I had seen the night before. He further told me to go home and get the shield.

I awoke in the morning and went home. I asked my people who took the shield from my father's grave, and they told me that some one had taken it from the grave. I told them who had it, and my mother went to the lodge of the man, who said, "Yes, I took it, but I threw the cover away, for I intended to make a new cover for it." The frame of the shield was given up by the man to me. I took it home, and I had my people make another cover, a cover I had seen myself upon my father's grave. You see the picture of the Bear as I saw it. It is throwing up white-dust. The left side of the shield is a Bear's ear. Inside of it are cedar berries. The right ear has pine cones in it. I hunted, and I killed a deer. The deer skin was tanned and these things were put upon the tanned buckskin—the picture of the Bear and Bear's ears. On a buffalo hunt I killed a buffalo bull and made the inner shield. This I did by getting the whole breast hide of a bull. After I got it I spread it upon the ground. I took all of the meat off. I then dug a hole and made a big fire in it. When the fire went down and there were only coals and hot stones I spread the hide over the bed of coals and drove stakes around the hide, so that the hide when it shrunk pulled the stakes up. As the hide shrunk it became thick. While hot, I cut around the rim until I got it of the right size. Now a ceremony was in order. Songs were sung while the covering of the shield was being painted as you now see. The red, downy eagle feather was put there for the first lightning, which was very red. The ears were put upon the shield, so the shield would have understanding. There are three songs that are sung when the shield is being made. The shield was made, and I hung it up. In the night I took it into the lodge. Before sunrise I would take the shield and hang it up so that it faced towards the east.

When I saw fifteen winters I joined a war-party. After we had gone several days we saw a Sioux coming. We hid away in a ravine and as he came near where we were I jumped up, holding the shield in front of me. Another man in our party shot and hit the Sioux in the breast. I struck the Sioux with my bow and counted my first coup. I returned to where the Sioux fell, for I had run beyond. I jumped upon the Sioux and took only his scalplock. This I took to my grandfather, who took the scalp to the lodge of the holy bundle. The ceremony of offering the scalp to the gods was performed. After this ceremony the chiefs had their ceremony, and I was made a chief. I was invited to sit among the great chiefs. An old man arose and, taking up a buckskin shirt, called me to him. He put the buckskin shirt upon me. He said: "My son, I put upon you a dress that is white; there are no marks upon the shirt. It is fringed upon the sleeves and body with ermine. You are now a young chief. See that you are always brave and as you strike enemies and scalp them make marks upon your shirt, so that these chiefs who are present here will be proud that you wear their shirt. When you come to old age this shirt will be covered with many marks, representing your deeds in battles." After this ceremony I again joined other war-parties. I gave many scalps to my grandfather. When the enemy attacked our village I wore my shield, and though the enemy shot at me I was never hit. When the battle would be over there would be young men brought in from the battlefield wounded.

Another time my people had what is now known as the "sun dance." My grandfather took me in and placed me upon the ground. He spoke to the old warriors, and said: "Medicine-men and warriors, I bring this young man into this lodge. I want you, medicine-men, to paint him and place this lariat rope upon the pole, and cut upon his back so that he will swing. Warriors, in cutting upon his back, tell of your great deeds, so that my grandson will overtake your great deeds in his life and become a great man. I have many ponies to give you, and his mother and relatives will give you presents." Two of the medicine-men arose and painted my body. Then one of the medicine-men spoke, and said: "Warriors, the young man is ready to be cut upon the back." One warrior arose and came to where I lay. This warrior told of his great deeds, then cut me upon my right shoulder-blade. It hurt, but I kept courage. The next man then came and put a stick through the cut and tied it with the buckskin string. The next warrior came and told of his great deeds, then cut upon my left shoulder and ran the stick through, tying the buckskin. Each of these men received a fine pony from my friends, also all the gifts brought in by my friends. The warriors now pulled the lariat rope, so that I now swung about four feet from the ground. I swung there one day and one night. One of my related warriors seeing me swing there so long arose, and said: "Medicine-men and warriors, this is the youngest man ever brought into such a lodge as this. I have a present of a fine racing pony for him. Now cut these strings." When he said this, many of my friends came in and spread presents of robes and other presents. No sooner would the giver place the presents than some one would come and take them away. A warrior arose and came where I hung. He told of fighting a duel with a Sioux and how he had cut him up with a knife. This man's name was Bloody-Knife. He cut the strips of skin, and I fell to the ground. I was taken out of the lodge. Then I was fed with pounded corn and tallow. A few days after, the Sioux attacked our village and again I counted coup and also struck the enemy. I had an easy time in battle; I think it was because of the sufferings I went through in the ceremony. I danced the sun dance many times after that, but always suffered, for the old medicine-men had died and young men took their places.

FOOTNOTES:

[73] Told by Strike-Enemy.

72.
THE CRUCIFIED ENEMY[74]

Many years ago there stood a village made of earth-lodges. In the village there were some people who wanted to go on a buffalo hunt. They were mostly young men and young women. The older people were left in the village. After many days the enemy were seen in the distance.

The old people who remained in the village were somewhat confused and frightened. When the enemy approached, the men marched out and fought them desperately. Finally the people of the village retreated. They all got inside of their lodges. The men stood by their doors, fighting the enemy. In one of the lodges sat an old man. He was putting on his medicine paint and costumes. After he had finished he went out, having a gourd in his hand, but no weapon. He went on top of the lodge and sang some of his most sacred songs, that there might come aid from some of the gods. When the enemy saw him they were much amazed, and very much afraid of him. Some one said that he knew the old medicine-man, and that they could not do anything to him, for he was a medicine-man who had the power to mesmerize. So they all ran, crying: "We can not do anything with him! Hurry on, before he works on us!" The old man ran behind them. One young man on the enemy's side was wounded and brought into the village. He was taken into the medicine-lodge, and they all saw him. He had been one of the bravest men, and had all kinds of medicines on his head and around his neck. Finally it was agreed that he should be tied up to a wooden cross and be placed outside of the village. They did this, and the man died. After a while he lost all of his flesh, but the bones were left on the cross.

Many young men used to go outside of the village near the cross to play at games. One day while they were playing, the bones of the man on the cross fell to the ground, rose up and ran toward the village. Everybody ran away, because of the ghost. The ghost ran toward the medicine-lodge and ran inside, but no one would go in, for everyone was afraid. At last one brave man came forward who dared to go in. He looked all around and found the man from the cross under some blankets upon the altar. He called to the others. They all came in and saw the ghost lying there. They gathered the bones and bundled them up in an old basket, then threw them away. After this had passed, the party that had gone on a buffalo hunt returned with lots of dried meat. Of course, the people who stayed were very glad to see them again. The happenings and results were told to them.

FOOTNOTES:

[74] Told by Hawk.

73.
HOW A SIOUX WOMAN'S SCALP WAS SACRIFICED[75]

In the fall there were five or six of us who went on the war-path. We came to the Pine Ridge Agency, and there hid, close to where the Sioux got their water. Two women came down to the spring to get water. We all ran towards the women. The women ran. One young man caught up with one woman, grabbed at her hair, took his knife, and took the scalp off from the right side of the woman's head. The woman ran into the camp.

We returned to our leader and gave the scalp to him. The leader then said, "We must hurry home." We walked all day and all night, and another day and night. The next day we found the thick timber, and there we lay down to rest. When we woke up, the leader took the fat off from the scalp. He then called one of the men. He then cut the fat, making it into five pieces. Facing the east, he placed four of the five pieces in his hand—one on each corner of his palm—and the fifth piece he placed in the center of the palm. He then took the pieces, one at a time, beginning with the one on the southeast corner, then the southwest corner, then the northwest corner, then the northeast corner, and placed them in a similar position upon the ground, which was to show that the scalp was to be offered to the gods. We then went home.

We gave the scalp to one of the high priests, who held the scalp ceremony. At this ceremony we used the fire-sticks to make the fire for burning this scalp. The scalp was burned. After the burning of the scalp the people turned out, passing their holy bundles and medicine bags over the smoke. The priest stood to the west of the burning scalp and recited a ritual, calling on the gods. The young men and children who wanted their names changed gave presents to the priests, who changed their names for them.

FOOTNOTES:

[75] Told by Sitting-Bear.

74.
THE WARRIOR WHO FOUGHT THE SIOUX[76]

When the Indians used to live at the Fort Berthold village a few of them moved about ten miles west of Fort Berthold, on the Missouri River bottom, in the timber. This was in the winter time. Strike-Enemy and some others went to the Fort Berthold village.

When Strike-Enemy was about a mile from the village he was attacked by a hundred or more Sioux. He held them back, for he had a rifle. He reached the fort; then the Sioux surrounded it. The people in the fort all fought the Sioux. It seems that one man had gone out to hunt antelope. He had killed one antelope, and was bringing it towards the fort. He could not see ahead, for he was carrying a whole antelope upon his back; but when he heard a noise he saw that the Sioux had attacked the fort. He threw down the antelope and ran. This all happened in the winter time when the snow was on the ground. The Sioux found the man's tracks, and they followed him. They caught up with the man about six miles west of the fort. Here he stopped, and the first Sioux he came to he killed. He then jumped on the enemy he had killed and cut him open with his knife, cut his arm off at the shoulder and commenced to hit the man on his head with his own arm. The Sioux were shooting at him from behind with their arrows. The hunter did not pay any attention to the shooting. He stood up, gave a big yell, like that of a bear, and the Sioux ran. Then the hunter again cut the Sioux upon the breast and began to put blood upon his face. When he straightened up, the Sioux saw that he had a piece of liver in his mouth. He chased them and took away all their ponies. He caught one pony, got on it, and ran after them. The Sioux say that they were scared, for they had never seen anybody acting in this way, for the hunter seemed like a bear. He gave them back their ponies, then went away, but the Sioux would not come near him. He took only one pony and went into some timber. That night a blizzard set in. The next day he was found frozen. He still had the arrows in his back. The Arikara and Sioux both tell this story.

FOOTNOTES:

[76] Told by Strike-Enemy.

75.
THE CAPTURE OF THE ENEMY'S BOWS[77]

In olden times the young men in a village went on the war-path. While they were gone the Sioux came down to the village and captured all their old women and children, killing many. A young man returned to the village and found out what had happened. He found his brother coming from a thickly timbered place, who told him that his father was in hiding in the timber. These three were the only ones around the village. The young man was angry. He told his father and brother that he wanted them to follow him to the Sioux. This they did.

One evening they came up with the enemy, who were in camp by a creek. The young man said, "We will attack this camp." The three went through the timber. They saw the big campfires, mostly of their people, but there were some Sioux warriors stationed out, watching. The young man looked up at the stars, then at the trees, and at everything. Then he said to the two—his father and brother—"We must make an attack, give a big war-whoop, and make it sound as if there were many people." So the three gave the war-whoop and attacked the camp. The oldest man, at the same time, yelled: "My people, do not run, but pick up your bows! We are here!" When they gave the war-whoop the trees all seemed to give the war-whoop—even the grass gave the war-whoop. The stars seemed to give the war-whoop. War-whoops sounded all through the timber. The birds and everything seemed to give the war-whoop. The enemy were frightened. They ran. The people stayed behind. They captured the enemy's bows and several of their people. Then they followed the enemy. The next day they came up with them and killed a great many. The people then took the enemy's bows and arrows and took them up on a high hill. They set them up, with one bow in the middle and all the other bows resting on it. So all the bows and arrows were set upon the high hill. The hill was known after that as "Enemy's-Bows-Upon-a-High-Hill."

FOOTNOTES:

[77] Told by Yellow-Bear.

76.
THE WOMAN WHO BEFRIENDED THE WARRIORS[78]

When the Arikara had their village on the Missouri River there were two boys who started out on the war-path. They went away up on the Missouri River. They went down to the fields and found a little earth-lodge. They went in and found an old woman, who was glad to see them. She gave them something to eat. She told them where to go. There they went, and found the enemy. They killed one or two, then went home. Again they went on the war-path. They visited the old woman's place again, and she fed them. After they had eaten she told them where to go to find the enemy. They went and found the enemy. They killed the enemy and took scalps home. At another time several other young men joined their war-party. They went up to the old woman's place and there they were again fed, and they were told by the old woman where to find the enemy. They found the enemy, killed several, took their scalps, and went home. After this, whenever the two young men wanted to go on the war-path, many young men joined them. They found that these two young men had a grandmother, who was helping them. In one of these war-parties against the enemy there were so many young men in the party that when the old woman saw them she felt ashamed; but she told the people to go on; that they would find the enemy and would kill and scalp them. The people did kill the enemy, took their scalps, and went home.

Again, another war-party went out to find the old woman, but the old woman had disappeared. The men came and told the two boys. The two boys hunted for her, and at last found her in the side of a cliff in the Bad Lands. Here the two boys visited her, and she helped them. Other men found out where she was and a great company of them went there, but she had again disappeared. Another party of warriors went out. They came to a big lake. The warriors made their camp there. In the night they heard a woman singing scalp-dance songs, and she danced and laughed. The warriors were scared. They wanted to return home, but the leader said, "No, she is rejoicing, for we are to kill the enemy." The warriors went on, found the enemy's camp, and they killed several and took their scalps. They took the scalps home, and they had a scalp-dance. Again, another war-party went out. They went and stopped opposite the lake. The dancing and singing was again heard. The leaders were glad to hear this. They went and killed the enemy and scalped them.

Another war-party went out. They stopped opposite the lake. The woman, instead of singing and dancing, began to mourn. But the warriors went on, notwithstanding, and when they attacked the enemy the enemy got the best of them, killed several of them, and only a few of them reached home to tell the story. After that, when a war-party went to the lake, whenever the old woman sang scalp-dance songs and danced, they knew that they were going to be successful. If the woman began to cry and yell, they knew that if they went on, the enemy would get the best of them. It was found out afterwards that this was the same old woman who had lived upon the Missouri River, and she had gone away from the people and had gone to the Bad Lands; and when she was found out there she went off to dwell in the lakes. The people used to give the old woman blankets, tobacco, and other things.

FOOTNOTES:

[78] Told by Enemy-Heart.

77.
THE ATTACK UPON THE EAGLE HUNTERS[79]

Many years ago it was a common practice for the Arikara to go upon the hills and dig holes in them and stay in the holes many days, to catch eagles. One young man went away off by himself. He climbed upon a high hill, dug a hole, and over the hole spread some dry limbs. On the limbs he placed some dead jack-rabbits and other small animals. Then he himself got into the hole. His bow and arrows were lying outside of the den. While he was lying there the Sioux came and found the hole. They marched down and came upon the man. They found his bow, arrows, and gun outside. They took the things off from the hole and told the man to crawl out. They then wanted to know where the other men were. He told them they were at another place. So they tied him up and he led them up to the spot where the other men were. They found that the party had lots of meat. They untied the man and told the Arikara to stand around the fireplace while they made the man cook the meat for them. The man cooked a lot of dried meat, and the first thing he did was to take a fire-stick, which he ran into a piece of buffalo tallow. This he held over the fire, and as the grease was dripping from it he whirled it around and burned the Sioux with the grease. The Sioux were all scared. The man went out of the tipi and walked a short distance, for he was very weak, for the Sioux had been torturing him. Now, he went a little way ahead into a ravine. The Sioux were all scared, for they thought that the man had gone outside and was waiting for any of them to come out, so that he might kill them. They stayed in the tipi all night.

That night the man went home and told the people all that had happened, and the warriors and braves got on their ponies and they found that the Sioux had just left the tipi. They caught up with the Sioux and killed three of them. The Arikara went home victorious with three scalps. So the people gave war dances.

FOOTNOTES:

[79] Told by Many-Fox.

78.
THE ATTACK UPON THE EAGLE HUNTERS[80]

There was a young man who understood the ceremony of catching eagles upon the hills. He invited six other young men to join him in catching eagles. They went west from their village, upon the banks of the Missouri. These men made their camp, then dug into the bank of the Missouri. They made a kind of cave. They spread limbs of trees upon the top of the opening. They then laid fresh meat of deer or rabbit, which had been skinned, upon the limbs. Here these people stayed several days, catching eagles. They would hide in the cave, while one man would watch out. The magpies were the first birds to come and eat of the meat that they had placed upon the top of the cave. Then, when the magpies flew away they knew that an eagle was coming. They caught several eagles.

One afternoon the Sioux marched down from the hills, where they had been discovered. The Sioux saw that they could not do anything to the eagle catchers, for they were in a cave, so they tried to be friendly with them. They asked them for some eagle feathers. The leader of the party now went out and gave them some eagle feathers, walking backwards when he left them. There were some young men among the Sioux who wanted to fight. The Sioux attacked the Arikara. The leader kept all the young men in the cave and made them load their muzzle-loading guns, while he stayed at a certain distance from the bank, and the first man to attack them on horseback he killed. He would throw away his empty gun and the boys would pass a loaded one to him. He would then start to another place on the bank, and again the first man on horseback to come toward him he would shoot and kill. Thus he kept up the fire, killing several. The Sioux finally gave up and retreated. In the night the hunters crawled out of the cave, took scalps from the Sioux, and returned to their village with scalps.

FOOTNOTES:

[80] Told by Elk.

79.
THE MOURNING LOVER[81]

A man named Rolling-Log courted an Arikara woman, but she would not have him. One day a whole lot of Arikara men got together, and prepared to go hunting. Rolling-Log was one of them. This woman whom Rolling-Log wanted to marry went to him and said, "If you will bring home to me enough sinew to last a whole year I will marry you." Rolling-Log said that he would try to get enough, for he wanted to marry this woman. He went south and killed many deer, black tails, and antelope. Rolling-Log got about twenty-four sinews, and he thought this was enough for the woman; so he went home.

While the hunters were on the chase Rolling-Log's girl had become sick and died. When Rolling-Log came home he at once went over in the evening, where the girl had lived. He had the sinew for the girl, and he stood outside in front of the entrance, waiting for the girl to come out. A man by the name of Red-Horse came out, and Rolling-Log asked Red-Horse if his girl was inside. Red-Horse stood still for some time, and said, "My friend, the girl that you speak of died while you were out hunting." Rolling-Log stood there, surprised to hear that his girl was dead. He went back to his lodge and scolded his people because they had not told him that the girl was dead. He felt so bad that he went among the hills and never returned to the Arikara camp.

FOOTNOTES:

[81] Told by Two-Hawks.

80.
CONTEST BETWEEN THE BEAR AND THE BULL SOCIETIES[82]

A long time ago, when the Arikara used to have the medicine ceremonies, there was the Bear family on the north and the Buffalo family on the south, inside the lodge. There were certain days and nights for the Bear people to perform their wonders; then there were days and nights for the Buffalo people to perform their wonders.

In this Buffalo society there were two buffalo scalps, with horns. The two Buffalo men who wore these buffalo scalps were painted up and medicine was put upon them. These scalps were put upon them. They went out of the lodge, and the people played with the Buffalo men through the village. On one of these occasions the Buffalo were running after the people in the village, and one young man in the Bear family filled up a pipe and gave it to the leader of the Bear family. This young man made a request of the leader of the Bear family that he would like to challenge the Buffalo to fight. The leader of the Bear family did not want to give his consent to do this, for it was not the right thing to do. But the man insisted, so the leader of the Bear family gave his consent to the young man to fight. The young man was told to fill the pipe with tobacco and to take the pipe to the Buffalo family; that in presenting the pipe he must first tell the Buffalo family that the pipe given to them was a challenge to fight the Buffalo man. The young man took the pipe over and presented it to the leader of the Buffalo society, telling him that he had come over there with a pipe to challenge the Buffalo to a fight with the Bear family. The Buffalo leader objected to this, telling the young man that it was something unusual, and that although they had always shown their powers to the people, this hidden mystery of having power of the animals would have to be given to the two fighters. The young man insisted until at last the Buffalo leader gave his consent.

The leading Buffalo man now sent for the Buffalo man, who was outside, who had the buffalo scalp on. This man with the buffalo scalp came into the lodge. He was told to go outside and wash himself and to take a sharp stick and get all the dirt out of his toenails and fingernails; then, after washing, he was to roll in the dust, then come into the lodge. After entering the lodge the Buffalo family took their drum and began to sing sacred songs, while the leading Buffalo man took his medicines and placed some of them upon hot coals that were brought by the errand man. The Buffalo man, who wore the buffalo scalp, was told to pass this smoke all over his body. Then medicines were put upon his body, and paint—even the scalp of the buffalo with the horns was passed through the smoke and medicines were put upon it. The singing continued, so that when they were through with the painting and putting upon the Buffalo of the medicine, a certain one was sent to the Bear family to say that all was ready. While the Buffalo people were carrying on their singing the Bear family were also carrying on their medicine preparations.

The Bear and the Buffalo family now went out of the lodge, each carrying their drums, their rattles, and all their medicines. The Bear family sat on the north side in an open place. The Buffalo sat on the south. Each family now sang its medicine song. Then the Bear man came forth with a bear robe over his body, growling and acting the part of a Bear. The Buffalo man went forth with a buffalo scalp upon his head. The Buffalo man rolled on the ground, shaking himself, so that the buffalo scalp stuck on to the head of the man, although it was not fastened on his head, causing him to act the part of a real Buffalo. The people could see the Bear when it stood up, and that the Bear man had made the tusks come out of his mouth. The Bear family had put on the greatest medicine that they had, and so had all the Buffalo family. While the Bear was sitting around trying to get a chance at the Buffalo, the Buffalo seemed to have been the quicker, for it ran up to the Bear and hooked it before it could turn around. Again and again it hooked the Bear, until the Bear man was killed.

The Bear people took their man into the lodge, and the Buffalo people also returned into their lodge. It was announced through the lodge of the Bears that the young man was killed for all time, and that the Bear family did not get mad about it, for it was his own fault, as he had wanted to challenge the Buffalo man. The young man was buried. Ever after that, when the people were holding their medicine-lodge and performing their mysteries, the chiefs of the animals in the lodge never challenged one another while the performances were going on.

FOOTNOTES:

[82] Told by Standing-Bull.

81.
HOW WHITE-BEAR CAME TO BELONG TO THE BEAR SOCIETY[83]

White-Bear is my son. He has the spirit of the Bear. I will tell you how it happened: I was in the medicine-lodge when my wife was pregnant. I used to put on the bear robe that was wonderful and I used to try to catch people, that I might cut them open, so I could get a piece of liver from them. My doing this made my son have the spirit of the Bear. So when he was born, in nursing, the boy's mouth showed froth, and he made a noise like a young bear. I went hunting and killed a young bear. I skinned the bear, took the hide home, and had it tanned. In the Bear dances the boy, White-Bear, wore the robe. White-Bear stayed in the medicine-lodge.

One time the Arikara were about to have their yearly medicine dance. As they had brought willows and Cottonwood branches to build their lodges White-Bear, who was then but three years old, picked up a butcher knife and went out to play. The boy fell upon the knife. The knife handle struck the ground, the point upward, striking the boy on the belly. The knife cut deep. White-Bear got up and ran to the tipi, crying. I saw the boy coming, holding his intestines in his hands. I picked up the boy and took him into the tipi. I now laid the boy across my lap, and with ease put the intestines back into their place. The relatives and mother were mourning. I took some medicine and put upon the cut place, and bandaged it with buffalo hide. I still held the boy upon my lap. The boy cried. The mother was called and nursed the child. The child nursed like a bear. Froth came out from his mouth, and I unbandaged the child. I took the froth from the child's mouth and put it upon the cut. The child became better. In a few days the child was much better. I then took the bear robe and put it upon the child's back. The child could not straighten out. The bear robe was left upon him for several days. As the child got better he got to making noises like a cat. Now, the child began to try to walk, and went out. Children were sent for, so that the boy might see them. They came and played with the boy, for the boy had on the bear robe. The child grew up and acted like a bear. In their Bear ceremonies the boy stayed with me and much sleight-of-hand was performed upon him. As he grew up he had ways like a bear.

One time the boy, while in the medicine-lodge, had visions of a bear. He told me, and I was glad of this and encouraged the boy to remain in the lodge. The boy is that young man sitting there. He is now a man and has a big scar upon his belly. He is a Bear by birth, but as we now have no more Bear dances he does not show the ways of a bear.

FOOTNOTES:

[83] Told by Strike-Enemy.

82.
THE TALE OF A MEMBER OF
THE BEAR SOCIETY[84]

You heard what my father said about my belonging to the Bear Society. It is true. I used to stay in the medicine-men's lodge and inside of the Bear's lodge. I learned many things about the mysteries of the Bear Society. My father gave me a bear skin that was stuffed, so that it was like a bear. When we had a Bear dance my little bear used to be placed on the south side of the lodge and I would be placed opposite. When the singing for dancing was begun I danced, and as I danced I would notice my little bear doing the same thing that I was doing. If I moved my head sidewise, it would do the same thing. If I raised up my arms towards the sky, the little bear would do the same thing. People saw it. I kept the bear a long time. Only a few years ago it became spoiled. The little bear, which was part of my life, was now old, so that the hide was easily torn. My father thought it was best to dispose of it, so one day we took the little bear yonder among those hills, and we placed it in a ravine, where there was a bush of choke-cherries, and there we left it.

Some years ago one of my friends, a young man who was a great hunter, asked me to go hunting with him, and I agreed to go. I caught my pony and saddled it. This pony was a good runner. At this time there were many Sioux in our country, so I had to be careful which pony I rode while hunting. I took upon my pony some things to eat, and a rifle that my father had given me. I had also many cartridges. The other young man came to my lodge, and I was surprised to see him upon a white pony, which I knew could not run. I tried to persuade him to get a better pony, but he would not change, for the white pony, he said, would not run away. We started and crossed the Missouri River. We went over yonder hills. We started early in the morning and we went far over those hills. We did not see any deer all day. Towards evening we got to a draw, where there were some trees. There we unsaddled our ponies and made camp. We lariated our ponies some distance from where we were. Far into the night I heard the horses snorting. I reached for my gun, went to the other man, and tried to wake him. He was sleeping soundly, so I left him and crawled up to where the ponies were, dragging my gun as I went on. I noticed that there was a man standing in the shadow of a hill. My pony kept on snorting. I saw the man, so I crawled back to our place and woke my friend. We crawled up to the ponies, and as we approached them we saw the man coming. The pony was now snorting furiously. I told the other man to have his gun ready; that I would go up and meet the man; that if he should see anything wrong he should shoot. I rose and walked toward the man. As I rose the man ran, and as it was moonlight we knew from his running that he was a Scalped-Man. We had heard of this man wearing a wolf hide, so we let him go, and we went back to our camp. I told my friend that he could sleep and I would watch the rest of the night, for I could not go to sleep. The next morning, while I was dishing out some pemmican, I told my friend that I had always had a liking for bears; and that I would like to see one. He promised to let me see one.

After we had eaten a bite we went on further west. We found some deer. My friend thought that he, being an experienced hunter, could kill where others could not. He shot at the deer several times, but he never killed any. He was discouraged. We saw a deer at a distance. I then asked if I might try my luck on this fine deer. He allowed me to shoot at it. We were out of meat, and I was very hungry for fresh meat. As I neared the deer I crawled up to it and shot it. I broke both of its hind legs, so that it could not run. We killed it, then went into camp again. That night we had to watch, for we were now in a country where there were many rattlesnakes. The next morning we went further west into canyons, where we had to watch every step we took, for there were many rattlesnakes. The other man did not seem to care about them, but I did. I would not go any further, for I was afraid of snakes. I returned to our camp. I heard several shots, and after a while I saw my friend coming. He had killed three deer. We took our ponies and brought the meat to our camp. The next day we started for home. On our way home I saw at long distance what seemed to be a horse. I told my friend. As we went nearer to the supposed horse I saw that it stood up like a man. I told my friend about it. He looked, and said that it was a bear, saying, "Here is a chance for you to see a bear." We now unloaded our ponies. He told me to remain behind with the meat and his pony, for he rode my pony, taking his rifle with him. I saw him coming back, for the bear was now after him. The bear ran back, and I saw a young bear sitting at a distance. The bear got to its young and embraced it, as much as to say, "My child, we are lost." Then my man went for it again. He shot at it, but still the bear would run after him. Finally the man ran the bear towards me, and I got upon the pony's back and I had to whip the pony hard to make it go. I felt scared, for if the bear had kept on after me it would have got me. The bear ran back to its young, so I felt safe. My friend now attacked the bear, and he shot at it, hitting it.

The bear ran after the man, but it turned back and went into the brush. We went down, and found a pond on the side of the brush, where the bear had gone. I undressed, took only my knife, and waded into the pond. My man remained on the side of the pond, ready to shoot the bear, and was telling me that as soon as the bear jumped at me I should dive, and keep on in the same direction. I crossed the pond and found the bear sitting in the bushes. The bear was dead. We skinned it, taking only the hide. When a bear is skinned and stretched out it is the perfect image of a man.

I mounted my pony and we went on. I attacked the young bear, ran into the brush and got hold of the bear. I tried to get my man to bring my lariat rope, so I could rope it and lead it to the village. I became tired, so I called out to my man to shoot it. He would not do it, so I took my knife and stabbed the young bear and killed it. I skinned it. Now I had two hides. I tried to put the large hide upon my pony, and the pony snorted at it. I finally gave the hide to my friend. I did wrong, for I should have asked him to put the hide upon his pony for me. He did not belong to the Bear Society, notwithstanding he was thankful for the hide. The little bear hide I put upon the pony. My father scolded me for giving the bear hide away. My little bear hide was of good size. My father had it tanned for me, and the hide was also decorated with paint. The bear hide also had a soft, feathery appearance about its head. I wore it in dances, and kept it by my pillow in our lodge. Only a few years ago I was visiting the Sioux, and while I was gone some white man came to our village. He saw the bear robe in our lodge. He asked how much they wanted for the hide, and my bear was sold to some white man. When I came back home I missed my bear, and asked where it was. My folks said, "We sold it to a white man." I was sorry, but it was all right, for we do not have any more Bear dances.

FOOTNOTES:

[84] Told by White-Bear.

ABSTRACTS

1. THE WOLF AND LUCKY-MAN CREATE LAND.

Wolf and Lucky-Man meet on shore of big lake, where two ducks are swimming. Wolf challenges Lucky-Man to see who can endure rain longest. Lucky-Man wins. Wolf sends Duck down to fetch dirt from bottom of lake. Duck brings up mud, which Wolf throws in north and forms into prairie. Lucky-Man sends Duck for more mud, which he throws on south side of Wolf's land. Hills and mountains are formed and buffalo are on land. There is channel between two countries created, occupied by Missouri River.

2. THE SPIDERS GIVE BIRTH TO PEOPLE.

Wolf and friend change Spider-Man and Woman by rubbing them with wild sage dipped in water and teach them how to lie together. Their progeny are human beings.

3. THE ORIGIN OF THE ARIKARA.

Large people on earth long ago destroyed by flood, by Nesaru. People turn into corn and are put into cave with animals. Nesaru turns ear of corn into woman and sends her to bring people from earth. People and animals know her. Badger, Mole, and long-nosed Mouse offer to help her to take people out. They dig in turns. Thunder opens earth. People go out upon earth, journey west, leaving behind Badgers, long-nosed Mice, Moles, and some people who turn back into earth and become animals. People come to great basin, which Kingfisher fills up by striking bill into banks. Journey is continued until people stopped by timber, which is removed by Owl. They come to big lake. Loon parts waters. Mother-Corn returns to heavens. People here make games, first shinny and then javelins, to catch ring with. Winners kill those of other side. Mother-Corn returns to give people rules to go by. Man is selected as chief. He instructs people as to scalping. Mother-Corn makes bundle, songs, ritual, and ceremonies. Man instructs medicine-man, teaches them sleight-of-hand, and tells them to make village. Mother-Corn leads people to Republican River, Kansas. Awaho people come last and receive ceremonies from Mother-Corn. They offer smoke to gods. Dog comes to village and complains that Mother-Corn has left out Dog and Whirlwind. Dog has come from Sun, who has given it curative power. Whirlwind is disease, and if dog meat first offered as sacrifice gods will send storm to drive away disease. Whirlwind comes and Dog appeases gods and says he will be people's guardian. Mother-Corn says gods in heavens are four world-quarters. They will send storm if smoke not given to them first. Mother-Corn is Cedar-Tree in front of lodge and Stone at right of her is man who established office of chief. Nesaru watches over them and gives them long life.

4. ORIGIN OF THE ARIKARA.

Mother-Corn is assisted by Badger, Gopher, long-nosed Mouse, and Mole to get people out of ground, as in No. 3. People see where other people helped out of ground by Buffalo. They start on journey and are stopped by obstacles, as in No. 3, and are helped by Kingfisher, Owl, and Loon. Some people stay behind as Worms, Birds, Fish, and Loons. [Mother-Corn offers smoke and sends animals for offerings to gods.] Prairie-Chicken kills wild-cat, which represents heavens, and brings it to Mother-Corn for offering. Three Stars in East bring Mother-Corn stone for pipe to form smoke. Pipe is made and filled with native tobacco. Prairie-Chicken takes pipe in succession to gods in Southeast, Southwest, Northwest, and Northeast, and to Nesaru, all of whom smoke the pipe. Prairie-Chicken says sand blown by wind made white spots on its feathers. Smoking by Nesaru is to show consent to Mother-Corn having people on earth and that gods are to protect them. Dog comes and tells Mother-Corn that Whirlwind is angry for being slighted in smoke ceremony. Mother-Corn appeals to Nesaru and the gods for assistance. Woman says she will protect the people, and turns into Cedar-Tree. Big-Meteoric-Star falls from heavens by Cedar-Tree to assist. Whirlwind comes and people all run in all directions, and when Whirlwind strikes them it changes their language. People who stand on Cedar-Tree and Rock are Arikara. Wind strikes Mother-Corn and she vomits four times, water and ears of corn of different color. Whirlwind tells Mother-Corn it has left behind diseases, but says when they offer smoke to the gods they are to give it smoke last, that it may not come very often. Cedar-Tree asks Mother-Corn that it may be known as "Wonderful Grandmother" and be placed in front of the medicine-lodge. Big-Meteoric-Star asks to be known as "Wonderful Grandfather" and sit by Wonderful Grandmother in front of medicine-lodge. Dog asks, as he brought the news, to guard camps and villages and to be offered in ceremonies, and his fat to be used by medicine-men. Mother-Corn gives corn for seeds that corn may be offered to gods. People who scattered to be their enemies—to the southwest, "Sahe;" to northeast, "Pechea;" to the east, "Wooden-Faces;" to south, "Witchcraft-People." Mother-Corn stays with people until she has taught them bundle ceremonies. She tells them to tie all children's moccasins together on her back. Then they are to take her to river and throw her in. People do not understand and keep up singing in night. At daylight they find Mother-Corn has turned to ear of corn, with buffalo robe tied to it. People place children's moccasins with corn and throw them with Mother-Corn and robe into river. Many years afterwards Mother-Corn returns and teaches more bundle ceremony songs and finally disappears.

5. THE ORIGIN OF THE ARIKARA.

Many people in cave under ground with Corn, Mother of tribe. Mother-Corn sends four birds to find better world, but they are unsuccessful. Long-nosed Mouse, or Mole, Skunk, and Badger work, and at last Badger goes through hole, but falls asleep. Returns in morning and Mother-Corn forces her way through hole followed by all people. They march westward. They come to wide water, thick forest, deep ravine in succession, which Fish, Owl, and Kingfisher help them to cross. They see Buffalo on open prairie and are afraid, but Mole, Skunk, and Badger make holes all around animal. His blood sinks into ground and becomes stone, from which pipes were made. Buffalo butchered and flesh divided among different sacred bundles, with animal's joints. People again go on westward and fowls, fishes, and animals separate from them and give Mother-Corn power. Mother-Corn separates from animals.

6. THE ORIGIN OF THE ARIKARA.

[Man Bear's-Tail relates killing of buffalo cow by father, who calls old woman and keeper of bundle, and describes ceremony of untying bundle. Old man tells origin of bundle and of people.] Nesaru makes giants, but being displeased with them turns them into stones. Nesaru again makes people, small and wonderful. They displease Nesaru, who tells animals to hide. He is going to make water rise from earth. Animals give power to Bear to take people under ground, with assistance of Badger, Mole, and long-nosed Mouse. Fox acts as runner and errand man. People live under ground many years. Animals decide to dig upward for land. Bears, Badgers, Moles, and long-nosed Mice dig and Mole first to get his head through. Badger enlarges hole. Fox goes through and reports what he sees outside. Bear makes hole larger and animals go through, followed by people. Woman, who says she is grain of corn, tells man they are on island. People taken under ground by Mice were grains of corn and now turned to people. Mouse leader. They cross water by aid of woman, who becomes gar-pike. Some fall into water and become fish. People pick up stones to cut with. Mouse leads people through thick timber. Some turn to owls. Earthquake forms deep chasm, which Bear enables people to cross. Whirlwind makes pathway through thick timber. People come to muddy water in "Pawnee" country. They find things to wear and eat. First bow made. Long-nosed

Mouse, Bear, Mole, Badger, and Fox die, and their skins with skulls are wrapped in bundles. They receive ceremony from Pawnee. Each bundle receives different ritual. Arikara dress ear of corn as woman and throw it into river. Many years afterwards strange woman comes into lodge where bundle ceremony. People take no notice of her and she goes to other bundle lodges. In last old man recognizes her and Muddy-River-Country ceremony performed. Woman says that four world-quarters are her father, and that she will come to them in dreams and tell them about things in bundle. They are to tie her on bundle and clothe ear of corn. She turns into ear of corn. They send for other old man and tie ears of corn upon the bundles.

7. THE ORIGIN OF THE ARIKARA.

Arikara live under ground. Long-nosed Mouse, Mole, Badger, and Fox agree to take people to top of earth. Mole digs first. Arikara come out, Fox leading. Earthquake, and other people held fast. People journey west and come to chasm caused by earth shaking, but Badger makes pathway. Mother-Corn in heavens asking gods to let people live. Obstructions arranged by being known as Sickness. People come to deep river and Loon sent by gods. Loon flies across river and back and dives. River is open and people cross over. Waters come together again and some people left on other side. Mother-Corn stops and says Black-Wind is angry, but Black-Meteoric-Star will help them. Tells people to get under cedar tree. Black-Wind comes and takes many people. They go on and come to steep mountain bank. Bear digs steps on both sides and people go across. Dog comes up and says his meat shall be offered to gods. His father is Sun, who has given him power.

8. THE ORIGIN OF THE AWAHO-BUNDLE PEOPLE.

People come out of ground, but some are cut off by earthquake. Heavens hear crying and send Mother-Corn to them. Badger digs through earth. People come out and walk westward until they come to thick timber. Screech-Owl flies through and makes pathway. Owl and Whirlwind are enemies. People followed by "Cut-Nose," an animal with long horns. People run until they come to chasm, which Badger enables them to cross. They then come to thick ice and deep water, which Loon enables them to cross. Mother-Corn teaches people ceremonies and rituals and gives them things to put in bundles. Mother-Corn disappears by ear of corn wrapped in her robe under bundle. Awaho last people to come out of ground, and where other bands have camped they find bits of meat offered to gods, which they use for food. They know all ceremonies and teach them to others. Nearly all are killed by enemies, but bundle hid under bank. Women go for bundle and contents are purified. Sacrifices of meat made the next day. Nesaru made animals to take kernels of corn under ground. They were people turned to corn by Nesaru. This is why animals brought them out of ground and why Mother-Corn was sent by gods in heavens, who had field of corn.

9. MOTHER-CORN'S VISIT TO THE ARIKARA.

Mother-Corn tells Arikara when journeying west to dress her up and put her in river. When Arikara make permanent village upon Missouri River old men think it time to send Mother-Corn down stream. She is taken from bundle, painted, and dressed. After reciting rituals, Mother-Corn, with children's moccasins tied about her waist, is thrown by priests into river, her head up stream. Many years afterwards woman comes to village and is recognized by man as Mother-Corn. She teaches them ceremonies and songs and that night disappears.

10. MOTHER-CORN'S VISIT TO THE ARIKARA.

In olden times, old man made offerings to gods and Mother-Corn. Mother-Corn is pleased to have smoke with people and starts from east to visit them. She goes into medicine-lodge. She stays many days and teaches them many lessons, but people are hungry for meat. Mother-Corn asks woman to make moccasins for her. She puts on moccasins and they wear out when she walks slowly twenty steps. This takes place four times, but fourth pair brings her back to altar. Her walk means that she has walked long way off in west, and way very hard. She tells people she has seen buffalo and that they will be seen in four days. In morning of fourth day they kill many buffalo, but while they are away, enemies attack village and Mother-Corn is killed. They bury her and from place where she is laid, grass, etc., springs up.

11. HOW THE PEOPLE ESCAPED THE BUFFALO.

When people came out through ground they were led by woman, "Mother." Among them were all kinds of animals except buffalo. Monster with horns like buffalo comes out of lake. They call him "Cut-Nose." As it comes along, buffalo come from under him. Buffalo catch up with people and kill some of them. People make canyons behind, which buffalo can not cross. Whirlwind comes. Mother tells people to give presents and smoke to it. Whirlwind scatters some of people. Buffalo with Cut-Nose come behind and people come to big timber. Owl and Badger try to make path through timber, but fail. Coyote and Dog come and open way through. Buffalo and Cut-Nose come again and kill people. They come to deep water. Dogs fail to make pathway, but Loons make opening through waters. They come to canyon and Badger makes banks fall, after Kingfisher and Mole have failed. They cross and make village near canyon. Mother holds ceremonies for different bundles. Awaho-bundle people come last, and they receive all ceremonies. Awaho had been left behind when people came out of ground, and they pick up meat offerings to gods left behind.

12. WHY THE BUFFALO NO LONGER EAT PEOPLE.

Young man goes to village at night and finds people are Buffalo. They are talking about killing people. He finds human head and meat. Hears people are to be got out of ground and killed. Near by sees hole cut in side of hill where bulls circle around and drive people into cut. He sees people running to cut from out of ground. He goes among hills. Strange man gives him bow and arrows and tells him to take young man with bows and arrows to kill and scatter Buffalo. They go to place and attack Buffalo and kill and scatter them, so that they become buffalo and never eat people any more.

13. WHY THE BUFFALO NO LONGER EAT PEOPLE.

People hungry and chief priest opens bundle and offers gifts to gods for them to send buffalo. Buffalo come three days after ceremony and old priest tells story. Buffalo are human, but have horns. When they want meat they recite ritual. When hollow tree is struck with pole four times people led by Cut-Nose come out and are killed, except Cut-Nose, who re-enters tree. Boy chased by Buffalo cow. He sees fine-looking woman wearing white buffalo robe. She goes west and boy follows. He finds woman at tipi. Woman says she has selected him to turn her people into real buffalo, so as not to eat his people. They go through four circles of Buffalo bulls stationed as sentinels and enter tipi, where woman's father lives. She covers young man with her robe. Buffalo are human, but have horns and tails. They cook and eat human meat. Girl shows him arbors with human bodies, and hollow cottonwood tree, with long stick, and tells him its use. Takes him to timber, where during three days he makes bows and arrows. Next morning they place bows and arrows at foot of tree. Woman tells young man what to do and they hide. When Buffalo come towards tree, young man jumps out. Cut-Nose comes out, and then people. Young man gives men bows and arrows and tells them to shoot and kill Buffalo. Buffalo run towards village, chased by people, and they finally become buffalo. Young man and Buffalo woman take bundle from tipi. They marry and teach people songs and ceremony of bundle. People become part of Arikara.

14. THE GIRL WHO MARRIED A STAR.

Girl says she likes Red-Star and would marry him if on earth. In morning girl sees Porcupine and climbs after it in cottonwood tree. Tree grows higher and girl reaches another world. Porcupine turns into man and says he is Star. She stays with him, but cries every night. She gives birth to male child, who has star on forehead. Son wants wild turnips and man tells her not to dig for them in valleys. She digs in valley and stick runs through earth. She looks down and sees she is far away from her people. Woman tells her to get from husband sinews of whole buffalo and she will make sinew string to reach ground below. Girl gets sinew from husband, who forgets two sinews in shoulder. Old woman makes string and girl also makes long sinew string. They go to valley and girl takes child on back under robe, slips down string fastened to stick across hole. She reaches height of highest tree from ground. Husband sees her hanging and kills her with stone. Boy slips out of robe and falls on ground, but is not hurt. Boy nurses at dead mother's breast. He goes to cornfield. Old woman catches him and takes him home as grandson. Grandmother scatters corn in lodge for blackbirds and places mush behind curtain. Boy calls blackbirds and kills them all with club. Grandmother brings them to life again and tells them to fly all over the world. She tells boy to throw wood into pond and next morning finds black bow and four black arrows. Boy sees big serpent behind curtain and kills it with bow and arrow and serpent slips into pond. Serpent is grandmother's husband. Next day old woman tells boy not to go to dangerous place. He goes and sees mountain-lion, which obeys him. He leads lion to old woman's lodge. The same occurs with a cinnamon bear. Boy sees four wonderful men killing buffalo. They frighten him with fœtus of calf. He climbs tree and they place fœtus in fork. They offer to take calf down if he will give grandmother to them. He returns and tells her he is satisfied, but says they would have to give him something in return. They promise him bow and arrows and old woman tells him to take middle bow of five leaning against wall of lodge. Men go to grandmother's lodge and stay with her. Old woman sends boy with flute to play around men's lodge. Men all scared and close up lodge with earth. They die of hunger. Boy goes to den of snakes. Snakes give him long gut to eat, but it is snake, and he twists its head off. Snakes go into ground and try to get into boy's rectum, but hit rock on which he sits. They tell stories. Snakes all go to sleep on long circular stick around den. Boy with flint knife cuts heads on stick, but last one wakes up and disappears in hole. When boy sleeps he places arrows so that they can fall on him when Snake approaches him. Boy is very sleepy and arrows cannot awaken him. Snake goes into his mouth and nestles in his skull, where it remains until boy becomes skeleton. Boy's father sends storm and skull is filled with water, but this does not drive out Snake. Father gets Sun to move nearer earth and heats skull until water boils, and Snake crawls out. Boy catches Snake by neck, hits its snout with stone, and rubs its teeth upon rock. He lets it go on promise not to bother people after. Boy returns to grandmother and tells her country is free from wild animals. She disappears, and boy goes to village and tells his story. He dies after clearing country of all wild animals.

15. THE GIRL WHO MARRIED A STAR.

Girl taken up to heavens by star digs turnip and sees people on earth. Old woman makes sinew rope and lets her and child down through hole, but rope too short. Husband kills her with stone, but boy safe. He goes to cornfield and is caught by old woman, who takes him home. He shoots huge serpent behind curtain, who was woman's husband. She plans for bear to kill him, but he captures bear. Boy finds tipi with four strong men playing dice game. He shoots through hole and cleans man's nose with arrow. He goes with them to hunt and they annoy him with elk's fœtus. He climbs tree and men remove fœtus from tree only on his promising them his grandmother. She goes with him to men's tipi and they teach boy ceremony of catching eagles and of hunting. Boy meets camp of Snakes, all of whom but one he kills, as in No. 14. Surviving Snake enters anus while he sleeps and gets into head, from which it is driven by water boiling. Boy seizes it and knocks its head on flat rock. Boy afraid of fœtus because cluster of stars to which boy's father belonged did not come up at that time with rest; so father not present to help him.

16. NO-TONGUE AND THE SUN AND THE MOON.

Young man goes upon high hill to mourn. Little bird takes him to another place. Man, painted red, comes and says he is going to be his son and asks for his tongue. Young man cuts off his tongue and gives it to man and then falls dead. Moon sees him and goes and touches his feet. Young man sits up and Moon tells him man to whom he had given tongue is Sun. Moon makes him his own son and warns him that when Sun offers him choice of weapons he is to take old ones. Sun takes him to sky in morning and cries because No-Tongue takes best things, as these give boy life. Sun asks No-Tongue to send him white buffalo robe. Moon tells him to get dark-brown robe for Sun and powder it with white clay. Sun hangs up robe and wind shakes all white clay out of it. Sun tells Moon his Little-Sun is going to kill No-Tongue. Moon warns No-Tongue and advises him what to do. No-Tongue goes with party on war-path and Sun plans for Little-Sun to kill him. Little-Sun with enemy and in morning asks No-Tongue to shake hands with him. No-Tongue goes and kills Little-Sun and his people defeat enemy. Sun sends son Big-Sun to kill No-Tongue, but is killed himself. Sun becomes Buffalo to kill No-Tongue, but falls into mud hole. No-Tongue makes fire on his back and Buffalo burns up. Sun tells Moon he will scalp No-Tongue. Moon tells No-Tongue to put false scalp over head with dog's blood inside. Sun comes and takes scalp. Seeing that No-Tongue is not really scalped, Sun leaves him alone. When old and blind No-Tongue goes to top of hill and makes circle of red sticks for Sun and circle of white sticks for Moon. Sun and Moon come and Sun takes old man to his home.

17. HOW BURNT-HANDS BECAME A CHIEF.

Poor boy, Burnt-Hands, lives with grandmother outside of village. Last-Child, daughter of chief, brings them food. Burnt-Hands follows trail of wounded elk and finds it dead. Chiefs Red-Bear and Black-Bear come. Red-Bear shoots boy and drops him into air-hole in ice. White-Bear's cub takes boy to father. Father pities and adopts him as son and teaches him Bear ceremony. Burnt-Hands receives bundle of medicine and goes home. Notice given for buffalo hunt and that Red-Bear wants hide of white buffalo. Burnt-Hands goes with young men to chase. He gets white buffalo robe, as Red-Bear afraid of him. When he reaches camp he eats meat prepared for Red-Bear. Burnt-Hands takes white buffalo hide to grandmother, who gives it to Last-Child. Elk chase is made to get teeth for Red-Bear. Burnt-Hands promises grandmother elk-tooth dress and tells her in case of trouble to flee to timber. Burnt-Hands goes to chase and collects-many elk teeth and so does Red-Bear. They meet at last elk. Burnt-Hands strikes Red-Bear on head with war-club and drags him to air-hole. Burnt-Hands finds grandmother and they perform Bear ceremony. They turn into Bears and attack warriors, killing many. Others send peace-pipe by Last-Child and it is accepted. Burnt-Hands makes grandmother thirty-eight years old and himself twenty-two, and marries Last-Child. Burnt-Hands becomes chief and has Black-Bear as slave.

18. HOW BURNT-HANDS BECAME A CHIEF.

Poor boy goes on war-path with warriors. Grandmother says he is not to tell coyote stories and gives him round burnt clay ball that has handle. When hungry he is to put kernels of corn on ball and roast them. Boy asked to tell coyote stories, but refuses. He roasts corn upon clay ball and then tells stories. Enemy comes and men are scared. When boy has finished eating corn he attacks enemy with clay ball, which is war-club, and kills many. Enemy run away. Burnt-Hands made chief and given good tipi and wife.

19. HOW BURNT-HANDS BECAME A CHIEF.

Poor boy tells grandmother to make him bow and arrows that he may join buffalo hunt. He says he will bring back some tongues and hearts. Boy sings about being selected to stand in front and make motions to direct hunters, and he is selected. He kills buffalo and turning back pulls out buffalo beards and bunch of hair from shoulder. His robe is taken and he sings about snowstorm coming. He goes to grandmother and throws hairs on ground and several tongues and hearts appear. Blizzard kills many men who had made fun of young man. On next buffalo chase he again stands in front and is first to kill buffalo. He takes hair as before and it becomes tongues and hearts. People find out boy is wonderful, and give him pony. He marries chief's daughter, and becomes great warrior and chief.

20. THE TWO BOYS AND THE WATER-SERPENT.

Two boys are accused of eating up pots of corn. They watch at night near inclosure surrounding village and see long serpent come and stick its head into smokehole of lodges. Next day they make many arrows and at night when serpent has its head in lodge they shoot at it. Serpent goes to river, water of which roars and rises, and serpent is found dead when river goes down.

21. THE BOY WHO BEFRIENDED THE THUNDERBIRDS, AND THE SERPENT.

Boy gifted with powers by four-world-quarter gods kills so many antelope he is called Antelope-Carrier. Wood-Rats have given him bow and four differently colored arrows. He wanders from home, and while asleep two Thunderbirds carry him up high mountain. He finds nest with four young Thunderbirds. Mother Thunderbird comes and tells him of serpent with two heads that lives in lake and eats her young. She promises him lightning and control of all birds if he will help to kill monster. He promises and Thunderbird, after telling him when serpent would come out of lake, flies away. Fog rises from lake one day and boy sees monster with two heads crawling out of lake. Storm comes from west and Thunderbirds return, making lightning, which strikes serpent. Lightning throws it back, but it again crawls up. Monster opens its mouth to swallow boy. He shoots black arrow into its mouth. Monster falls and bursts open. Other head comes and boy shoots red arrow into its mouth and head broken in pieces. Thunderbirds come with all kinds of birds, which feast upon serpent. They give boy power as objects which he swallows. Boy chief of all birds and kills all bad animals. Two boys, joined together with rawhide, go to shoot birds. One shoots at white object, like mushroom, moving up and down and strong wind carries them far away to an island. They go west and come to lodge of old woman. She makes cakes, four for the great serpent, who will carry them across by water. Serpent comes and carries them across, stopping each day when hungry. They give it cake and soft-shell turtle (lice) from its head. Wild boy jumps before they come to land and is swallowed by serpent. Other boy asks serpent to open its mouth wide and he drags swallowed boy out. Boys travel to Missouri River bottom. They put log of wood on fire and it is serpent. Foolish boy eats chunk of meat and he gradually turns to serpent. Other boy takes him to Missouri River and turns him loose there. Antelope-Carrier hears of serpent and hunts him with all his birds. Serpent uses his power and carries him into his den. Antelope-Carrier is made to vomit up all his power, except lightning in his eyes. Serpent remains in river and gives its powers to people, and songs and medicine-men's ceremony.

22. THE BOY WHO TURNED INTO A SNAKE.

Idiot boy and son of chief go on war-path. They have to return through want of food, and come to water-serpent. It is so big they can not get around it, and idiot proposes to burn it. Serpent burns in two. Idiot eats of serpent meat and his body gradually becomes colored red and blue. By fourth day his legs are grown together and become snake's tail. Other boy carries him to lake, where fishes object to him, and finally they come to the Missouri River. He rests in middle of river and people by giving him presents cross over without danger of drowning.

23. THE BOY WHO RECEIVED THE MOUSE POWER.

Young man stays behind when people go hunting. He goes through village and hears crying. He goes to lodge and sees woman wrapped in buffalo robe, who tells him people have taken her children. She says they are in sacred bundle robe, and asks him to go and bring her children back. He does so and gives nest with children to woman. She tells him to return at night and then becomes mouse. Young man goes to lodge at night and finds woman there. Rats come in human form and priest gives him war-club and power to become mouse at any time, and little box of medicine. Woman tells him he is now her son and says they are not to kill mice as they are his relatives. Young man becomes great warrior. In enemy's camp he turns into mouse and drives ponies out of camp after cutting ropes. He becomes so bold that people become afraid of him, but finally he and young man who has power of Bear fight and kill one another.

24. THE BOY AND THE YOUNG HAWKS.

Small boy discovers hawk's nest with four eggs. Eggs are hatched and boy feeds birds with insects. Boy goes to take birds home when he sees man who calls birds his sons and says he will be rewarded for taking care of them. Boy takes feathers from young birds to put on his arrows. He becomes good hunter and on war-path fights where the arrows are thickest. He becomes known as brave, but finally does wrong among his people. Many try to kill him, but always forget, until one man capable of killing him does so.

25. THE END OF THE ELK POWER.

Four strong young men, of whom only oldest is married, go to trap eagles, leaving woman and child at home. On their return woman is missing. Eldest unmarried brother is filled with pity for child and goes to cry near timber, where is old skull of buck elk. On second night voice tells him woman and three others captured by Bear and that he has received

Elk power. He is to go again and receive instructions. Pretty-Voice goes again and learns ceremony of Elks. He is to blow whistle and all females will come to him. He goes near Bear's home and whistles four times. Women run out of den and they go away with Pretty-Voice. Bear follows and he orders party to stop. Pretty-Voice shoots arrows at Bear without effect. He then throws himself on ground and becomes Elk. Elk and Bear fight, and Bear admits his defeat. Elk again becomes man and Pretty-Voice wins great honor by capture of women. He causes ill-feeling by using his magic whistle to attract girls and then married women. Men shoot at him, but nothing can harm him. Sioux attack village, but they can do nothing while Pretty-Voice is living. Men come on friendly visit and Pretty-Voice secures Sioux girl by his ceremony. She gets to know secret of his power and then runs away. She obtains necessary things and then starts at head of war-party to kill Pretty-Voice. Inhabitants of village are defeated and Pretty-Voice finally falls. His mother wishes to collect his flesh, as he had told her, but men will not let her. They make big fire and destroy his body. White fog seen to arise from place for many days after.

26. THE ELK RESCUES A WOMAN FROM THE BEAR.

Poor young man and chief's daughter run away together. They live alone and man kills deer and elk. He goes to catch eagles and while away Bear comes and takes wife away. Elk tells man and teaches him how to transform himself into Elk. Gives him whistle to attract female elk. Bear leaves den and man blows whistle. Wife and other women rush out to him. Bear comes and attacks Elk, which puts its head down and sticks horns into body. Man shoots and kills Bear. Man takes his wife and Elk other women, who become Elk.

27. THE BOY AND THE ELK.

Young man goes to place where animal skull near lake to cry because no girl will marry him. He hears flute and Elk comes. Elk tells boy to take teeth from skull and gives him flute which will attract girls to him. He goes home, tries flute, and girls come. After he is married, women also come and men kill him. One of his relatives takes teeth and flute. Boy is left unburied and several days afterwards he goes to mother's tipi. He sends mother to society of Young-Dogs for tobacco. Men afraid of him. Boy goes away followed by relatives. They go into river and all turn into animals. Young man who had flute and elk teeth does not go and is the only one who lives.

28. THE COYOTE, THE GIRL, AND THE MAGIC WINDPIPE.

Beautiful girl lives alone in timber. Has plenty of buffalo meat and some wonderful bundles. Coyote becomes her errand man. When out of meat girl tells Coyote to cover his head up as her brothers are coming. Girl waves buffalo windpipe over smoke and dust in it turns to her seven brothers. They take bows and arrows and girl goes on to lodge, yells and waves towards west and south. Buffalo come and brothers kill them. They return to lodge and girl puts them again into windpipe as dust. Coyote sees performance and decides to steal windpipe. Coyote goes away with windpipe, and while he sleeps girl has brothers bring him back again. This occurs three times. Fourth time girl lets Coyote carry thing off. He goes up hill near village and howls for people to come and kick with him. Several young men go and Coyote turns windpipe upside down, but, instead of dust and boys, swarm of bumblebees come out. Young men run into timber, bees go into hollow tree, and Coyote goes away as coyote.

29. THE BUFFALO-WIFE AND THE JAVELIN GAME.

Young man out hunting dreams of two buffalo bulls turning into sticks and of buffalo cow turning into ring. In morning he sees cow and lies with her. Finds ring in grass and wears it on his wrist. He makes sticks and plays game with young men, winning many things. Goes hunting and sees old woman, who induces him to carry her across river on his back. He can not throw her off and he goes home with her fast to his back. Medicine-men are sent for, but they can do nothing. Poor boy puts on old robe and goes to young man's lodge with bow and four arrows of different colors. He shoots black arrow and splits woman in two. With red arrow he takes her off boy. The other arrows he places on boy's back to remove sore place. Old woman is then burned. Next day crying and voice are heard near where woman burned. Young man finds ring has gone. White tipi with woman and child inside appears where others were. Young man goes to see it and woman with new buffalo robe passes by him, having child. Young man makes bundle of eagle feathers and follows them. They become buffalo. Calf communicates with father, and woman finally becomes reconciled to him. They come to hill on which Buffalo bull, boy's grandfather, is waiting for them. Man puts two eagle feathers on his horns. He sends them on to next hill and at last they come to hill with four Buffalo bulls, chiefs of Buffalo camp. Man puts feathers on their heads. They are sent into village and Buffalo become mad because man has not feathers enough to go around. Man made to sit on hill until they decide what to do with him. He sticks flint knife into ground and asks gods to form stone around where he sits. Buffalo devise various ways for killing him, but do not succeed in doing so. They decide to send man with Buffalo cow and calf to Indian village for presents. Buffalo bull turns man into Buffalo. Buffalo follow them. Man finds village and tells errand. People bring eagle feathers and native tobacco, which man takes to Buffalo. Buffalo willing to be slaughtered and man tells chiefs. Four times people go and kill Buffalo. Leader of Buffalo gives man sticks to play with. Sticks and ring different kinds of people. Man lives long life. Buffalo calf starts Buffalo ceremony among people.

30. THE ORIGIN OF THE WOLF DANCE.

Young man, son of chief, refuses to marry and seven girls plan to put him into hole. They spread weeds over hole and young man falls in. Girls promise to take him out if he does certain things, but finally they leave him. He cries and gray Wolf hears. Wolf says he will help him, and while he is gone Bear comes. Wolf returns and they quarrel about boy, but finally agree that whoever digs through to boy first shall claim him. Wolf gets to boy first, but Bear says he shall be his son. Wolf takes boy among Wolves and he comes to act like wolf. Afterward Buffalo hunters see him, but they cannot catch him. They make trap and place buffalo meat inside inclosure. Wolves are run into trap and four strong men with rawhide leggings are put in. Other Wolves are let out, but Wolf man caught. They tie him, put him into sweat-lodge, and make him vomit. Wolf man recovers and has tipi made. Seven girls who had put boy into hole are invited. Man goes and calls for Wolves and Bears. They come, and he places them about tipi. He tells girls, who try to escape, but Wolves eat them. Father tells people boy's story and girls' relatives do not offer to save them. Young man finally becomes chief. He starts Wolf dance.

31. MEDICINE DANCE OF THE BEAVER, TURTLE, AND WITCH-WOMAN.

Animals meet for sleight-of-hand performances. Only Beaver, soft-shell Turtle, and Witch-Woman are to perform. Beaver gnaws nearly through three of lodge posts and people ask him to stop, as they think lodge will fall. Turtle sticks knife near left collar-bone and water pours out all over lodge. People are afraid and Turtle takes all water back again. Witch-Woman plays with gun, but calls for help and gives birth to child, who is to be great medicine-man.

32. THE VILLAGE-BOY AND THE WOLF POWER.

Four girls are made fun of for dancing with their brother. "Village-Boy" has never gone on war-path. Boy goes to graveyard to mourn. Wolf comes and asks why he is crying. Wolf tells boy to join next war-party and he will lead him to enemy's camp. War-party starts and Village-Boy follows in three days. Wolf has taught him secret powers and when he comes to ravine he rolls on the ground and becomes wolf. He barks and friend brings him burnt bones, which he gnaws. Next day he tells friend enemy's camp is near. He drives in ponies. When enemy is attacked Village-Boy is in lead and takes scalp. He gives scalp to leader and returns ahead of war-party, but says nothing. Leader gives all credit to Village-Boy. Scalp-dance held. Young man's sisters dance without fear of ridicule. He goes east with warriors and takes head of medicine-man of Dumb People. Head dries and is used for medicine purposes. Now about size of hen's egg.

33. THE RABBIT-BOY.

Young man who has not been on war-path mourns on graveyard hill. Remains there several days in storm. Jack-Rabbit crawls under his robe. Eagle comes and asks for Rabbit. Rabbit promises him powers if he will save him. Eagle promises him scalps if he will turn Rabbit loose. Boy refuses and Eagle flies away. Rabbit says he will make young man great warrior and gives him war-club, rabbit-skin, and medicine paints. Boy returns home. He follows war-party and acts as scout. Goes and brings ponies from enemy's village. Attack is made on enemy's camp. Rabbit-Boy kills old man and goes through village and escapes. Sees pretty girl who watches him. Soon after they go again to village. Boy kills man and again sees girl. Girl gives Arikara woman captive moccasins, beaded bracelets, and beaded armlet to take to young man. Woman gives him things and young man at once starts for enemy's camp. He goes to girl's tipi, puts in his hand, and she recognizes him by bracelet. He sleeps with girl and father finds them in bed together. Father sends for warriors, who prepare to kill young man. He is saved by new-comer, who is glad he has married one of their girls, as he will now lead their people. They go on war-path to young man's country. He kills captive woman and gives her scalp to chief. This happens several times and young man never kills members of his own tribe. The two tribes make peace.

34. THE MAN AND THE WATER-DOGS.

People in large village are afraid of man who commits evil deeds. They make plot to seize him. They attack him and he walks towards river. He steps in and walks on bottom and sees tipi. He goes in and sees many dogs. Leader tells him not to be afraid of any man and if hurt he is to come to them. Man returns home and men afraid. He commits worse acts than before and his relatives and his wife's relatives separate from the village. People dare not fight with man.

35. THE FIVE TURTLES AND THE BUFFALO DANCE.

Five soft-shell Turtles go to village. Four of them have eagle feathers on head. Fifth has black feather and is so angry it goes to river. Four turtles die and they are made into drums, which are afterwards changed for rawhide drums. Buffalo dance organized. Mysterious being with magpie feathers growing on his head et qui falsum penem inter crura habebat dances. Girl not permitted to leave lodge while mysterious being dancing. She goes out and et monstrum fecit quasi cum illa concumbere vellet. Girl becomes pregnant and gives birth to child like father. People kill it and throw it into river. Father goes to medicine-man, who throws rock into river and waters part. They see child in water and man pulls him out. Medicine-man breaks big stone in two with club and they bury child between stones. Mysterious being then marries girl who gave birth to mysterious boy.

36. THE NOTCHED STICK AND THE OLD WOMAN OF THE ISLAND.

Notched stick for rubbing other sticks on and dried buffalo hide used to make rain during medicine-men's ceremony. At end of ceremony notched stick and buffalo hide are taken to island. Man goes to island and sees old woman sitting. He tells father, who says objects are put on island because they are old woman.

37. THE MAN WHO MARRIED A COYOTE.

War-party is attacked by enemy. One man killed and others return home. Man only stunned, and year after he comes to. He falls in with Coyotes and marries one. Warriors hunting surround and capture him. He becomes well by taking medicine. He shouts for coyote wife from top of lodge. Coyotes come and wife goes into lodge. They smoke her, but she goes away and joins other Coyotes. Man finds one of his baby coyotes in snow bank. He goes home to warm himself and on return baby is gone.

38. THE MAN WHO TURNED INTO A STONE.

Old man with great reputation as medicine-man goes with people to meet hunting party. He sits on hill waiting for dried meat to offer sacrifice to gods, but no one presents any. Last young man gives him dried buffalo tongue, but old man sits with head down. Feasts and councils are held, but old man absent. They go in search of him and he tells them it is too late. His legs have turned to stone and next day he is a rock in form of man.

39. THE WOMAN WHO TURNED INTO A STONE.

Daughter of chief refuses to marry, but at last is persuaded by mother. Husband fails to have connection with wife, who has only sunflower. She goes away and turns to stone through shame.

40. THE POWER OF THE BLOODY SCALPED-MAN.

Young man goes to hill to obtain power. Bloody scalped-man comes and young man runs away. Friend goes and when scalped-man comes he closes his eyes, but does not run. Man takes him to cave. There men are seated in circle, but none are scalped. Leader tells young man how to make himself look like scalped-man; gives him war-club, and root to make him run swiftly. Enemy comes and young man makes himself look like bloody scalped-man. He attacks enemy and kills one. Enemy retreats and while his people run after them he smokes body, washes in creek, and returns to lodge. In night he goes to place where he received power. He becomes great medicine-man and brings home many pieces of scalps, which he makes himself.

41. THE BOY WHO CARRIED A SCALPED-MAN INTO CAMP.

Party of warriors on war-path run into lake by enemy and all killed and scalped. Another war-party starts from same village. Camp near lake. Poor boy goes at night to get water from lake. Voices tell him to go further into lake for water. By light of moon sees leader of first war-party scalped, with hands and feet cut off. Boy carries scalped-man on his back to camp. They kill number of enemy equal to number in lake and return home.

42. THE GIRL WHO WAS BLEST BY THE BUFFALO AND CORN.

Mother while busy puts baby girl on buffalo skull at altar. Skull thinks baby given to him. Child grows and shows signs of having power from gods. When grown to womanhood famine prevails. Medicine-men can do nothing. Woman tells people to clean cellars. They do so and give her their seed corn. Woman throws little seed into each cellar, which is covered up, and after fourth day cellars filled with corn and other things.

43. THE FIGHT BETWEEN THE ARIKARA AND THE SNAKES.

Arikara go to hunt and see pretty little snake by path. They give it presents. Two foolish boys come along and kill snake. They tell people, who turn back from hunt and climb upon high arbors. Many snakes come. Arikara kill snakes with clubs, but many Arikara are killed, among them the two foolish boys.

44. THE FIGHT BETWEEN THE ARIKARA AND THE BEARS.

Young wife has garden in woods. She goes every day in spring and takes much food. Husband secretly follows her. He sees man with bear's claws about neck come and help wife and afterwards lie with her. Next day husband pretends to go hunting, but hides in garden. Man again comes to wife and while they are lying together husband shoots man with arrow. He then clubs woman, who tells him man is bear. Three days afterwards bears attack Arikara camp and kill husband and all people who do not hide in cellars.

45. THE WIFE WHO MARRIED AN ELK.

While man goes hunting men come to see wife. She goes away with one. Husband follows and sees wife walking with Elk. He shoots at it, but arrows do no harm. Elk and woman go into lake. Man stays there crying. Woman comes and tells him to go home and that when he starts upon war-path to come to lake. Man goes on war-path, first going to lake. Sees woman, who tells him that they would kill people in three tipis and capture their ponies. They do so. Next time man goes on war-path he again visits lake. Woman tells him she can not leave lake any more and that in fight he will see woman like her. He is to catch her and she will become his wife. It happens as she said.

46. THE FOUR GIRLS AND THE MOUNTAIN-LION.

Mountain-lion tells four girls who are gathering wood he wants them for wives. They run to different wonderful beings for protection, but none can help them. They come to Hair-Cut-in-Notches and offer to live with him as wives if he will save them. He sends them into lodge and then sings about his head and hair—his hair is his arrows. Mountain-lion comes and man shoots and kills him. Hair-Cut-in-Notches tells girls he is not human being and sends them home.

47. THE DEEDS OF YOUNG-EAGLE.

Chief of north village of Arikara has beautiful daughter, Yellow-Calf. Chief of south village has handsome son, Young-Eagle, who does not look with favor upon women and has not been on war-party. Young-Eagle starts for north village to see Yellow-Calf, and same day Yellow-Calf starts for south village to see Young-Eagle. They meet on hill half-way between villages. They make pile of stones on hill and start for Yellow-Calf's home. They come to lake and Young-Eagle says they must wash before going to village. Yellow-Calf washes first. Young-Eagle wades into water with clothes on and when he comes out he is quite changed in appearance. He is like "Burnt-Belly" boy. Girl takes him home and they lie together. In morning Yellow-Calf's parents are ashamed of him and so is she, but he remains. Boy hears that war-party is going out and tells girl that in three days her youngest brother is to get buffalo intestines and bones and that he will come. Young-Eagle takes wife to lake and after she has washed he wades into lake. He comes out same man she had first met. He sends wife home and turns to young eagle, which flies to where warriors gone. Brother-in-law hears eagle's cry and takes him intestines and bones. Young-Eagle brings in ponies and then kills several men and takes their scalps, which he sends by brother-in-law to leader. He goes to lodge, but does not tell wife what has happened. War-party returns and tell story of Young-Eagle's doings. Scalps are put upon pole at entrance of old woman's lodge. This occurs on several occasions, and once Young-Eagle goes with wife to lake and gets his own likeness. They go with scalps Young-Eagle has taken to village of his father, Black-Sun. Black-Sun sings scalp songs and braves and warriors decide that Young-Eagle shall lead people to girl's village. Arikara become one tribe again.

48. THE GIRL WHO BECAME A WHIRLWIND.

Woman has boy and girl on travois drawn by pony. Children fall off unknown to mother and wander away to cave. Girl goes to find something to eat and is taken far away by Whirlwind. She soon returns, but afterward goes away. She brings brother bow and arrows on two occasions. Owl tells boy sister is Whirlwind and is planning to kill him. Owl says she cuts off men's testes and eats them. Boy watches for sister. Sees her do what Owl says. She goes away again and Owl comes and takes boy into Owl's den. They say that sister wants woman and he is to tell her he will give her first woman he marries. Whirlwind comes and demands boy, but says she will let him go on his promising to give her the first woman he marries. Boy goes to his people. Tells chief that buffalo not far away. Many are killed. Enemy attack village and boy makes way to kill them. Chief's daughter given him for wife. Boy goes out and calls sister. She comes and boy tells her of his marriage. She and the girl lie together. Sister gives brother club and medicine, with power of Whirlwind. He becomes warrior and then chief.

49. COYOTE AND THE MICE SUN DANCE.

Coyote hears noise of dancing in elk skull. Mice run away, but finally they agree to let Coyote see dancing. He puts his head through skull and Mice run away. Coyote's head fast in skull and as Mice do not help him he goes away with skull on his head. He goes to water and people on other side think he is wonderful animal and are scared. Coyote promises they shall all live if they give him chief's daughter. They agree and Coyote swims across. They make tipi and he stays with girl all night. Boy sees that it is Coyote and people break skull and catch Coyote. They tie him fast to pegs. They urinate and defecate on him. He plays mean trick on old woman and thereby frees himself and then runs away.

50. THE COYOTE BECOMES A BUFFALO.

Buffalo asks Coyote why he is not Buffalo. He consents to be made one and Buffalo rushes at him. There are then two Buffalo bulls. They go to herd controlled by Buffalo bull and kill him. Each bull takes many cows to look after. Herd goes away leaving Coyote-Buffalo behind. He meets Coyote and says he is going to make him into Buffalo. He runs into him and there are two coyotes instead of Coyote-Buffalo and Coyote.

51. THE COYOTE AND THE ARTICHOKE.

Coyote digs up Artichoke plant and asks if it has another name. It answers "Take-a-Bite." Artichoke repeats same four times and Coyote takes bite each time, eating it all. He goes and expels flatus. He gets worse and carries tree up in air. He takes hold of stone which goes up with him. Stone falls on Coyote and kills him.

52. THE COYOTE RIDES THE BEAR.

Coyote meets Bear, makes all kinds of threats, and finally rides on his back. He jumps off and runs to top of hill. Not seeing Bear he yells derisively at him. Bear hears, runs after Coyote, and kills him.

53. THE COYOTE RIDES THE BUFFALO.

Pretty girl does not care to marry. Buffalo comes and girl becomes attached to him. Coyote visits girl, but she repulses him. Coyote tells her that Buffalo is his horse and girl says she will marry him if he will ride Buffalo there. Coyote goes home and strikes himself hard with club on the knee. Girl tells Buffalo what Coyote said and Buffalo says he will bring Coyote and kill him. Coyote tells Buffalo he is cripple, but says he will go if Buffalo will carry him. Buffalo agrees and Coyote sits on his back, with cane to hit Buffalo with. Coyote runs back to village and marries girl. Buffalo so ashamed he never came back.

54. THE COYOTE AND THE BUFFALO RUN A RACE.

Coyote tells Buffalo he cannot run fast and Buffalo challenges him to run race. Coyote accepts and goes off to select place. He sets landmarks near steep place. He tells Buffalo that at landmark they are to close their eyes and run fast. They race and Buffalo with eyes closed jumps over deep bank. Coyote goes down, skins and cuts up Buffalo, and takes meat to creek. While roasting meat Fox comes and Coyote sends him with Buffalo's pouch for water. Fox eats up pouch and tells Coyote something came and took away pouch. This happens four times and Coyote throws coals in Fox's face, sending him off. Fox tells story to every animal he meets and they all go to Coyote's lodge while he is asleep and eats all he has. When he wakes up he finds all his meat gone and goes away crying.

55. THE COYOTE AND THE DANCING CORN.

Two hungry Coyotes go to village in search of pounded corn. They separate and leader sees pounded corn, in lumps, running into mortar. Coyote begs lumps to come out. He sings and walks around fireplace. Lumps of pounded corn come out and dance with Coyote. He tells them to close their eyes. He runs to mortar and gets his head fast in bowl. Brother comes and captive tells him to cut bowl open with axe. He does so, but cuts Coyote on head so that he dies.

56. THE COYOTE AND THE TURTLE RUN A RACE.

Coyote boasts of his swiftness and Turtle says he can beat him running. They agree to run race. Turtle gets other Turtles to assist him. They go to course, place one Turtle at end, others at different distances back. Each Turtle carries pole and hides in ground. Next morning Turtle meets Coyote. Turtle gives command to start. Coyote runs and Turtle crawls into hole. When Coyote gets over little ridge he sees Turtle ahead of him. He catches up with him and Turtle throws away pole and crawls into ground. This happens several times and at end Turtle is at goal. Coyote says he is beaten, and running kills him.

57. THE COYOTE AND THE STONE RUN A RACE.

Coyote asks Stone its name. Stone says, "Run-Fast." They agree to run race. Coyote places Stone upon hill and starts him rolling. Coyote passes Stone, but Stone catches up with him and rolls upon his back. Stone won't get off and grows heavier. Coyote calls to Bull-Bats and tells them Stone has been calling them names. Bull-Bats fly at Stone until they break it in two and it falls from Coyote. Coyote makes fun of Bull-Bats and they separate.

58. THE COYOTE AND THE ROLLING STONE.

Coyote sees Jack-Rabbit men dancing around fire and eating intestines. He offers them his warrior headdress if they will tell where they get them. Rabbits send him to get red willows, which they put into fire. They dance around and as willows burn they turn into large intestines. Coyote then by trickery gets back his war-bonnet and runs away chased by Rabbits. He is too swift for them, but they tell him he cannot do the trick four times. He succeeds three times, but the fourth time willows burn into ashes. Coyote has stomach ache and defecates rabbits. He tries to catch them in robe, but they turn to excrement. Coming to big Stone he gives it soiled robe. Storm comes on and he returns for robe, which he finds clean. He takes it and storm passes. He hears something coming behind him and sees it is big Stone. Stone chases him, and he is about to give out when Bull-Bats fly around. Coyote appeals to them for assistance on ground that Stone had spoken against them. Bull-Bats break Stone up with flatus. Stone thus spread all over world. Coyote puts white clay on Bull-Bats' heads and bodies.

59. THE COYOTE AND THE ROLLING STONE.

Coyote and Rabbit agree that one who goes to sleep first shall be covered by other one. Rabbit sleeps with eyes open and Coyote thinks he is awake. Coyote goes to sleep by morning and Rabbit covers him and goes away. Coyote defecates rabbits. He gives robe to Stone, as in No. 58. He takes robe away from Stone four times and then Stone runs after him. Stone broken up by Bull-Bats as in No. 58. Coyote eats young Bull-Bats and Bull-Bats kill him with flatus.

60. HOW THE SCALPED-MAN LOST HIS WIFE.

Girl climbs tree to get grapes and Scalped-Man finds her. She goes with him and at creek she tells Scalped-Man she will be his wife if he washes his head. While he is diving she runs away and crawls under grapevine. He follows her, but at last gives her up. Woman runs home.

61. THE GENEROUS SCALPED-MAN AND HIS BETRAYER.

Man hunting sees Scalped-Man kill and carry off antelope. Man follows and enters Scalped-Man's cave. They become friendly and man remains four days. Scalped-Man goes away for several days, and brings ponies, which he gives to man, who returns home. Man obtains ponies in this way several times, and then tells Scalped-Man he wants scalp. Scalped-Man gets scalps for him twice. Man takes several others on war-path guided by Scalped-Man. They return with scalps and ponies. Man becomes chief and thinks he will capture Scalped-Man, but he fails, as Scalped-Man has heard his plans and gone away.

62. THE SCALPED-MAN.

Scouts see mysterious beings, who disappear in side of steep bank, where entrance to den is found. Man is seen in cave crying. He is dressed in Coyote skins and his head tied with white sheeting. There is Buffalo skull in lodge. Men agree to ask Scalped-Man to help their war-party.

63. THE DEAD MAN'S COUNTRY.

Man faints and afterwards dies. He sees path leading east. There is inclosure with little hole through which he goes and is in dead man's country. Man tells him not to go into village and directs him to lodge of dead people, which he is not to enter. He sees many people in lodge, and black drums. Men are painted red. Seven men stand out. Drummers sing in low voice. Dancers have dried willow sticks, as representatives of their living relatives, whom they call to them. Man is told to go to his country, and wakes up.

64. THE COYOTE WHO SPOKE TO THE EAGLE HUNTERS.

Young men go to hills to catch eagles. While sitting in cave telling Coyote stories, Coyote walks in and says they tell many things about him that are not true. Coyote goes away and party is so dazed they return to village.

65. THE GIRL AND THE ELK.

Men hunting hear Elk whistling across river. Girl wants to go and find out what it is, but people prevent her. This happens many days. Men agree to kill Elk, but they can not shoot it. Man puts medicine in cartridge and then kills Elk. Girl tries to run away, and is put into sweat-lodge many times until she gets over crazy spell.

66. HOW THE RABBIT SAVED A WARRIOR.

Arikara follow Ojibwa horse thieves. They overtake different band of Ojibwas and attack them. Brave man is shot through neck by bullet. He seems about to die from loss of blood, when Jack-Rabbit tells him he will not die. Man is attended by Rabbit medicine-man and in less than four days is well. He becomes one of the leading medicine-men of Rabbit band.

67. THE WOMAN WHOSE BREASTS WERE CUT OFF.

Man with beautiful woman and little boy goes hunting. Young man comes and courts woman. She feigns sickness and pretends to die. She is placed on arbor. Lover unties girl and places bodies of three dogs upon arbor. Girl is dressed as boy and breasts tied with wide strings. They go to another village where young woman passes herself for young man. Woman is anxious to see child. They paint up as men and watch for child near spring. They see boy and woman asks him for drink. He goes to lodge and tells father he has seen his mother. Father sends invitation to young men to eat in his lodge. They come and husband knows one of them is woman by her ways. He says she is his wife. Young man runs away. She asks forgiveness, but husband cuts off her breasts and woman dies.

68. WATER-DOGS.

Poor boy sees dog come out of river and carry little ones to spring. He dies shortly afterwards. Old woman near same place hears dogs chattering in water and soon afterwards dies.

69. TWO-WOLVES, THE PROPHET.

Two-Wolves left by himself in storm after buffalo chase has life saved by Prairie-Chicken. "Waruhti" gives him power to understand speech of Thunder. Long afterward he practices power. Man Two-Bears has herd of ponies which are disturbed by horse owned by Roving-Coyote. Two-Bears throws pointed stake at horse and kills it. Roving-Coyote goes to Two-Wolves to know who did it. Two-Wolves performs ceremony to father, Thunder, who comes and tells him. Two-Wolves sends for Two-Bears, who confesses and makes reparation. Wolf-Chief does not believe in Two-Wolves' power. Thunder tells Two-Wolves to speak to Wolf-Chief and have him kill his black dog and perform ceremony. Two-Wolves sends for Wolf-

Chief, who goes to him and promises to do as asked. Two-Wolves sends out one war-party and it is a failure. He lives long, discovering thieves and prophesying wonderful things.

70. HOW THE MEDICINE-ROBE SAVED THE ARIKARA.

When Arikara living in Nebraska young woman alone in lodge while medicine-men's ceremony is performing. She sees enemy looking at her through top of opening. He digs at side of lodge and she puts out fire. Next day husband hides in lodge, and when enemy comes he catches him from behind. Woman gives alarm and men come and overpower enemy. He says southern tribe are coming to kill them. Man is tied upon scaffold and left to die. He breaks loose several times by shaking his arms, so he is stabbed to death. During ceremony this man comes into lodge. All medicine-men run out. Keeper of wonderful robe goes and wraps man in robe and throws him into river. Afterwards so many Sioux come that people are scared. Keeper of holy robe wraps it round body and taking eagle wing and gourd climbs upon top of lodge. He then shakes himself and shakes robe towards sun. Enemy are so scared they give way and there is great slaughter. Scalps are brought in and there is great rejoicing.

71. THE MEDICINE BEAR SHIELD.

Boy's father dies and is buried. Boy goes to grave to cry and dreams that Bear tells him that woman has removed shield from grave. During storm he crawls into crevice and watches grave. He sees Bear with paws toward sky. Lightning forms appearance of shield with bear for black center mark. Boy returns to grave and when asleep he dreams his father tells him shield taken by Howling-Wolf and that he must get it. Howling-Wolf gives boy frame. Boy has another shield made like that he had seen on father's grave. Kills buffalo and makes inner shield. When fifteen, boy joins war-party. He strikes Sioux with bow and takes his scalplock. Scalp is offered to gods and boy made chief. Old man puts buckskin shirt on him and tells him as he strikes enemies and scalps them to make marks on shirt. When enemy attacks Village-Boy wears shield and is never hit. At sun dance boy swings day and night by buckskin strings tied to sticks run through his back. Sioux again attack village and boy again counts coup and strikes enemy. He dances sun dance many times afterward, and suffers because old medicine-men dead.

72. THE CRUCIFIED ENEMY.

People go on buffalo hunt, leaving old people in village. Enemy come and people retreat to lodges. Old man puts on medicine and costumes and, gourd in hand, goes to top of lodge and sings sacred songs. Enemy see him and are much afraid, as he has power to mesmerize. They all run with old man after them. One of enemy's bravest men captured and tied to wooden cross outside of village. Man dies, loses his flesh, and only bones left. When young men playing near cross, bones fall and run toward village and into medicine-lodge. Man is found under blankets on altar. His bones are gathered and thrown away.

73. HOW A SIOUX WOMAN'S SCALP WAS SACRIFICED.

Men go on war-path and hide near where Sioux get their water. Two women come to spring and as they run away one is seized, and scalp taken from side of her head. Men hurry back, and when they come to timber, leader takes fat from scalp and divides it into five pieces, which he places in four directions with one in center, first on his hand and then on the ground, to show that scalp is offered to gods. Scalp ceremony used when they get home. Fire-sticks are used to burn scalp. Holy bundles and medicine bags are passed through smoke and priests change names of young men and children who give them presents.

74. THE WARRIOR WHO FOUGHT THE SIOUX.

In winter Sioux attack Fort Berthold. Man coming with antelope on back does not see Sioux until he hears noise. He runs and is followed by Sioux. Man kills first Sioux and cuts him open with knife. Sioux shoot at him from behind with arrows. Man stands up and yells like a bear and Sioux run away. Man has piece of liver in his mouth. He chases Sioux and takes ponies and runs after them. He goes into timber and next day is found frozen, with arrows in his back.

75. THE CAPTURE OF THE ENEMY'S BOWS.

Young men go on war-path and Sioux come and capture old women and children. Young man returns and finds what has happened. He, his brother, and his father follow Sioux to creek where they are in camp. Young man looks at stars, trees, and everything and says they must attack and give big war-whoop. When war-whoop given, trees and everything seem to join. Enemy are frightened and run away. They capture enemy's bows and kill many people. Bows and arrows are set upon high hill.

76. THE WOMAN WHO BEFRIENDED THE WARRIORS.

Two boys on war-path find earth-lodge where old woman lives. She feeds them and tells them where to go. They kill enemy. This occurs several times, but once there are so many young men in party old woman is ashamed. Next time war-party goes old woman has disappeared. Two boys hunt for her and find her inside of cliff in Bad Lands. Great company of men go there, but she again disappears. Party of warriors come to big lake and hear woman singing scalp-dance songs. Warriors scared, but leader says she is rejoicing, and they go and take enemy's scalps. This occurs again, but next time instead of singing and dancing, woman mourns. Warriors go on and are beaten by enemy. She is found to be same old woman that lived in Bad Lands. People give her blankets, tobacco, and other things.

77. THE ATTACK UPON THE EAGLE HUNTERS.

Arikara go to hills to catch eagles. Young man prepares and baits hole and then gets into it, leaving weapons outside. Sioux find hole and tell man to crawl out. He takes them where other men are. They make Arikara stand around fireplace while man cooks meat for them. He holds piece of buffalo tallow over fire and whirls it around and burns Sioux with grease. They are scared and man, though weak through torturing, walks away. Sioux stay in tipi all night. Man goes home and tells people. They go after Sioux and return with three scalps.

78. THE ATTACK UPON THE EAGLE HUNTERS.

Young men go eagle hunting and while in cave Sioux come. Sioux ask for eagle feathers, which leader goes out of cave to give them. They attack Arikara, whose leader kills several Sioux, and others retreat. Hunters at night return to village with scalps.

79. THE MOURNING LOVER.

Man called "Rolling-Log" courts Arikara woman, who says she will marry him if he will bring her enough sinew to last her a whole year. He goes south with hunters and gets twenty-four sinews. He returns home and goes to see girl, but finds she is dead. He feels so bad he goes among hills and does not return to Arikara camp.

80. CONTEST BETWEEN THE BEAR AND THE BULL SOCIETIES.

During medicine ceremonies Bear family is on north and Buffalo family on south inside lodge. Buffalo Society has two buffalo scalps with horns. These are worn by two Buffalo men who play with people of village. Young man of Bear family tells leader he wants to challenge Buffalo to fight. Leader finally consents and sends pipe to leader of Buffalo Society as challenge. He objects, but finally consents and sends for Buffalo man. Men are prepared by medicines of their respective societies for fight. Societies meet and fight takes place. Buffalo hooks Bear, who is killed. Bear lodge announces that Bear killed for all time, but they do not get mad, as it was his own fault.

81. HOW WHITE-BEAR CAME TO BELONG TO THE BEAR SOCIETY.

When White-Bear's mother is pregnant his father puts on bear robe and tries to catch people to cut them open and get piece of liver. So his son has spirit of Bear. In nursing boy's mouth shows froth and he makes noise like young bear. In Bear dances boy wears robe of bear hide. When three years old, White-Bear falls on knife, cutting belly so that intestines come out. Father restores them to place and bandages child. In few days child is much better and bear robe is put on its back. Child cannot straighten out and makes noise like cat. As he grows up he acts like Bear. In Bear ceremonies sleight-of-hand ceremonies are performed by him. In medicine-lodge he has visions of bear. When no more Bear dances he does not show ways of bear.

82. THE TALE OF A MEMBER OF THE BEAR SOCIETY.

Boy stays in medicine-men's lodge and learns mysteries of Bear Society. Father gives him stuffed bear skin. In Bear dance little bear dances and imitates boy. When worn out little bear is placed in ravine. Some years ago great hunter asks young man to go hunting. At night pony snorts furiously and Scalped-Man is seen. After killing deer they start for home. They see bear, which stands up like man. Bear embraces young one. After being shot bear goes into brush, where it is found sitting, dead. Young one also killed and both are skinned. Man gives large hide to friend and keeps little bear's hide. He wears it in Bear dances. Afterwards it is sold, in his absence, to white man.